CROSSROADS OF CONFLICT

A publication of the
Georgia Civil War Commission

Published in association with
the Georgia Department of
Economic Development and the
Georgia Humanities Council

The University of Georgia Press
Athens and London

Barry L. Brown and Gordon R. Elwell   Foreword by Vince Dooley

CROSSROADS OF CONFLICT

A GUIDE TO CIVIL WAR SITES IN GEORGIA

Published by The University of Georgia Press
Athens, Georgia 30602
www.ugapress.org
© 2010 by the Georgia Department of Economic Development
All rights reserved
Edited, designed, and typeset by Jennifer Evans Yankopolus
Printed and bound by Transcontinental/Interglobe
The paper in this book meets the guidelines for
permanence and durability of the Committee on
Production Guidelines for Book Longevity of the
Council on Library Resources.

Printed in Canada
14 13 12 11 10 P 5 4 3 2 1

Library of Congress Cataloging-in-Publication Data
Brown, Barry L., 1958–
    Crossroads of conflict : a guide to Civil War sites in Georgia /
    Barry L. Brown and Gordon R. Elwell ; foreword by Vince Dooley.
        p.   cm.
"A publication of the Georgia Civil War Commission."
Includes bibliographical references and index.
ISBN-13: 978-0-8203-3730-2 (pbk. : alk. paper)
ISBN-10: 0-8203-3730-7 (pbk. : alk. paper)
1. Historic sites—Georgia—Guidebooks. 2. Georgia—Guidebooks.
3. Georgia—History—Civil War, 1861–1865—Battlefields—Guidebooks.
4. United States—History—Civil War, 1861–1865—Battlefields—Guidebooks.
5. Battlefields—Georgia—Guidebooks. 6. Georgia—History—Civil War, 1861–1865.
I. Elwell, Gordon R. II. Georgia Civil War Commission. III. Title.
F287.B76 2010
975.8'03—dc22   2010013130
British Library Cataloging-in-Publication Data available

*Frontispiece: Fort Pulaski,
Savannah, Georgia
(Photo: Cara Pastore,
Georgia Dept. of Economic
Development)*

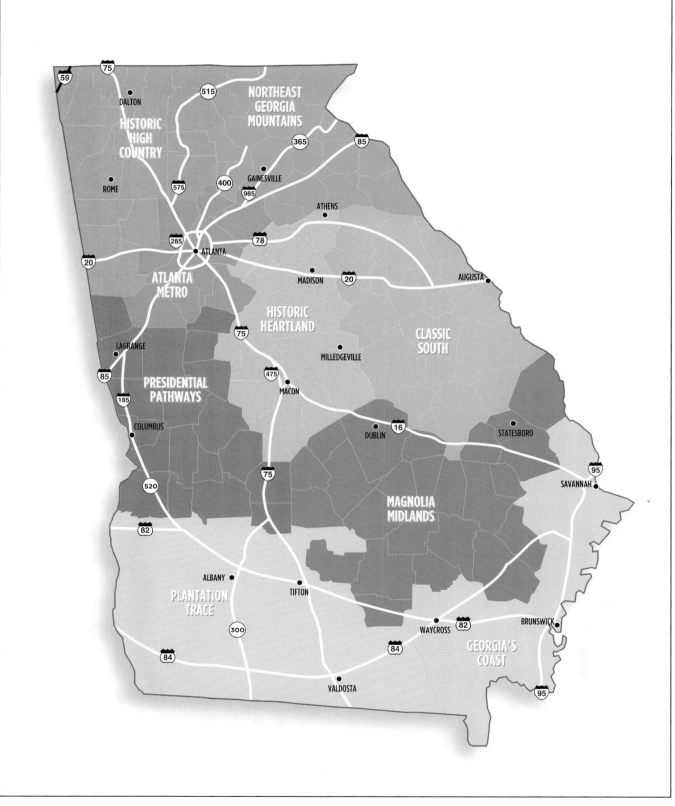

Tourism Regions of Georgia

Contents

Foreword

With the commemoration of the 150th anniversary of the American Civil War, it is a distinct privilege to be asked to write the foreword to the revised edition of the state's Civil War sites guidebook, *Crossroads of Conflict*. The war's sesquicentennial has stimulated added interest both here in Georgia and throughout the nation regarding our country's "greatest national crisis." This revised edition reminds us of the significant role played by Georgia in the Civil War; almost every part of the state was touched by this greatest tragedy in our nation's history.

Crossroads of Conflict chronicles the remarkably rich and varied history of the Civil War in Georgia. During the four years of warfare between 1861 and 1865 there were 550 raids, skirmishes, and battles (27 major). There were eleven POW campsites and numerous hospitals scattered throughout the entire state. Some areas of the state never saw battle, but all sent men (over one hundred thousand) and supplies. Georgia ranks second only to Virginia in the number of soldiers provided for the Confederacy.

Considering the importance of Atlanta as an industrial and railroad center and the effect of the Atlanta Campaign on the reelection of President Abraham Lincoln, the significance of the historical sites in the state is arguably at least as important as those in Virginia, if not more.

The role of Union Major General William T. Sherman not only was paramount in many of the battlefield sites in Georgia, but his total war philosophy that targeted civilian resources during his March to the Sea had a significant social and cultural effect on the homefront. Love him or hate him, Sherman's role and legacy make him one of the main tourist personality draws to the Peach State.

As a history and Civil War enthusiast, I found that *Crossroads of Conflict* provided me with fascinating and previously unknown facts about Georgia's role in the conflict. Buried in Oak Hill Cemetery in Cartersville is Major General Pierce M.B. Young, a West Point graduate who served with Major General J.E.B. Stuart's cavalry in Virginia. Young became the first Georgian seated in Congress after the Civil War and was the youngest major general in either the Confederate or Union army. Buried in West Point (Georgia) is Brigadier General Robert C. Tyler, the last Confederate general to die in combat in the Civil War. Tyler, who had lost a leg at Missionary Ridge, gallantly defended a small earthwork with a handful of "extra-duty" men and militia against a full brigade of Federal cavalry. After being overwhelmed and killed, the heroic general was honored when the area became known as Fort Tyler.

As one who likes to read historical markers, I was unaware that in LaGrange there is one for the Nancy Hart Rifles, a militia unit of women "who practiced military drills in preparation to defend the town." Union cavalry commander Colonel Oscar H. LaGrange (no connection to the town) spared the city after meeting with the ladies, who impressed him with their "fearless spirit and fine martial air."

In reviewing the book, a headline entitled "Moore's Bridge Park and Horace King Historic Site" got my attention. One of the first African American athletes to play football for me at the University of Georgia was Horace King from Athens, Georgia, who became a great running back for the Bulldogs and afterwards played ten years with the Detroit Lions in the NFL. The Horace King of the Civil War era interestingly was a free black master builder of covered bridges throughout the Southeast. He built (with two white partners) and managed a toll bridge across the Chattahoochee River, connecting Carroll County to Coweta County. Union cavalry General George Stoneman captured the bridge and later burned it. I was happy to learn that Carroll County plans to build a replica of the bridge and turn the site into a park.

I have long enjoyed walking in the footsteps of history. I did so recently while visiting Washington-Wilkes County, the home of Brigadier General Edward Porter Alexander, the artillery commander of Lt. General James Longstreet's corps of General Robert E. Lee's Army of Northern Virginia. What prompted me to visit the site was reading the book edited by noted Civil War historian Gary Gallagher, entitled *Fighting for the Confederacy: The Personal Recollections of General Edward Porter Alexander*. Robert K. Krick, a leading authority on the Army of Northern Virginia, encouraged Gallagher to edit the work; most Civil War experts believe the book is the newest and "richest personal account of the vast literature of the Civil War." It is the best I have ever read on the eastern campaigns. General Porter is buried at Magnolia Cemetery in Augusta along with six other Confederate generals.

History is important because it helps us to better understand the present. Civil War history is important because, despite the fascination, valor, and utter tragedy it holds, the outcome set forth precisely the type of nation that we have become. The noted late Civil War historian Shelby Foote said, "The Civil War defined us as what we are and it opened us to being what we became, good and bad things. And it is very necessary, if you're going to understand the American character in the twentieth century, to learn about this enormous catastrophe of the mid-nineteenth century."

The study of history and the Civil War is important, but it is also fun. There is a joy to learning, and by directing visitors to the multitude of Civil War sites in our state this Georgia guidebook is about historic education and making history come alive in an exciting and meaningful way for students of all ages.

It is also about linking education with economic development. This publication will increase visitation to the state and create an economic impact. The casual tourist will pick up the book or go online for the various Civil War sites and click on the *New Georgia Encyclopedia* on the World Wide Web. While the casual tourist will bring some dollars to the state, it is the Civil War buffs who will make the most significant financial impact. They too will walk in the footsteps of some of the major battlefields and visit many of the small towns where a lot of exciting hidden Civil War history took place.

I commend the Georgia Civil War Commission and the Georgia Department of Economic Development Tourism Division for updating and revising *Crossroads of Conflict*. This in-depth guide will advance the historical interpretation of Georgia's Civil War era and at the same time bring visitors here, raising the visibility and enhancing the economy of many communities.

I have toured a lot of Civil War sites in Georgia, and *Crossroads of Conflict* has stimulated my interest and afforded me a bucket list of many more sites to visit. I am looking forward to extending my Civil War journey throughout the state.

Vince Dooley

Preface

Georgia is rich in historic resources from the Civil War era, many of which are not widely known. *Crossroads of Conflict: A Guide Civil War Sites in Georgia* is intended to help you in planning visits to Georgia's many significant Civil War sites. It was prepared by the Georgia Civil War Commission under the auspices of and with the technical assistance of the Tourism Division of the Georgia Department of Economic Development.

Originally published in 1994 by the Georgia Civil War Commission; the Historic Preservation Division of the Georgia Department of Natural Resources; the Tourist Division of the Georgia Department of Industry, Trade, and Tourism; and the Georgia Battlefields Association, the first edition of *Crossroads of Conflict* covered 155 Civil War sites and was reprinted, with only minor revisions, several times. This new edition contains significant revisions and updates and now encompasses 350 sites. Portions of the book are available online at www.exploregeorgia.org.

SCOPE AND LIMITATIONS

The Civil War sites covered in *Crossroad of Conflict* range in size from the five-thousand-acre battlefield at Chickamauga to the thirty-foot-wide crossing at Sope Creek and are as diverse as battlefields, markers, houses, relief maps, monuments and statues, museums, mills, churches, depots, and cemeteries and grave sites. Also included are bridges, forts, parks, visitors centers, ferries, courthouses, capitols, prison sites, campsites, trenches and Shoupades, plantations, archives, arsenals, and lighthouses. Travelers can visit an iron works, a foundry, a factory, an armory, and a hotel; stroll in a garden and walk through a tunnel; take in a cove and a canal; see the only double-barreled cannon known to exist; and view what many consider the finest cyclorama painting in the world.

However, the many places covered in *Crossroads of Conflict* do not represent all of the Civil War–related sites in Georgia. For example, many more cemeteries, markers, and monuments exist than are included here. Additional sites will surely come along as new museums are opened, new markers and monuments are erected, and historic houses and pieces of remaining battlefields are acquired for preservation, education, and tourism.

Access by the public to certain sites may be subject to change. For example, a historic house currently open for touring may become privately owned and closed to the public. We ask that you respect private property and only enter with owner consent.

It should be emphasized that this publication is not intended as a comprehensive history, although the authors attempt to place the tourism sites in their historical context. Also, everything one can see at each site is not fully described here. We hope the descriptions will motivate you to visit and experience all that is there, as well as hear the insights and behind-the-scenes stories from the staff and volunteers at the site.

Every effort has been made to obtain permission to use private or copyright material. The authors apologize for any errors or omissions and would welcome these being brought to their attention.

To help us keep the information up to date, please notify us of any corrections. We would also appreciate any suggestions about the content of future editions.

For more information about Georgia's Civil War attractions, please contact:

Georgia Civil War Commission
georgiacivilwar.org

Tourism Division
Georgia Department of Economic Development
www.exploregeorgia.org

Acknowledgments

For their contributions to this book the authors wish to express their gratitude to the late Dr. Philip Secrist, whose enthusiasm and knowledge about Civil War history was infectious; to Jennifer Yankopolus, whose effort on this project represents the apex of dedication, patience, and skill; to all of the Georgia Civil War Commission past and present and especially members Kelly Barrow, Dan Childs, John Culpepper, Doug Davis, Debra Denard, and Mauriel Joslyn and with special thanks to Tommy Barber, whose prodigious grasp of facts and generous help and guidance kept the project on course; to all the dedicated people at Georgia Department of Economic Development with special thanks to Charlie Gatlin, Bruce Green, Fred Huff, Kevin Langston, Ellen Stone, Avon Thompson, Greg Torre, and Fay Tripp; to photographer/historian Bob Price, who allowed us to freely use his vast photographic archive and gave selflessly of his time and gas mileage; to Marla Bexley-Brown for her photographs and encouragement; and to photographer Philip Lovell, who got up early for the cause and always managed to catch the best light.

We would also like to thank those who supported the project: Dr. Brandon Beck, John and Dorothy Brown, Dr. George Coletti, Roberta Cook, Charlie Crawford, Dr. David Evans, Charlie Geiger, Dr. W. Todd Groce, Allison Turner-Hansen, Dr. Ray Luce, Alphonso Murchison, Cara Pastore, Ken Thomas, Jr, and Dr. Jamil S. Zainaldin. This book is dedicated to the Georgia Civil War Commission members who are no longer with us: Tom Watson Brown, Oliver Keller, and Philip Secrist.

Members of the Georgia Civil War Commission included Tommy Barber, Charles Kelly Barrow, John Culpepper, Douglas R. Davis, Debra Denard, Hugh K. "Rusty" Henderson, Mauriel Philips Joslyn, Jan Burroughs Loftis, Eunice Mixon, John Odom, Olin Pound, Jimmy Rhodes, R. Edward Shelor, Dr. Melvin T. Steely, and James Yancey.

Authors always face the risk of omitting the names of some who have helped, and for this we apologize. At nearly every site included in *Crossroads of Conflict* a staff person or local expert provided information culled from a wealth of local knowledge.

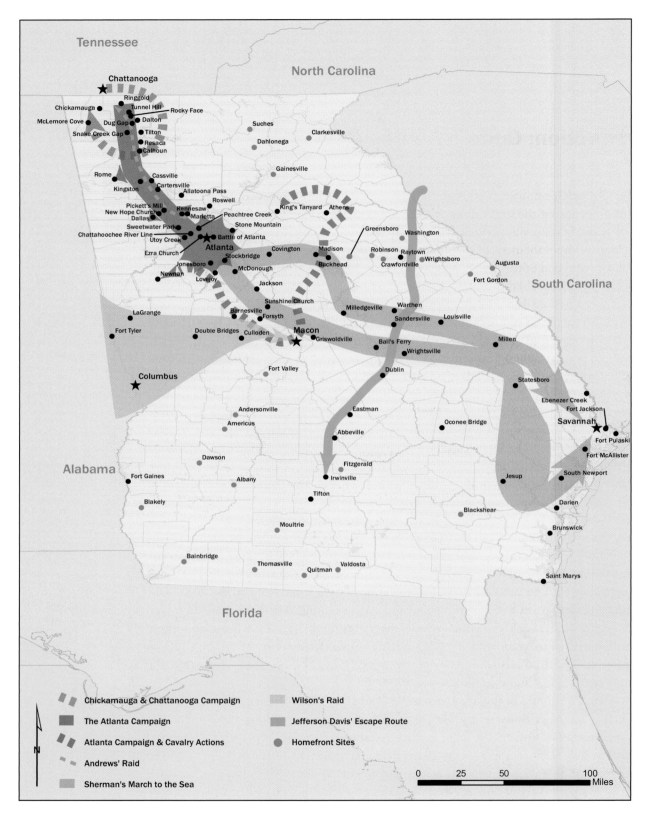

Military Campaigns in Georgia, 1861 – 1865

Introduction: Georgia during the Civil War

Georgia's geographic position in the heart of the Confederacy kept the state almost immune from invasion during the early years of the Civil War, with the exception of its coastline. For two years fighting was concentrated in Virginia, Tennessee, and the Mississippi Valley before Union forces focused on Georgia. Nonetheless, Georgians fought in almost every battle and, by the end of the war, had supplied approximately 112,000 soldiers to the Confederate cause. Former slaves, many of whom were native Georgians, served in the 44th United States Colored Infantry, which was garrisoned at Rome in the summer of 1864. Black soldiers served in other USCT commands too, and some white Georgians fought for the Union.

A number of civil officers and members of President Jefferson Davis' military staff were from Georgia: Vice President Alexander H. Stephens, First Secretary of State Robert Toombs, Assistant Secretary of the Treasury Philip Clayton, Assistant Secretary of War John Archibald Campbell, Quartermaster-General of the Confederate States Alexander Robert Lawton, Commissary-General Isaac Munroe St. John, and Assistant Secretary of State William M. Browne, naval agent to England James D. Bulloch, as well as Phoebe Yates Levy Pember, the first female administrator of Chimborazo Hospital in Richmond, Virginia, the world's largest military hospital at the time. You will find the homes of some of these people listed in this guidebook.

One of Georgia's best-known Civil War stories, the Great Locomotive Chase, occurred in April 1862 when James J. Andrews and his raiders seized the *General* and three box cars at Big Shanty (now Kennesaw). They headed north toward Union lines on their mission to disrupt the Western and Atlantic Railroad, which supplied Confederate forces at Chattanooga, Tennessee. The *Texas*, manned by Georgians, entered the chase about thirty-four miles north of Big Shanty and ran fifty-one miles in reverse in pursuit of the other locomotive. When the *General* was abandoned by the raiders, the *Texas* towed the damaged engine back to Ringgold. The *Texas* continued to serve the Confederacy throughout the war. The Union soldiers involved in the chase were the first recipients of the Congressional Medal of Honor, the nation's highest military honor.

From the early months of the war, the coast of Georgia saw much activity, with the Union navy blockading the coastline to prevent blockade runners from supplying the Confederacy. In early 1862, Union forces laid siege to Fort Pulaski, and on April 10 the four hundred defenders of the fort surrendered. Unable to invade Savannah, Federal forces continued to raid the sea islands and coastal plantations in the vicinity. In 1863, the Union made three naval attacks against Fort McAllister but was defeated each time. The Federals did capture and destroy the coastal town of Darien, which was occupied by the 54th Massachusetts Colored Infantry, in some of the war's first action involving African American troops.

Union forces invaded Georgia in September 1863 at the Battle of Chickamauga. Two

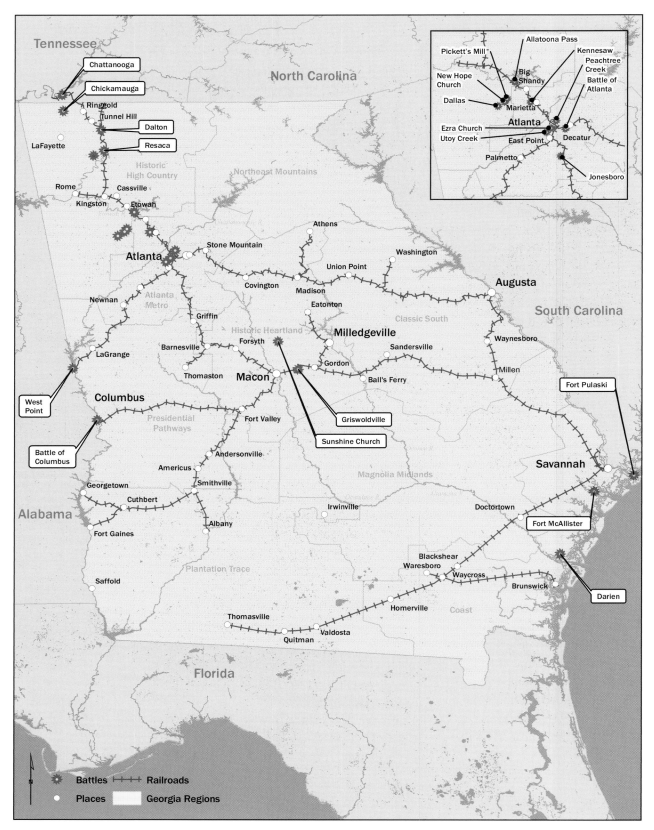

Battles and Transportation Routes in Georgia, 1861–1865

days of hard fighting between Major General Braxton Bragg's Confederate forces and General William S. Rosecrans' Federal army ended with Rosecrans retreating to Chattanooga. Chickamauga, an Indian word for "River of Death," was among the ten bloodiest battles of the war. The price the Confederacy paid for this victory was one from which they never recovered.

The next spring Major General William T. Sherman invaded Georgia, and his one hundred thousand men repeatedly outmaneuvered General Joseph E. Johnston's seventy thousand troops. The war came to the heart of Georgia with engagements at Rocky Face Ridge, Resaca, New Hope Church, Pickett's Mill, and Kennesaw Mountain. After being outflanked at numerous positions, including his Chattahoochee River Line, Johnston was replaced by Lt. General John B. Hood.

During the Civil War, Atlanta was a strategic supply and communications center for the Confederacy. With no troop reinforcements available, Atlanta's fortifications were hurriedly strengthened by thousands of impressed slaves. Twelve miles of heavy fortifications surrounded the city from which General Hood launched attacks on the Union forces during three major battles in July 1864. At the conclusion of these battles and after a forty-day siege, Hood was forced to retreat from Atlanta to avoid entrapment by Union flanking movements. After the Battle of Jonesboro, August 31–September 1, Hood rested his men near Palmetto. On September 2, the mayor of Atlanta formally surrendered Atlanta to the Union army. Sherman's successful Atlanta Campaign assured the reelection of Abraham Lincoln in November 1864, ultimately resulting in a preserved Union rather than an independent Confederate States of America.

In early October, Hood turned north, hoping to cut Sherman's supply lines and lure him away from Atlanta. Sherman then detached part of his army to follow Hood northward. The Battle of Allatoona Pass on October 5, 1864, was fought as part of this maneuver. By the middle of November, Hood was well on his way to Tennessee. After Hood's departure, Sherman ordered the evacuation of Atlanta and set much of what was left on fire, destroying a large number of Atlanta's forty-five hundred houses and commercial buildings. Atlanta was in flames as Sherman departed southward November 15 on his March to the Sea. After many skirmishes with Confederate cavalry and a clash with Georgia home guard militia at Griswoldville on November 22, he arrived in Savannah on December 22, having first captured Fort McAllister on December 13.

With the war nearly over, a large Federal cavalry force under Brigadier General James H. Wilson launched a month-long series of lightning-quick raids in Alabama and Georgia. The raids successfully destroyed the remaining productive capacity in the Deep South. The end of the war came with a series of surrenders. In April 1865, General Robert E. Lee surrendered at Appomattox, Virginia. Two weeks later, on April 26, General Joseph E. Johnston surrendered at Durham Station, North Carolina. President Jefferson Davis hoped to continue the war from the Trans-Mississippi region. However, he was pursued across Georgia and captured near Irwinville in southern Georgia on May 10, 1865.

HISTORIC HIGH COUNTRY

The most widespread military action Georgia saw during the Civil War occurred in the northwest Georgia mountains, the region referred to today as the Historic High Country, between September 1863 and July 1864 as Confederate forces tried to fend off Major General William T. Sherman's advance on Atlanta. The Chickamauga and Kennesaw battlefields are major sites in this area.

Georgia was spared invasion during the first two years of the war, although in 1861 and 1862 engagements occurred on the coastline and Federal agent James Andrews led a daring raid in northwest Georgia resulting in a rousing locomotive chase. Union forces first invaded the state in September 1863 at Chickamauga, causing the bloodiest two-day battle of the war, after which the Federal army withdrew to Chattanooga, Tennessee.

Early in May 1864, Sherman launched his Atlanta Campaign through northwest Georgia beginning at Ringgold and relentlessly throwing his 100,000-man force against 70,000 Confederate defenders. His first objective was to destroy the Confederate Army of Tennessee under General Joseph E. Johnston.

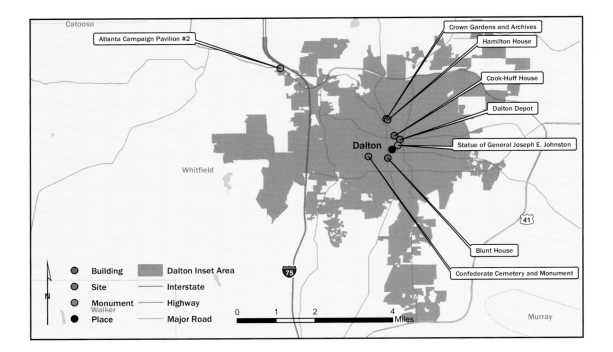

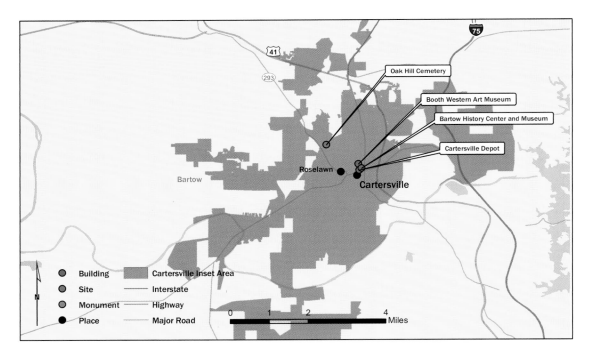

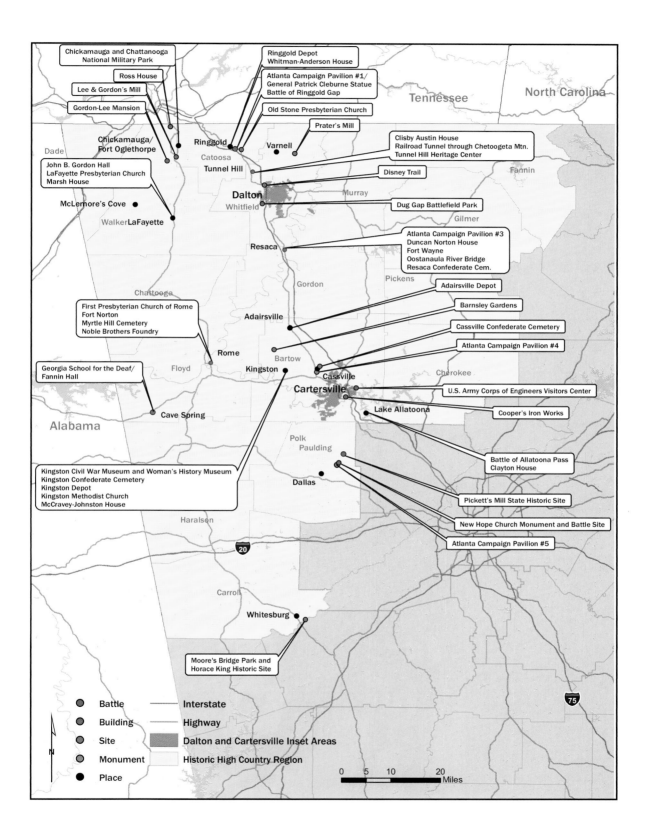

Chickamauga and Chattanooga
National Military Park

Ross House

Lee & Gordon's Mill

Gordon-Lee Mansion

Chickamauga/
Fort Oglethorpe

Dade

John B. Gordon Hall
LaFayette Presbyterian Church
Marsh House

McLemore's Cove

WalkerLaFayette

Ringgold Depot
Whitman-Anderson House

Atlanta Campaign Pavilion #1/
General Patrick Cleburne Statue
Battle of Ringgold Gap

Old Stone Presbyterian Church

Prater's Mill

Ringgold

Varnell

Catoosa

Tunnel Hill

Tennessee

North Carolina

Clisby Austin House
Railroad Tunnel through Chetoogeta Mtn.
Tunnel Hill Heritage Center

Fannin

Disney Trail

Dalton

Whitfield

Murray

Dug Gap Battlefield Park

Gilmer

Resaca

Gordon

Pickens

Atlanta Campaign Pavilion #3
Duncan Norton House
Fort Wayne
Oostanaula River Bridge
Resaca Confederate Cem.

Adairsville Depot

Barnsley Gardens

First Presbyterian Church of Rome
Fort Norton
Myrtle Hill Cemetery
Noble Brothers Foundry

Chattooga

Adairsville

Cassville Confederate Cemetery

Atlanta Campaign Pavilion #4

Rome

Floyd

Bartow

Kingston

Cherokee

Georgia School for the Deaf/
Fannin Hall

Cassville

Cartersville

U.S. Army Corps of Engineers Visitors Center

Lake Allatoona

Cooper's Iron Works

Cave Spring

Alabama

Polk
Paulding

Battle of Allatoona Pass
Clayton House

Kingston Civil War Museum and Woman's History Museum
Kingston Confederate Cemetery
Kingston Depot
Kingston Methodist Church
McCravey-Johnston House

Dallas

Pickett's Mill State Historic Site

Haralson

New Hope Church Monument and Battle Site

Atlanta Campaign Pavilion #5

20

Carroll

Whitesburg

75

Moore's Bridge Park and
Horace King Historic Site

● Battle   Interstate

● Building   Highway

● Site   Dalton and Cartersville Inset Areas

● Monument   Historic High Country Region

● Place

N

0   5   10   20
                      Miles

CHICKAMAUGA/FORT OGLETHORPE,
Catoosa County and Walker County

Catoosa County Area Chamber of
Commerce
P.O. Box 52
Ringgold, GA 30736
706-965-5201
www.gatewaytogeorgia.com

Walker County Chamber of
Commerce
P.O. Box 430
Rock Spring, GA 30739
706-375-7702
www.walkercochamber.com

In the fall of 1863, some of the hardest fighting of the Civil War occurred in the fields and thick woods of northwest Georgia. The prize was Chattanooga, Tennessee, a key rail center and gateway to the heart of the Confederacy. On September 19, 1863, sixty-five thousand Confederate forces under General Braxton Bragg attempted to dislodge fifty-eight thousand Federals under Major General William S. Rosecrans south of Chattanooga at Crawfish Springs, Georgia. The ensuing battle became known as Chickamauga. The opposing armies fought desperately all day, often hand-to-hand, resulting in no clear advantage.

During the next day's fighting, a gap opened briefly in the Federal line just as Confederate Lt. General James Longstreet's corps, transferred from General Robert E. Lee's army in Virginia, attacked that very point. Longstreet's men smashed through the hole routing half of Rosecrans' army. However, Union Major General George H. Thomas rallied some Federals and formed a new battle line on Snodgrass Hill. The Union troops held their ground against repeated assaults, earning Thomas the nickname "Rock of Chickamauga."

After dark on September 20, the Union army withdrew from the field and retreated into Chattanooga. The next day, the Confederates pursued and occupied Lookout Mountain, Missionary Ridge, and the Chattanooga Valley. However, in November 1863 Union forces under Lt. General Ulysses S. Grant defeated Bragg's army at Missionary Ridge in Chattanooga, thus opening Georgia to invasion.

Chickamauga was the bloodiest two-day battle of the war, costing the South eighteen thousand and the North sixteen thousand casualties. One Confederate regiment, the 20th Georgia, lost seventeen of its twenty-three officers. Chickamauga Creek had lived up to its Indian name, the "River of Death."

Right: *A war-era depiction of the Battle of Chicamauga (Courtesy of the UGA Hargrett Rare Book and Manuscript Library)*

Chickamauga and Chattanooga National Military Park (NRHP)

In 1892 Congress purchased fifty-two hundred acres of land in northwest Georgia that now forms the Chickamauga and Chattanooga National Military Park. This was the first major Civil War battlefield set aside as a memorial to the soldiers who fought there. The park was officially dedicated in 1895 by veterans from both the North and the South. The battlefield's visitors center offers interpretive exhibits, a large bookstore, and a twenty-six-minute multimedia program that gives a unique orientation to the battle. The Fuller gun collection features many rare items among the 355 weapons on display. Outside, an artillery display illustrates the various types of light field artillery used at Chickamauga and Chattanooga. The battlefield contains numerous monuments, historical tablets, wayside exhibits, and hiking trails.

Visitors should also visit the nearby Missionary Ridge and Lookout Mountain Battlefield in Tennessee, which includes Point Park and a visitors center. The center features James Walker's impressive *Battle of Lookout Mountain* painting that measures thirteen by thirty-three feet.

3370 Lafayette Rd.
Fort Oglethorpe, GA 30742
706-866-9241
423-821-7786 (Point Park)
www.nps.gov/chch

Daily: 8:30 a.m.–5:00 p.m.

Right: *Snodgrass Cabin on Snodgrass Hill, the site where Federal General George H. Thomas rallied the last defense at Chickamauga (Photo: Marla Bexley-Brown)*

Gordon-Lee Mansion (NRHP)

In September 1863, James Gordon's mansion, which was built in 1847, served as headquarters for Union Major General William S. Rosecrans and his chief of staff, future president of the United States James A. Garfield. Today, the Gordon-Lee Mansion is the only structure used during the Battle of Chickamauga that is still standing.

Although Rosecrans came to occupy the house just before the battle, his troops were spread out across fifty miles. Ironically, Confederate General Braxton Bragg, who was headquartered in the John B. Gordon Hall in LaFayette twelve miles away, was closer to Rosecrans' men that Rosecrans himself. During the Battle of Chickamauga, the Federals used the Gordon-Lee Mansion as a hospital with wagons placed outside the windows to collect amputated limbs. After the battle, thirty Union doctors were permitted to stay to continue tending to the enormous numbers of wounded from both sides.

The mansion was also the site of the 1889 Blue and Gray Barbeque hosted by the Honorable Gordon Lee, the Seventh District U.S. congressman from Georgia, who now owned the home. The event was attended by fourteen thousand Civil War veterans, including generals John B. Gordon and William S. Rosecrans.

The Gordon-Lee Mansion, now restored to its antebellum splendor and furnished with museum-quality period antiques, currently functions as a special events facility.

217 Cove Rd.
Chickamauga, GA 30707
706-375-4728
www.gordon-leemansion.com

Below: *Gordon-Lee Mansion (Photo: Barry Brown)*

Lee & Gordon's Mill (NRHP)

71 Red Belt Rd.
Chickamauga, GA 30707
706-375-6801
www.roadsidegeorgia.com/site/
leeandgordonmill.html

Lee & Gordon's Mill, one of the oldest mills in Georgia, is located near the Chickamauga and Chattanooga National Military Park, at the confluence of Chickamauga Creek and Crawfish Springs. Landowner and entrepreneur James Gordon, who came to the area in 1836 and built his palatial estate now known as the Gordon-Lee Mansion, owned the mill with his son-in-law James Lee.

On September 9–10, 1863, the mill served as headquarters for Confederate General Braxton Bragg's Army of Tennessee. When Bragg subsequently moved his headquarters south to LaFayette, Georgia, Union troops occupied the mill. Skirmishes occurred here between the opposing forces on September 13–18 prior to the Battle of Chickamauga. During the battle the mill served as a point of reference for both sides. At the start of the Atlanta Campaign in 1864, Union Major General James B. McPherson used the mill as a staging area for his move south to Snake Creek Gap west of Resaca.

Below, left to right: War-era view of Lee & Gordon's Mill, Wartime image of the Ross House (Courtesy of the Library of Congress)

In 1993, the mill was restored to its Civil War–era appearance and still functions as a mill. A museum in the front displays photos and artifacts from the Civil War, including the Battle of Chickamauga.

Ross House (NRHP)

Spring St. west of U.S. 27
Rossville, GA
http://roadsidegeorgia.com/
site/rosshouse.html

Open: June–Sept.
Call the John Ross Association,
706-861-3954, for exact dates
and hours

Built in the late 1700s, the Ross House is the oldest remaining structure in northwest Georgia. John Ross was an influential Cherokee leader, who became the first and only elected chief of the Cherokee nation in 1828. His home is a featured Native American site in north Georgia.

During the Battle of Chickamauga, Union Major General Gordon Granger used the Ross House as his headquarters. For most of the day, Granger's troops, designated as a reserve corps, held a position near the house observing the battle. When Granger saw Union Major General George Thomas holding a thin line around Snodgrass Hill, Granger, on his own initiative, ordered Brigadier General James Steedman's division to advance, reinforcing the desperate Union army.

RINGGOLD, Catoosa County

Ringgold, the seat of Catoosa County, is located just south of the Tennessee border in the northwest Georgia mountains. It played an important role during the War Between the States due to its proximity to the Western and Atlantic Railroad and the pass through the mountains directly to the south of town. From early 1862 through late 1863, the town was an important Confederate supply and hospital center. During the Great Locomotive Chase in April 1862, when James J. Andrews and his raiders abandoned the hijacked engine the *General*, having exhausted its fuel supply, they escaped to the woods two miles north of Ringgold near Graysville at a site noted by a historical marker. After the Federal army arrived on November 27, 1863, Ringgold remained in Union hands for the remainder of the war.

A number of state historical markers and monuments at the Catoosa County Courthouse describe Ringgold's role as an important hospital center able to care for several thousand patients. Fannie Beers and Kate Cummings, pioneers in the nursing profession who helped pave the way for women in the medical field, worked in the Ringgold hospitals, including the General Bragg, the General Buckner, and the Foard. However, in October 1863 the hospitals were moved south to avoid capture by advancing Union forces. Large hospitals on the outskirts of Ringgold at Cherokee Springs and Catoosa Springs were also moved south ahead of the Union advance.

www.cityofringgold.com

Catoosa County Area
Chamber of Commerce
P.O. Box 52
Ringgold, GA 30736
706-965-5201
www.gatewaytogeorgia.com

Left: *James J. Andrews' raiders abandoning the hijacked engine the* General *at Ringgold. Painting by Wilbur Kurtz. (Courtesy of the Atlanta History Center)*

Atlanta Campaign Pavilion #1

The Atlanta Campaign Pavilion #1 is the first in a series of five interpretive pavilions erected under the Works Project Administration during the 1930s. A relief map describes the positions of the opposing armies in the Ringgold area during the early stages of the Atlanta Campaign and the scope of the entire campaign. Plaques set atop fieldstone bases, along with several state historical markers, describe the nearby action. A trail behind the pavilion leads to a marker showing the farthest position reached by Federal Colonel David Ireland's brigade during the Battle of Ringgold Gap. A parking area/pull off and picnic tables are available at the pavilion.

U.S. 41 approx. 1 mile south of
Ringgold

Battle of Ringgold Gap

Above: *Major General Patrick R. Cleburne (Photo: Allison Turner-Hansen). Below: Ringgold Depot (Photos: Bob Price)*

After General Braxton Bragg's Confederate Army of Tennessee was driven from strong defensive positions along Missionary Ridge on November 25, 1863, the defeated army practically lost all cohesion as a fighting force. Many soldiers turned and ran in the face of the Federal assault to avoid being flanked and captured. However, Major General Patrick R. Cleburne's division, the last to retreat after successfully defending its sector along Missionary Ridge, left in good order and by default became the army's rear guard unit.

The defeated Bragg, taking the last option open to him, ordered Cleburne to make a stand against Major General Joseph Hooker's fifteen-thousand-man corps, which was then pursuing the retreating Confederates and their slow-moving wagon supply train. On November 27, Cleburne, with forty-one hundred men and two artillery batteries, set up a well-positioned ambush on the unsuspecting Federal forces from the top of Taylor's Ridge and across the gap on White Oak Ridge. As Hooker's vanguard marched through Ringgold toward the narrow gap, Cleburne's men let loose a destructive crossfire from rifles and artillery, first stunning and then repulsing the Federal column. For the next four hours Hooker attempted to break the Confederate line at a number of points but was effectively repulsed every time.

Cleburne reported 222 killed, wounded, and missing following the fighting of November 27. Hooker's casualties, at 501 killed, wounded, and missing, were considerably higher, having lost more men at Ringgold than in his celebrated Battle Above the Clouds on Lookout Mountain.

The Battle of Ringgold Gap assured Cleburne's status as a hero of the Confederacy. He earned the sobriquet "The Stonewall of Our Armies" from the *Atlanta Intelligencer.* The Confederate Congress passed a resolution of thanks on February 9, 1864, citing his act of saving Bragg's army from destruction.

The site of the Battle of Ringgold Gap can be viewed from the rear of the Ringgold Depot, where both slopes of the gap are visible. Attempts by preservation groups to purchase the battlefield and surrounding area have been unsuccessful, though a National Register of Historic Places listing is pending.

Ringgold Depot (NRHP)

155 Depot St.
Ringgold, GA 30736
706-965-5201
www.cityofringgold.com

Built in 1849 for the Western and Atlantic Railroad with locally quarried sandstone blocks, the Ringgold Depot is one of the state's oldest depots. It was used for the shipment of wheat and other staples during the antebellum period and was the receiving point for sick and wounded soldiers during the War Between the States. It was also the last depot Andrews' Raiders passed before their capture in the Great Locomotive Chase.

Damage from artillery fire inflicted during the Battle of Ringgold Gap is still evident, especially on the south side and along the roofline where light-colored limestone was used to repair the damaged sandstone blocks. The depot recently underwent renovation and can be rented for events. The building is also on the National Register of Historic Places.

Old Stone Presbyterian Church (NRHP)

Although the congregation was organized in 1837, this small stone church was not constructed until 1850. The walls, composed of locally quarried sandstone, are over a foot thick and are topped with a hipped roof. The building was used as a Confederate hospital after the nearby Battle of Ringgold Gap on November 27, 1863, and as a Federal hospital when Major General William T. Sherman moved south toward Tunnel Hill and Dalton in May 1864. Bloodstains can still be seen in the wood floor dating from its use as a hospital. The church, which is on the National Register of Historic Places, still contains the historic altar and pews.

U.S. 41 approx. 3 miles south of Ringgold

Left to right: *Old Stone Presbyterian Church, Whitman-Anderson House (Photos: Bob Price)*

Whitman-Anderson House (NRHP)

Constructed in early 1863 with handmade red brick, the two-story Whitman-Anderson House is of a classic Doric-order Greek Revival design. After the nearby Battle of Ringgold Gap, Union Lt. General Ulysses S. Grant used the house as his headquarters for the night of November 27, 1863. The next day he left with Major General William T. Sherman for Graysville, Georgia, where the decision was made to end the pursuit of the retreating Confederate army. Legend states that upon his departure from the home, Grant offered Mrs. Whitman fifty dollars in U.S. greenbacks as payment for lodging. She refused the offer, wanting Confederate currency instead. When he heard her request Grant said, "She certainly is not whipped yet," and his soldiers cheered her as they departed.

The Whitman-Anderson home is privately owned and not open to the public. It is easily viewed from Tennessee Street.

309 Tennessee St.
Ringgold, GA 30736

VARNELL, Whitfield County

During the Civil War, the town of Varnell in Crow Valley was called Varnell's Station. It was the site of a clash on May 9, 1864, where Confederate Major General Joseph Wheeler with nine hundred cavalrymen routed five thousand Federals under Brigadier General Edward M. McCook. Ten Confederates and one hundred fifty Federals were killed, and Wheeler captured more than one hundred prisoners.

Dalton CVB
288 Clisby Austin Rd.
Tunnel Hill, GA 30755
706-270-9960/800-331-3258
www.visitdaltonga.com

Prater's Mill (NRHP)

452 Varnell School St.
Varnell, GA 30756
706-694-6455
www.pratersmill.org

At various points during the Civil War, both armies camped at Prater's Mill, which Benjamin Franklin Prater built in 1855. In February 1864, six hundred Union soldiers under Colonel Eli Long camped at the mill after skirmishing near Dalton. Then in April 1864, twenty-five hundred Confederates under Major General Joseph Wheeler set up camp here en route to Tunnel Hill, where a major engagement occurred in May 1864. While occupied by Union forces, the mill was considered a valuable resource for food and was not destroyed. On some Civil War maps, Prater's Mill is listed as Barrett's Mill or Russell's Mill. Barrett was a former owner of the property, while Russell was probably a Prater relative hired as a miller. Today, the mill still grinds corn into meal.

The grounds of Prater's Mill are open to the public. An annual Country Fair and Festival is held the second weekend in October and features art, crafts, music, and food as well as a living-history Civil War encampment.

TUNNEL HILL, Whitfield County

Dalton CVB
288 Clisby Austin Rd.
Tunnel Hill, GA 30755
706-270-9960/800-331-3258
www.daltoncvb.com

Tunnell Hill is west of I-75 off exit 336, Dalton/Rocky Face, Hwy. 41
www.tunnelhillheritagecenter.com

On May 7, 1864, the opening shots of Major General William T. Sherman's Atlanta Campaign occurred at Tunnel Hill, named for the 1,477-foot railroad tunnel running through Chetoogeta Mountain. Dismounted Confederate cavalry under Major General Joseph Wheeler stoutly defended the tunnel until infantry and artillery from Major General John M. Palmer's XIV Corps forced Wheeler to abandon the position. The tunnel became an important link in the Union's vital supply line as Sherman's campaign thrust deeper into Georgia.

The town of Tunnel Hill was important in supplying both armies, first the Confederates during the fighting at Chickamauga in 1863 and then the Federals during 1864. Tunnel Hill was contested on four different occasions and throughout the war was the site of camps and hospitals for both sides. Several antebellum homes and buildings still exist along with Civil War breastworks and gun placements constructed by both armies. The railroad tunnel has been restored and is open to the public. A local heritage center features a museum. In addition, the 1852 stone depot, which was built by the Western and Atlantic Railroad, is still standing. William Whitten is believed to have been the first station agent. Local historians are planning a restoration of the depot.

Above: *Prater's Mill (Photo: Bob Price)*. Right: *The Confederate engine the* Texas *approaching the railroad tunnel at Chetoogeta Mountain in reverse while in pursuit of Andrews' Raiders in the engine the* General. *Painting by Wilbur Kurtz (Courtesy of the Atlanta History Center)*

Clisby Austin House

Following the Battle of Chickamauga, the Clisby Austin House was used as a Confederate hospital, which treated Confederate Lt. General John B. Hood after his right leg was amputated during the battle. Major General William T. Sherman also used the house as his headquarters in early May 1864. Sherman's first dispatch to mention a "push to salt water" following the capture of Atlanta was written from here. Today, the grounds of the now-restored house are the site of the annual reenactment of the Battle of Tunnel Hill. The house is privately owned, and tours are not currently available.

Clisby Austin Rd.
(adjacent to the tunnel)
Tunnel Hill, GA 30755

Left to right: *Clisby Austin House, Railroad tunnel through Chetoogeta Mountain (Photos: Bob Price)*

Railroad Tunnel through Chetoogeta Mountain

Built in 1850, the 1,477-foot tunnel through Chetoogeta Mountain was an engineering marvel of its time, linking the Atlantic coast to the western frontier via rail and the Tennessee River. Early in the Civil War, Confederate President Jefferson Davis gave a rousing speech at the depot in Tunnel Hill. In 1862, the Great Locomotive Chase passed through the tunnel, ending a few miles north at Ringgold. The tunnel, the oldest in the southeastern United States, has been restored. Visitors to the Tunnel Hill Heritage Center can walk its length.

Clisby Austin Rd. (adjacent to the Tunnel Hill Heritage Center)
Tunnel Hill, GA 30755
www.tunnelhillheritagecenter.com

Tunnel Hill Heritage Center

The Tunnel Hill Heritage Center, which opened in 2004, offers visitors displays about the railroad tunnel through Chetoogeta Mountain, the Dixie Highway, Cherokee heritage, notable families from the area, and the Civil War, including a mountain howitzer and uniforms.

215 Clisby Austin Rd.
Tunnel Hill, GA 30755
706-876-1572
www.tunnelhillheritagecenter.com

Mon.–Sat.: 9:00 a.m.–5:00 p.m.
(Closed Mondays in the summer)

DALTON, Whitfield County

Dalton CVB
288 Clisby Austin Rd.
Tunnel Hill, GA 30755
706-270-9960/800-331-3258
www.daltoncvb.com

The northwest Georgia city of Dalton played a conspicuous part in the state's Civil War history following the Chickamauga/Chattanooga Campaign of 1863. Located along the Western and Atlantic Railroad, Dalton served as a hospital center and supply base. Furthermore, the surrounding mountainous terrain provided natural defensive barriers, making it an opportune location to begin the defense of Georgia.

Following the Confederate Army of Tennessee's disastrous defeat at Missionary Ridge and subsequent retreat into Georgia during late November 1863, Dalton became the Confederate army's winter quarters. From this position it could rebuild and prepare for the difficult task of defending Georgia from the inevitable Federal offensive that would begin with the coming campaign season. Soon after arriving, General Braxton Bragg, the controversial and long-standing commander of the Army of Tennessee, resigned his commission and was replaced by General Joseph E. Johnston on December 16, 1863. The choice of Johnston over other possible candidates had long been a topic for debate due to the antagonistic relationship between Confederate President Jefferson Davis and Johnston. Possibly the result of a feud going back to their days at the United States Military Academy at West Point, their relationship was strained at best and always seemed to be based on a mutual mistrust. This dynamic was a key factor in setting the tenor of the Atlanta Campaign and ultimately affected its outcome.

Johnston, once apprised of the situation in Dalton, began the task at hand by initiating a rebuilding process for the Army of Tennessee. His goal was to return the army to its former stature as a cohesive and effective fighting force devoted to its commander and mission. He furloughed the entire army in rotation, granted a generalized amnesty to deserters, and obtained new clothing, equipment, and improved rations. Discipline and training were also stressed. Johnston was well aware that in the coming campaign season he would be facing a worthy adversary in Major General William T. Sherman and his enormous and determined Federal army.

Below: *Confederate monument in Dalton's Confederate Cemetery (Photo: Bob Price)*

The Atlanta Campaign officially began (according to the *Official Records of the War of the Rebellion*) with a skirmish at the Old Stone Presbyterian Church near Ringgold on May 1, 1864. However, the first major fighting occurred in the immediate vicinity of Dalton. Major combat got underway at Tunnel Hill on May 7, 1864, and at Rocky Face Ridge's Dug Gap and Mill Creek Gap on May 8–11, 1864.

Following Atlanta's fall in September 1864, the area around Dalton again played a role in Georgia Civil War history. The Western and Atlantic Railroad became a Confederate target as it was being used to supply Sherman's armies from the North.

On October 13, 1864, during General John B. Hood's march north through Georgia preceding the Campaign for Tennessee, the Confederate army of approximately 35,000 surrounded and forced the capitulation of the Federal garrison of 751 officers and men of the 44th U.S. Colored Infantry at Fort Hill near Dalton. The garrison's white commander, Colonel Lewis Johnson, feared for his soldiers' safety but received no promise of good treatment and was forced to submit to an unconditional surrender.

The garrison's more than six hundred African American soldiers were turned over to Major General William B. Bate's division. Their shoes and personal belongings were taken, and they were ordered to tear up the railroad tracks. Any soldier that refused to work was summarily shot on the spot. Although such treatment was not unusual for prisoners of war during the Civil War, these men faced the additional hardship of a return to slavery. The Federal garrisons manning the blockhouses at Tilton, as well as Mill Creek Gap, were also forced to surrender.

Many earthen fortifications from the Atlanta Campaign still exist in the Dalton, Mill Creek Gap, Rocky Face Ridge, and Tunnel Hill areas of Whitfield County. Most of these remaining historic resources are located along high ridges and in precarious out-of-the-way locations unsuitable for development. If earthworks are located on private property, they should only be visited with the landowner's permission.

Atlanta Campaign Pavilion #2

This picnic area and pavilion, the second in a group of five, contains a relief map built by workers in the 1930s under President Roosevelt's WPA program. This pavilion describes military events that occurred in the area on May 7–13, 1864, including Union Major General William T. Sherman's feint attacks on Mill Creek Gap, Crow Valley, and Dug Gap Mountain; Union Major General James B. McPherson's successful flanking movement to the southeast; and Confederate General Joseph E. Johnston's retrograde movement from Dalton.

U.S. Hwy. 41 in front of the Georgia State Patrol building
Dalton, GA

Blunt House (NRHP) and Cook-Huff House

Built in 1848 by Dalton's first mayor, Ainsworth Emery Blunt, the Blunt House was used as a Federal hospital and headquarters for General Joseph E. Johnston's staff. The soldiers damaged the house, and following the war, Blunt applied for and received compensation from the federal government due to his reported Union sympathies. The house is on the National Register of Historic Places.

While in Dalton, Johnston used the Cook-Huff House as his headquarters. It was also here, during the winter of 1863–1864, that Major General Patrick R. Cleburne presented his controversial proposal to emancipate slaves and arm them for service in the Confederate army.

Blunt House:
506 S. Thornton Ave.
Dalton, GA 30720

Cook House:
314 N. Selvidge Ave.
Dalton, GA 30720

To visit, contact the Whitfield-Murray Historical Society:
706-278-0217

Confederate Cemetery and Monument

Throughout much of 1862 and until being forced to move south during the spring of 1864, hospitals in the Dalton area cared for thousands of Confederate casualties from battles in Tennessee and northwest Georgia. Many who died in the hospitals are buried in the Dalton Confederate Cemetery. Interments include 421 unknown Confederates, 4 known Confederates, and 4 unknown Federal soldiers. A monument to the Confederate dead from the battles of Dalton, Rocky Face, Chickamauga, and Resaca was erected in 1892. The United Daughters of the Confederacy, the Sons of Confederate Veterans, and the Dalton Civil War Round Table hold a memorial service here on Confederate Memorial Day.

At Cuyler St. and Emory St.
(to the right of the chapel)
Dalton, GA

Above: *Blunt House (Photo: Bob Price)*

Crown Gardens and Archives (NRHP)

715 Chattanooga Ave.
Dalton, GA 30720
706-278-0217

Tues.–Fri.: 10:00 a.m.–5:00 p.m.
Sat.: 10:00 a.m.–2:00 p.m.

Originally the antebellum office of the Crown Cotton Mill, this building is now occupied by the Whitfield-Murray Historical Society. It houses Civil War relics, many uncovered at period campsites and battlefields in Whitfield County. The museum also features a quilt exhibit displaying antique and unique examples of this vernacular art form. Research and genealogical material is available upon request.

Dalton Depot (NRHP)

110 Depot St.
Dalton, GA 30720
706-226-3160

Built in 1852, the Western and Atlantic Railroad Depot in Dalton served as a Confederate ordnance depot in 1862–1864. During the Great Locomotive Chase, it was from here that Edward Henderson, Captain William A. Fuller's seventeen-year-old telegraph operator, sent a wire to the Confederate commander of Chattanooga, Brigadier General Danville Ledbetter, reporting that the *General* had been stolen and was heading his way. The depot, no longer used by the railroad, currently houses a restaurant.

Disney Trail

U.S. 41 behind the Nazarene
Church

This steep, challenging hiking trail ascends Rocky Face Mountain west of Dalton through the area where the Battle of Rocky Face Ridge occurred on May 8–10, 1864. The Disney Trail provides access to the north end of the mountain, which was defended by entrenched Confederates along the ridge.

At the trail's end is the grave of the British national and Confederate volunteer George Disney, a member of the 4th Kentucky, Orphan Brigade of Major General William B. Bate's division. The 4th Kentucky was deployed in a line from the base of the mountain to the summit of the ridge in order to view Federal troop movements and convey the information back down the line. Disney was killed by a random shot during the fighting on February 25, 1864, and was buried where he fell. The grave was discovered by a Dalton Boy Scout troop in 1912, and through their efforts the wooden war-era grave marker was replaced by the marble marker seen today.

Dug Gap Battlefield Park

W. Dug Gap Battle Rd.
Dalton, GA 30720

Once an important pioneer trace, the road through Dug Gap passed through Dalton on its way to the Western and Atlantic Railroad. The Federal army made unsuccessful attempts to capture the gap on February 25, 1864, and May 8, 1864.

The February 1864 fighting, relatively minor, occurred after General Joseph E. Johnston sent two of his divisions to the Trans-Mississippi Department to reinforce Confederate forces against a Federal offensive. Union Major General George Thomas probed Johnston's line hoping to exploit the weakened Confederate army.

The major fighting at Dug Gap occurred on May 7–12, 1864, when Federal troops under the command of Brigadier General John W. Geary engaged in a feint assault against the well-entrenched Confederates on the precarious and easily defended mountainside. The Federals' attack was intended to draw Confederate attention away from Major General James B. McPherson's flanking movement through Snake Creek Gap to the outskirts of Resaca. The movement was intended to place his army in a position to block the Confederate line of retreat. During the fighting, the Confederate defenders launched boulders from their stone breastworks on top of the attacking Union soldiers.

After McPherson's failure to take Resaca on May 9, 1864, Major General William T. Sherman began a generalized withdrawal from the outskirts of Dalton to join McPherson at Resaca. When Johnston discovered the Federal army's move, he too retired south to Resaca and arrived first.

The Dug Gap Battlefield Park has a small parking area directly off Walnut Avenue. A path from the parking area leads to almost fifteen hundred feet of Confederate breastworks constructed of large boulders where visitors can view the precarious conditions faced by the attacking soldiers from General Geary's division.

Hamilton House

John Hamilton built this house and stone springhouse in the early 1840s. During the Civil War, Confederate Brigadier General Joseph H. Lewis of the famed Kentucky Orphan Brigade used this house for his headquarters in the winter of 1863–1864. His tent was pitched at a site near the springhouse. Located on the grounds of the Crown Gardens, the house contains a museum that highlights the early history of Dalton, including a Civil War artifacts room.

701 Chattanooga Ave.
Dalton, GA

To visit, contact the
Crown Gardens and Achives:
706-278-0217

Statue of General Joseph E. Johnston (NRHP)

The only statue in the United States honoring Virginia-born Confederate army commander General Joseph E. Johnston is located in downtown Dalton. Johnston had largely been responsible for the Confederate victory at the First Battle of Manassas early in the war. However, a strained personal relationship with President Jefferson Davis and a cautious nature hampered Johnston's effectiveness throughout the war. The United Daughters of the Confederacy dedicated this statue on October 12, 1912. Artist and sculptor Belle Kinney designed the bronze statue, which is on the National Register of Historic Places.

Hamilton St. and Crawford St.
Dalton, GA

Left: *Statue of General Joseph E. Johnston in downtown Dalton (Photo: Bob Price)*

LAFAYETTE, Walker County

Walker County Chamber of
Commerce
P.O. Box 430
Rock Spring, GA 30739
706-375-7702
www.walkercochamber.com

Below: *John B. Gordon (Courtesy of the Library of Congress).* Right: *John B. Gordon Hall (Photo: Bob Price)*

In September 1863, Union Major General William S. Rosecrans advanced into Georgia from Chattanooga, Tennessee, in pursuit of General Braxton Bragg's Confederate army. From his headquarters in LaFayette, Bragg learned that the Federals had divided their forces. Union Major General George H. Thomas' twenty-thousand-man XIV Corps had crossed Stevens Gap over Lookout Mountain and marched into the confined McLemore's Cove. Bragg ordered an attack to destroy Thomas' vulnerable corps, but poor coordination by the Confederates resulted in inaction and a missed opportunity. Fighting occurred at Davis Crossroads on September 10, but Federal forces were able to strengthen their position, making Bragg's attacks unsuccessful.

In June 1864, 450 Union soldiers were quartered at the old courthouse in LaFayette. Just before daylight on June 24, a Confederate cavalry force of one thousand troopers launched a surprise attack. The intense fighting went building to building until Federal reinforcements arrived to drive off the attackers. This little-known but bloody struggle was one of the few Civil War conflicts fought in a town.

John B. Gordon Hall (NRHP)

306 North Main St.
LaFayette, GA 30728
www.roadsidegeorgia.com/site/
gordonhall.html

Built in 1836, the two-story red-brick Chattooga Academy, now the John B. Gordon Hall, is believed to be the oldest brick schoolhouse still standing in Georgia. Confederate General Braxton Bragg used the school as his headquarters on September 10–17, 1863. Under a large oak tree in front, Bragg and his officers formulated the plans that resulted in the Battle of Chickamauga. The tree later became known as the Bragg Oak, which was destroyed in 1920 after being struck by lightning.

The school was also the scene of fierce fighting on June 24, 1864, during the Battle of LaFayette. A Confederate force under Captain William V. Harrell attacked the Union troops occupying the building, which housed commissary stores.

On November 15, 1936, the old school building was renamed for one of its early pupils, John B. Gordon, a Confederate major general and governor of Georgia. The building is currently owned by the City of LaFayette, which received a preservation grant in 2005 to restore the building. A Confederate monument and stack of cannonballs can also be found on the grounds.

LaFayette Presbyterian Church

107 North Main St.
LaFayette, GA 30728
706-638-3932

The LaFayette Presbyterian Church was organized in 1836; the present brick building was built in 1848. During the Civil War, the church served as a field hospital for both armies; surgeries were performed on planks laid across the pews. The Confederate dead were buried in the LaFayette Cemetery a few blocks from the church.

Marsh House

Spencer Stewart Marsh built the Marsh House, now the Marsh-Warthen-Clements House, in 1836. When the Civil War came to northwest Georgia, he moved his family south to Cassville, Georgia, and Union troops occupied the house. The family returned to LaFayette after the war to find the furniture and household items missing and the downstairs floors stained with blood and marked with hoofprints. Many bullets were lodged in the outer walls, and bullet holes pierced the glass, remnants from the battle fought in downtown LaFayette on June 24, 1864.

Walker County purchased the house in 2003, and a restoration is in progress. The Marsh House is also undergoing the approval process to be listed on the National Register of Historic Places.

308 North Main St.
LaFayette, GA 30728
706-638-5187
www.marshhouseoflafayette.com

Open weekends or by appointment

Left: *Marsh House (Photo: Jim Lockhart, Historic Preservation DIvision, Georgia Dept. of Natural Resources)*

McLemore's Cove (NRHP)

McLemore's Cove, a broad, beautiful valley with pristine grasslands between Lookout Mountain and Pigeon Mountain, was the site of a failed attempt to trap twenty thousand Federal troops of the Army of the Cumberland in September 1863. Union Major General George H. Thomas' corps escaped the cove before the disorganized Confederates could strike. The skirmish at Davis Crossroads occurred near the present-day intersection of GA Hwy. 193 and Hogjowl Road on September 10, 1863.

GA Hwy. 193
LaFayette, GA

RESACA, Gordon County

Resaca, a small village along the Western and Atlantic Railroad where the railroad crosses the Oostanaula River, was named in honor of the U.S. victory at the Battle of Resaca de la Palma during the Mexican-American War. Resaca again became associated with warfare when the first large-scale battle of the Atlanta Campaign, the Battle of Resaca, occurred here on May 14–15, 1864.

On May 9, 1864. Major General James B. McPherson's Army of the Tennessee made a flanking maneuver through Ship's Gap, Villanow, and the Snake Creek Gap. This was an attempt to get behind General Joseph E. Johnston's army in Dalton to block an escape route and cut the railroad supply line, thus opening a clear, unimpeded path to Atlanta. Major General William T. Sherman, who ordered the movement, stressed its importance to McPherson, "Strike hard as it may save us what we have most reason to apprehend, and a slow pursuit, in which he gains strength as we lose it." It would have been a brilliant movement had it been carried out as ordered.

Near the present intersection of I-75 and Lafayette Road/State Highway 136, a force of approximately four thousand Confederates, a combination of two Confederate brigades and a handful of Georgia Military Institute cadets, were stationed at Fort Wayne and the surrounding hills to guard the railroad in Johnston's rear. They were all that

Calhoun-Gordon County CVB
300 South Wall St.
Calhoun, GA 30701
706-625-3200/800-887-3811
www.exploregordoncounty.com

stood between the Federal army and Confederate defeat. McPherson could have easily taken their position and gained the advantageous plateau of Fort Wayne, a hilltop earthwork controlling the railroad. Furthermore, the Snake Creek Gap should never have been left undefended, an oversight that could have cost the Confederates the campaign. McPherson, plagued by indecision and a lack of reconnaissance, chose to do nothing, when with aggressive leadership he could have exploited a great advantage. By the time Johnston's army withdrew from Dalton to march the short distance to Resaca and meet the threat, the Federal opportunity was lost.

On May 12, Lt. General Leonidas Polk's Army of Mississippi arrived in north Georgia with a force that included the troops sent west by Johnston in February, which added considerable strength to the Army of Tennessee for the coming campaign. Johnston designated Polk's force as the III Corps. The combination of forces now under Johnston's command totaled approximately sixty-six thousand men. The Confederate lines in the hilly country surrounding Resaca could easily accommodate this number. The left end of their line was anchored on the Oostanaula River near the present-day intersection of I-75 and Highway 136. The right end, Lt. General John B. Hood's corps, was anchored to the northeast by the Conasauga River.

Skirmishing began on May 13, two miles to the west of Resaca. A cavalry fight between Major General Joseph Wheeler and Federal Brigadier General Judson Kilpatrick resulted in the Confederates giving ground while Kilpatrick received a serious thigh wound. The Federal Army of the Tennessee passed the now-stationary cavalry and occupied a small range of hills (visible today looking west from the I-75 off-ramp at Highway 136) that gave them an advantageous view of the Confederate positions. The Army of the Cumberland was stationed on McPherson's left, thus holding the center, while the Army of the Ohio held the far left, partially encircling the village of Resaca.

Johnston, realizing the precariousness of his position, moved the rest of his army from Dalton to Resaca on the wagon road he had improved during the preceding weeks for just such a maneuver. With the arrival of the entire Confederate army, the two forces occupied opposing lines on generally high ground facing each other across the Camp Creek Valley and the Conasauga River Valley.

The Battle of Resaca began in earnest on May 14, 1864, with fighting breaking out over much of the line. The heaviest combat took place between McPherson's and Polk's forces on the southern end of the field and between Major General John Schofield's and Lt. General William Hardee's forces farther to the north. Hard combat also occurred at a salient held by the renowned Kentucky Orphan Brigade. Constant Federal assaults eventually forced the Confederates out of the hilltop redoubt, giving the Federal artillery a position within range that could threaten Fort Wayne and the Western and Atlantic Railroad bridge over the Oostanaula River. Artillery fire drove the Confederates to erect a temporary bridge about a mile upriver, out of gun range. While this was occurring, Hood's corps on the right was ordered to attack a gap between the divisions of Federal generals David S. Stanley and Thomas J. Wood. The movement got underway too late and was not well coordinated. Part of the line made contact with elements of Major General Stanley's troops but was unable to break through and ground to a halt as darkness intervened.

On May 15, 1864, the second day of fighting, Federal Brigadier General Thomas W. Sweeny's division crossed the Oostanaula River on a pontoon bridge near Lay's Ferry. Sweeny was attempting a movement around the Confederate army's left flank since Johnston's line could not be broken by direct frontal assault.

Below: *The Resaca battleground (Courtesy of the Library of Congress)*

While Sweeny was crossing the river to the southwest, bitter fighting was taking place to the north, where the Federal brigades of Colonel David Ireland and William T. Ward were assaulting the Confederate four-gun battery of Captain Maxillian Van Den Corput's Cherokee Artillery. The attackers, led by Colonel Benjamin Harrison, who replaced Ward in command after the latter was wounded during the attack, managed to overrun the battery driving away the gunners. The costly attack accomplished nothing beyond forcing the battery to cease its destructive fire. That evening the Federals dug through the battery's earthen wall and, using rope lassos, captured one of Van Den Corput's guns. Harrison would later gain fame as the twenty-third president of the United States.

Sweeny had gained a strong bridgehead on the south bank of the Oostanaula at Lay's Ferry below Johnston's army, putting the Confederates in a perilous position with the river at their backs. Because Sweeny could easily cut the railroad near Calhoun and since McPherson was threatening the railroad bridge at Resaca, Johnston was forced to withdraw his army and move south. The Confederates retreated from Resaca to Cassville, a distance of thirty miles, and took up strong positions north of the Etowah River. Sherman's army followed in close pursuit.

Practically the entire force of both armies was present during the fighting in and around Resaca, entrenched in parallel fishhook-shaped lines. The casualties were almost equal, with the Federals suffering 2,747 and the Confederates losing 2,800. Though the Confederates were not defeated in combat, technically the battle was a Federal victory because the Union army was left in control of the field as a result of its flanking movement while the southern army retreated. The ferociousness of the fighting was an indication of the combat that was to come during the Atlanta Campaign, which was later dubbed the Hundred Days Battle.

From 1997 to 2000, the Georgia Civil War Commission and the Friends of Resaca preservation group spearheaded an effort to acquire the well-preserved Resaca Battlefield. With donations and help from numerous private organizations, 506 acres were purchased with the intention of making the site into a state battlefield park. As of this writing, the plans for a park have not yet been realized.

Atlanta Campaign Pavilion #3

U.S. 41 approx. 2 miles north of Resaca

This is the third in the series of WPA-era markers. The pavilion, surrounded by a stone wall and containing metal topographic maps, is located behind the historic position of the Confederate lines and at the opening of the road to the Resaca Confederate Cemetery. The fighting at and around Resaca, as well as the flanking movement and rear guard action at Lay's Ferry, is explained in detail at this pavilion.

Duncan Norton House

Walker St.
Resaca, GA

This architecturally unusual brick house with strong Gothic Revival elements is one of the few structures in Resaca that remains from the time of the Battle of Resaca, when it served as a hospital. The house is also visible in the distance in a period photograph taken by George N. Barnard after the battle. The Duncan Norton House is currently undergoing an extensive rehabilitation. Although it is not open to the public, the home is in a quiet residential neighborhood with little automobile traffic and can be easily viewed from the street.

Right: *Duncan Norton House*
(Photo: Barry Brown)

Fort Wayne

U.S. Hwy. 41 at the Oostanaula River

Originally a Confederate training camp and staging area constructed in 1862, Fort Wayne consists of two separate earthworks placed several hundred yards apart. Strategically located, Fort Wayne sits on a high ridgeline overlooking Resaca and the Western and Atlantic Railroad bridge across the Oostanaula River, the site it was intended to protect. By May 1864, Confederates had heavily fortified the area around the earthworks and placed several batteries at the position. The first artillery shots of the Battle of Resaca were fired from here at the advance elements of Major General James B. McPherson's army on Bald Hill.

Following the Battle of Resaca, after General Joseph E. Johnston moved his army south of the Oostanaula River, the Federals occupied the earthwork and strengthened the position by constructing a large redoubt encircled by a double line of trenches. A Federal garrison was stationed at Fort Wayne from May 1864 through the early stages the Reconstruction period and was withdrawn in 1868.

In 2003, the Friends of Resaca in conjunction with the Gordon County Commission acquired the sixty-seven additional acres of the Resaca Battlefield that contain Fort Wayne. Though not currently open to the public, plans are underway to make the area part of a Gordon County Battlefield Park along with the 506 acres to the west that were acquired by the state in 2000.

Oostanaula River Bridge

Although the current CSX railroad bridge over the Oostanaula River is of a more recent era, it was built atop the supports from the original Western and Atlantic Railroad bridge that was constructed c. 1850. During the Great Locomotive Chase in April 1862, Andrews' Raiders considered this bridge a prime target and tried to set it on fire. Their attempt was foiled by recent rains, which had saturated the bridge's timbers and prevented their being ignited.

During the Battle of Resaca, the bridge was once again the focus of Federal efforts to capture it, but to no avail. After the battle, both armies crossed the bridge as they moved south. Worth noting: the fine ashlar granite stonework by the Irish stonemasons who constructed the prewar bridge is still visible at either end.

U.S. 41 south of Hwy. 136 at the present CSX bridge over the river

Left: *Andrews' Raiders crossing the Oostanaula River Bridge. Painting by Wilbur Kurtz (Courtesy of the Atlanta History Center)*

Resaca Confederate Cemetery

Shortly after the war, town resident Mary J. Green and her sister Pyatt Green organized an effort to rebury the Confederate dead, moving them from their crude battlefield burial sites to proper graves in the Resaca Confederate Cemetery. Today, graves of 420 unknown Confederate soldiers are arranged in concentric circles around a large cross. Mrs. E.J. Simmons, a member of one of the committees that worked with Mary Green to establish the cemetery, is buried here as well. A stone arch tops the cemetery entry gate, and large stately oaks shade the grounds. Confederate Memorial Day services are held here annually.

U.S. 41 at County Rd. 297 on the right at the end of the road

Daily: Daylight hours

Left: *Resaca Confederate Cemetery (Photo: Barry Brown)*

ADAIRSVILLE, Bartow County

Cartersville-Bartow County CVB
One Friendship Plaza, Suite 1
Cartersville, GA 30120
770-387-1357/800-733-2280
www.notatlanta.org/adairsville
.html

Adairsville had its first brush with Civil War action during the Great Locomotive Chase in April 1862, when the pursuers appropriated the southbound engine *Texas*, disconnected the cars, and quickly steamed in reverse in pursuit of the northward bound Andrews' Raiders.

During the Atlanta Campaign on May 17–18, 1864, General Joseph E. Johnston's army, after departing Resaca and fighting the Lay's Ferry rear guard action, attempted to establish a defensive line across the Oothcaloga Valley, in which Adairsville is located. However, the valley was too wide to accommodate his army and lacked natural anchors to protect his flanks. Combat did occur on the outskirts of Adairsville between cavalry units and at the Robert Saxon House, also known as the Octagon House. Here Major General Oliver Otis Howard's IV Corps attacked Confederates from Major General Benjamin F. Cheatham's division. The commanding officer of the attacking force was Major Arthur MacArthur, the father of future U.S. Supreme Commander of the Southwest Pacific Forces during World War II General Douglas MacArthur. The attack was called off due to the onset of darkness, and the Confederates withdrew. The Octagon House no longer exists.

Right: Painting by Wilbur Kurtz depicting Andrews' Raiders destroying railroad tracks and telegraph lines (Courtesy of the Atlanta History Center)

Adairsville Depot (NRHP)

Adairsville Square
Adairsville, GA

Right: A display in the Adairsville Depot commemorating Andrews' Raid (Photo: Bob Price)

Before the Civil War, the 1845 Adairsville Depot was at the center of a major Western and Atlantic Railroad repair facility. During the war, it played an important part in the Great Locomotive Chase on April 12, 1862. Captain William A. Fuller was forced to abandon the engine *William R. Smith*, which he had commandeered outside Kingston, when he ran into track destroyed by the raiders. Fuller and his crew traveled the last three miles to the Adairsville Depot running on foot. At

Adairsville, the raiders in the *General* were forced to wait for the southbound engine the *Texas* to pass before they could continue. When Fuller arrived in Adairsville, he commandeered the *Texas* by standing in the middle of the tracks brandishing a pistol. He and his men unhitched the freight cars, letting them off at a siding, and continued their pursuit of the Andrews' Raiders. However, they had to spend the rest of their northward chase traveling in reverse, mostly at full throttle.

The Adairsville Depot is at the center of Adairsville's annual Great Locomotive Chase Festival held on the first weekend in October.

Barnsley Gardens (NRHP)

Godfrey Barnsley, an English-born Savannah-based cotton merchant, built Barnsley Gardens in 1840 on land ceded by the Creek nation. He believed this land in the north Georgia piedmont would be a healthier climate than the hot, mosquito-laden low country along the coast. Barnsley intended the house to be a gift for his wife, Savannah socialite Julia Scarborough. The house, known as the Woodlands, was architecturally quite different from the typical prosperous Georgia plantation of the period. Designed with Italianate as opposed to Greek Revival influences, the magnificent landscaping and intricate boxwood parterre garden showed the influence of Andrew Jackson Downing, one of America's early landscape architects and horticulturalists.

597 Barnsley Gardens Rd.
Adairsville, GA 30103
877-773-2447
www.barnsleygardensresort.com

Barnsley, a man with obvious Southern sympathies, had two sons in the Confederate army and a daughter married to a Confederate officer. On May 18, 1864, while attempting to warn Barnsley of the Federals' approach, Confederate cavalry officer Colonel Richard G. Earle was shot dead in the yard. This precipitated a cavalry skirmish on the grounds between Earle's men and advance units of Federal cavalry. The skirmish was depicted on the pages of the Northern newspaper *Harper's Weekly*.

Charles Wright Willis, of the 103rd Illinois Infantry, wrote this account of the event in his book *Army Life of an Illinois Soldier*: "May 18, 1864. Our cavalry had a sharp fight here this P.M. and on one of the gravel walks in the beautiful garden lies a Rebel colonel, shot in five places." Colonel Earle was laid to rest in a prominent place in the perennial garden and remains there today.

Below: *The ruins of Woodlands and the boxwood garden* (Photo: Marla Bexley-Brown)

Major General James B. McPherson spent the night of May 18 in the home. Although he forbade any looting, Barnsley's Irish maid Mary Quinn is recorded to have referred to McPherson as a gentleman surrounded by rogues and thieves as statuary was smashed, windows and china broken, and wine and stored foods consumed or stolen. Woodlands, however, remained intact until a 1906 tornado tore away the roof of the main house, leaving only the kitchen wing untouched.

Today, the estate is an upscale golfing destination with outstanding dining and fine accommodations. It also houses the Barnsley Family History Museum and world-class gardens.

ROME, Floyd County

Greater Rome CVB
402 Civic Center Dr.
Rome, GA 30161
706-295-5576/800-444-1834
www.romegeorgia.org

Below: *Confederate Women's Monument in Rome's Myrtle Hill Cemetery (Photo: Mauriel Joslyn)*

Rome, founded shortly after the Land Lottery of 1832, is at the convergence of the Etowah and Oostanaula rivers and the headwater of the Coosa River. Like its European namesake, it is surrounded by seven hills. A prime site for water-powered manufacturing, it supplied military goods, such as cannons, munitions, and haversacks, to the Confederacy. Because of this, Rome was the target of two Federal initiatives during the War Between the States.

In late April and early May 1863, Federal raider Colonel Abel D. Streight, in command of seventeen hundred men and seven hundred mules, set out on a raid across northern Alabama, intending to destroy the industrial capacity of Rome. Riding through the frontier wilderness of northern Alabama, Streight and his men held a five-day running battle with Major General Nathan Bedford Forrest and his cavalry, beginning at the western Alabama border and ending near the Georgia border. After an almost superhuman contest of endurance, Streight and his superior force were driven to complete exhaustion and finally surrendered to Forrest and his battalion of less than five hundred mounted soldiers. Forrest had used a ruse to fool Streight into thinking he was outnumbered. The chase ended at the Lawrence Plantation between Gadsden, Alabama, and Rome, Georgia, saving Rome from capture and destruction. Forrest received a hero's welcome when he arrived in Rome on May 3, 1863, while Streight was sent to Richmond, Virginia's infamous Libby Prison.

Even though it failed, Streight's raid brought the reality of the perils of war to the people of Rome. The city appropriated three thousand dollars for the construction of a line of fortifications on three of the seven hills around the city, using slave labor for the project. On August 21, 1863, the *Rome Weekly Courier* wrote, "The fort in Desoto shall be known as Fort Attaway. The fort in Hillsboro (now Myrtle Hill) shall be known as Fort Stovall. The fort between Rome and Woodville shall be known as Fort Norton on Jackson Hill."

On May 15, 1864, Federal Brigadier General Jefferson C. Davis' division, which was detached from the main army, marched on Rome. Before reaching the city limits, Davis' soldiers were met by Major General Samuel G. French's Confederate division arrayed in line of battle and ready to defend their ground. Fighting ensued and on May 17, 1864, Davis drove French into Rome but was halted after sharp skirmishing by the guns of Fort Attaway. Entrenched on the opposing Shorter Hill, Davis constructed battery positions within range of the Coosa River and fired on Confederate supply ships. Starting at three o'clock in the morning on May 18, 1864, the Confederates began evacuating Rome. By dusk on May 19, 1864, only the local militia remained to guard the city. Davis easily took the city's forts, and shortly thereafter, Rome fell. The city was garrisoned by Federal troops until November 10, 1864, when the war industries were burned as the Union army moved south as a prelude to the March to the Sea.

First Presbyterian Church of Rome

101 East Third Ave.
Rome, GA 30161
706-291-6033
www.fpcrome.org

The First Presbyterian Church of Rome, one of the city's oldest churches, was built in 1856. The building was used by Federal soldiers to store food and supplies during their May–November 1864 occupation of Rome. The soldiers also removed the original pews to build horse stalls and a pontoon bridge and poured molasses down the organ's pipes.

Fort Norton

Following the panic produced by the failed Abel Streight Raid on July 13, 1863, the Rome City Council allocated three thousand dollars to build a string of forts on the hills surrounding the city. General Braxton Bragg ordered that the fortifications "be completed in proper military style and manned with siege guns." Over the next few months the forts were constructed using slave labor under the authority of West Point–trained engineer Confederate Major General Gustavus W. Smith. Fort Attaway sat on Desoto Hill along the west bank of the Oostanuala River; Fort Stovall was on the south bank atop Myrtle Hill; and Fort Norton was constructed on Jackson Hill on the east bank north of the city.

When Union Brigadier General Jefferson C. Davis approached Rome on May 15, 1864, he reported, "Two formidable fieldworks, one situated on the east bank of the Oostanaula and the other on the south bank of the Coosa. The works look too strong I thought it imprudent to storm them hastily." Although shelling from Fort Attaway stalled Davis, the Confederates, under orders from General Joseph E. Johnston, pulled out of Rome within the next two days, leaving the city open to the Federal invaders. Today, the well-preserved earthworks are protected in the Rome City Park atop Civic Center Hill.

On Jackson Hill overlooking the visitors center
Rome, GA

Below, left to right: *Fort Norton, one of the ring of forts constructed in 1863 to protect Rome from invasion; Rome's tribute to Nathan Bedford Forrest in Myrtle Hill Cemetery (Photos: Bob Price)*

Myrtle Hill Cemetery (NRHP)

Much about the Civil War history of Rome can be found in the picturesque Myrtle Hill Cemetery. During the war, the site was known as Hillsboro and served as one of Rome's hilltop defensive fortifications, named Fort Stovall, guarding the southern approaches to the city. Today, a monument to the Floyd County Confederates who fought for the defense of Rome marks the site of the fort. At the base of Myrtle Hill is the city cemetery, which dates from 1857. It is the final resting place of 363 Confederate and 2 Union soldiers who died in Rome hospitals. Rome native John Wisdom, considered a Civil War Paul Revere who rode from Alabama to warn Rome of the approach of Colonel Abel D. Streight's raiders, is buried here.

Monuments to honor Confederate Major General Nathan Bedford Forrest and the perseverance and sacrifice of Confederate women are also located in Myrtle Hill Cemetery.

South Broad St. and Myrtle St. at the Coosa River
Rome, GA

Noble Brothers Foundry

On Civic Center Hill
Rome, GA
800-444-1834

Open daily

The Noble Brothers Foundry, a major machine shop and foundry that manufactured arms during the war, was one of the objectives of Colonel Able D. Streight's failed raid. Opened by the Noble Brothers in 1847, the foundry was located at First and Broad streets, a site convenient to both the railroad and the Etowah River. In 1861, cannon production increased along with other war-related materiels. The giant lathe turned out many cannons for the Confederacy until the Confederate government halted operations due to charges that the foundry was manufacturing inferior product. The investigation into the matter was never completed as the Federal army occupied the town and later burned the foundry on November 10–11, 1864. The marks visible on the lathe's faceplate were made by sledgehammers wielded by Union soldiers attempting to destroy it.

Today, the lathe is displayed outside the Rome Visitors Center at the base of Civic Center Hill, along with a Corliss steam engine, the type used during the war to power the foundry machinery. A trail next to the lathe leads to Fort Norton at the top of the hill.

CAVE SPRING, Floyd County

www.cityofcavespring.com

Greater Rome CVB
402 Civic Center Dr.
Rome, GA 30161
706-295-5576/800-444-1843
www.romegeorgia.org

Cave Spring, named after the picturesque mineral spring emanating from a limestone cave, was established in 1832 as a health resort. In 1846, the Georgia Asylum for the Deaf and Dumb (later the Georgia School for the Deaf) opened in Cave Spring and is still in operation today. Temporarily closed in 1862–1867 due to the Civil War, the school's Fannin Hall was used as a hospital by both Confederate and Federal forces. Confederate General John B. Hood met with his superior, General P.G.T. Beauregard, in Cave Spring for a conference on October 9, 1864, to discuss Hood's plan for the invasion of Tennessee. Today Fannin Hall serves as the Cave Spring city offices.

KINGSTON, Bartow County

Cartersville-Bartow County CVB
One Friendship Plaza, Ste. 1
Cartersville, GA 30120
770-387-1357/800-733-2280
www.notatlanta.org/kingston
.html

Kingston, a town whose history is inextricably tied to the Western and Atlantic Railroad, experienced a number of noteworthy events during the Civil War. Kingston was a major center for the shipment of potassium nitrate, or saltpeter, used for the production of gunpowder at the Confederate Powder Works in Augusta, Georgia. The mine near Kingston was taken over by the Confederate Nitrate Bureau early in the war and operated until the Federal army forced it to cease operation in May 1864.

The Great Locomotive Chase came through Kingston on April 12, 1862. Andrews' Raiders were forced to wait for over an hour on a sidetrack in Kingston while several southbound freight trains steamed through town. It was also in Kingston that Captain William A. Fuller and his party abandoned the small Cooper's Iron Works yard engine *Yonah* to continue their pursuit with the more powerful engine *William R. Smith*.

Both Confederate and Federal armies marched through Kingston on the way to Atlanta. When Major General William T. Sherman spent May 19–23, 1864, in Kingston, he developed a plan to move his army off of the railroad supply line and to the west towards Dallas

Above: *Noble Brothers Foundry*
(Photo: Bob Price)

in Paulding County. With the Confederate army entrenched in the natural fortification of the Allatoona Mountain range, a direct assault would have been suicidal. Sherman was familiar with the terrain, having years before worked as an engineer on the construction of the Western and Atlantic Railroad. By moving around the Confederate army's left, Sherman's continual flanking movements would force the Confederates to either retreat or fight at a disadvantage, a strategy that became known as the "red clay minuet."

After the armies moved south, Kingston served as a supply base for the Federal army. In November 1864, while General John B. Hood's army marched north for the Tennessee Campaign, Sherman was in Kingston conducting much of his telegraph correspondence with Lt. General Ulysses S. Grant on the strategies that would end the Civil War. He ultimately wrote his final orders for the March to the Sea while occupying the V.B. Hargis House, which the Federals burned upon departing.

Prior to Federal occupation, Kingston served as a Confederate hospital center. A monument honoring the women who cared for thousands of Confederate and Union sick and wounded at the eight Confederate hospitals in Kingston can be seen at the southern end of the city park. Kingston was also the site of the last surrender of Confederate troops east of the Mississippi on May 12, 1865, by their commander, Brigadier General William T. Wofford.

Below: *Kingston after having recently been occupied by Sherman's troops (Courtesy of the UGA Hargrett Rare Book and Manuscript Library)*

Kingston Civil War Museum and Woman's History Museum

Both the Kingston Civil War Museum and Woman's History Museum are housed in the same building. The Civil War Museum portrays Kingston's role in the War Between the States, along with memorabilia from past Confederate Memorial Day observances.

The Woman's History Museum, the newest museum in the Martha Mulinix Annex Building, displays information about the varied history of Kingston and the surrounding area through artifacts, scrapbooks, and photographs. For additional information call the Welcome Center at 770-387-1357.

13 East Main St.
Kingston, GA

Sat.–Sun.: 1:00 p.m.–4:00 p.m.

Kingston Confederate Cemetery

Johnston St.
Kingston, GA

In the Kingston Confederate Cemetery a Confederate monument marks the graves of 250 Confederate soldiers, only one of whom is known. Two unknown Federal soldiers are also buried here, and a large obelisk honors the dead from both armies. The soldiers interred here were wounded in most of the major battles of the Western Theater and died in Kingston hospitals between 1862 and May 1864.

The cemetery is the site of one of the nation's earliest Decoration Day ceremonies, where the occupying Federal troops under Brigadier General Henry M. Judah allowed local women to decorate the graves of the war dead provided that the Federal graves were also decorated. Held on the last Saturday in April throughout Georgia, this ceremony eventually evolved into Confederate Memorial Day, observed as a state holiday.

Left: *Kingston Confederate Cemetery (Photo: Bob Price)*

Kingston Depot

Downtown Kingston
Kingston, GA

The stone foundation is all that remains of the Kingston Depot, where during their pursuit of Andrews' Raiders Captain William A. Fuller, Jeff Cain, and Anthony Murphy exchanged the small underpowered yard engine *Yonah*, which they borrowed from the Cooper's Iron Works in Cartersville, for the locomotive *William R. Smith*. This engine, which was located a short distance north of town, took the pursuers as far as Adairsville on this leg of the Great Locomotive Chase.

The Federals burned the Kingston business district and the depot upon departing the area on November 13, 1864. This wanton destruction was seen as a prelude to the total warfare methods Major General William T. Sherman inflicted on the civilian population on the March to the Sea.

Right: *Wilbur Kurtz painting depicting Andrews' Raiders bluffing their way through Kingston (Courtesy of the Atlanta History Center)*

Kingston Methodist Church

The only church to survive the town's burning, the 1854 Kingston Methodist Church was used as a hospital during the war. Afterward, former Army of Northern Virginia brigade commander Brigadier General Clement Anselm Evans entered the Methodist Episcopal ministry and served as a pastor here.

Church St.
Kingston, GA

Left: *Kingston Methodist Church (Photo: Bob Price)*

McCravey-Johnston House

Bartow County native Brigadier General William T. Wofford used the McCravey-Johnston House, which survived the Federal burning of Kingston in November 1864, as his headquarters. There on May 12, 1865, he surrendered approximately four thousand troops to Federal Brigadier General Henry M. Judah. This was the last Confederate surrender of troops east of the Mississippi River.

Church St. opposite the City Park
Kingston, GA

CASSVILLE, Bartow County

A thriving town during the antebellum period, Cassville was founded in 1833. With a prewar population of fifteen hundred, this Etowah Valley village in the northwest Georgia mountains was the seat of Cass County. It was also an educational and cultural center, including the site of the Cassville Female College. After the First Battle of Manassas in Virginia in 1861, the state legislature voted to change the county's name to Bartow in honor of Georgia Colonel Francis S. Bartow, killed in the battle.

During the Atlanta Campaign, while the opposing armies were marching through Bartow County, Major General William T. Sherman sought an opportunity to flank the Confederate army out of its position at Kingston. At the time, the retreating Confederate army divided temporarily at Adairsville and regrouped at Cassville. General Joseph E. Johnston hoped Sherman would divide his army, which would give the Confederates an opportunity to attack and destroy a portion of the Federal army before reinforcements could arrive. Fulfilling Johnston's wishes, Sherman did divide his force, ordering generals John Schofield's and Joseph Hooker's corps to Cassville in an attempt to flank the Confederates and force their retreat farther south. The divided Federal army was vulnerable to attack from its flank and front. However, Johnston's carefully laid plan unraveled when Lt. General John B. Hood failed to move his corps on the offense, thus losing the opportunity. His hopes dashed, Johnston had his army dig in on a ridgeline with the idea of making another stand, but well-placed Federal artillery fire made the position untenable. At Hood's urging, Johnston again moved his army south toward the Allatoona Mountain range. By dawn on May 20, 1864, Johnston again retreated to a new defensive line centered on the deep railroad cut at Allatoona Pass.

Cassville survived the first Federal occupation in May 1864 relatively unscathed. However, in October 1864 while the Union army was following Hood on his march

Cartersville-Bartow County CVB
One Friendship Plaza, Ste. 1
Cartersville, GA 30120
770-387-1357/800-733-2280
www.notatlanta.org/cassville
.html

through northwest Georgia into Alabama, Cassville would not fare well. The Federal army again used Cassville as a base of operations. Sherman did much of the planning for the March to the Sea from here. Upon departing, the Federals burned the town and many surrounding structures, sparing only the churches. In fact, almost all structures within a five-mile radius of Cassville were destroyed.

The reason for this scorched-earth policy remained unknown for more than a century until a Federal officer's diary came to light with an explanation. According to the diary, Cassville and the area around it was a center of Confederate partisan guerrilla activity where Federal patrols had been ambushed and some of the soldiers killed. On the evening of November 5, 1864, the town was razed in retaliation for these deaths.

Right: The site marker for Cassville, one of the Georgia towns that ceased to exist after Sherman's army marched through the area (Photo: Bob Price)

After the war, Cassville was never rebuilt, and today, much like the once thriving mill town of New Manchester in Douglas County, it is a lost community. The ruins of the Cassville Depot are still evident. A stone WPA roadside marker on the Cassville/White Road marks the location of the former town's courthouse square.

Atlanta Campaign Pavilion #4

U.S. 41 and Cassville/White Rd.

This is the fourth, and the largest, of the five Atlanta Campaign Pavilions erected as part of the New Deal's Works Progress Administration. It was constructed in the 1930s under the National Park Service. Currently, the steel topographical map showing the troop movements around Cassville is missing, and the pavilion is in need of repair. However, the state historical marker provides information about the activities that occurred in the area.

Cassville Confederate Cemetery

Pinelog Rd.
Cassville, GA

A large obelisk placed in the Cassville Confederate Cemetery in 1878 by the Ladies Memorial Association recounts the burial of approximately one known and three hundred unknown Confederate soldiers who died of disease or wounds in the several Confederate hospitals in Cassville. However, these burials represent only a portion of the patients who died in Cassville during the war as many bodies were later claimed by relatives and were relocated.

Outstanding Mexican-American War veteran and Army of Northern Virginia Confederate Brigadier General William T. Wofford is also buried here. Wofford served in Lt. General James Longstreet's corps of General Robert E. Lee's Army of Northern Virginia from May 1862 to May 1864. Wofford assumed command of fellow Georgian T.R.R. Cobb's legion after the latter was fatally wounded at Fredericksburg, Virginia, in December 1862. Wofford died near Cassville on May 22, 1884.

Left to right: Cassville Confederate Cemetery and the grave of Brigadier General William T. Wofford (Photos: Bob Price)

CARTERSVILLE, Bartow County

On May 19, 1864, Confederate General Joseph E. Johnston established a rear guard force in Cartersville. Barricading themselves inside the Cartersville Depot, the troops knocked out blocks in the walls for firing ports. Major General William T. Sherman's forces attacked on May 20, burning the building's wood roof and floors.

Cartersville-Bartow County CVB
One Friendship Plaza, Ste. 1
Cartersville, GA 30120
770-387-1357/800-733-2280
www.notatlanta.org/cartersville
.html

Bartow History Center and Museum

The Bartow History Center and Museum documents over two hundred years of Bartow County's history, beginning with prehistoric aboriginal occupation. Civil War displays include weapons, artifacts recovered from nearby battlefields, photos, and maps. An archive is available to researchers.

13 North Wall St.
Cartersville, GA 30120
770-382-3818
www.bartowhistorycenter.org

Mon.–Sat.: 10:00 a.m.–5:00 p.m.
(open until 8:00 p.m. Thursdays)

Booth Western Art Museum

The Booth Western Art Museum, which opened in August 2003, features a permanent collection of contemporary western American and Civil War art. The large Civil War gallery showcases original art depicting Georgia campaigns and battles, including the Atlanta Campaign and the Battle of Allatoona Pass. Special exhibitions and visits by Civil War artists are featured during the year.

406 Old Mill Rd.
Cartersville, GA 30120
770-387-1300
www.boothmuseum.org

Tues.–Sat.: 10:00 a.m.–5:00 p.m.
(open until 8:00 p.m. Thursdays)
Sun.: 1:00 p.m.–5:00 p.m.

Cartersville Depot

Main Street at 1 Friendship Plaza
(GA Hwy. 113)
Cartersville, GA 30120
800-733-2280/770-387-1357
www.notatlanta.org

Mon.–Fri.: 8:30 a.m.–5:00 p.m.
Sat.: 11:00 a.m.–2:00 p.m.
Sun.: 1:30 p.m.–4:00 p.m.

The Cartersville Depot is the site of General Joseph E. Johnston's rear guard action against Federal forces on May 19–20, 1864. A large section of the original depot, approximately 40 feet wide and 124 feet long, survived the Federal attack on May 20. The restored depot is now home to the Cartersville–Bartow County Visitors Information Center.

Outside the depot stands the Cooper Friendship Monument, the only monument known to be erected by a debtor to honor his creditors. In 1860, iron mogul Mark Anthony Cooper built the monument to honor thirty-eight friends who aided him in a financial crisis.

Cooper's Iron Works (NRHP)

River Rd.
Cartersville, GA 30120
678-721-6700 (Corps of Engineers office)

(There is a walking trail to the iron works from the Corps of Engineers Visitors Center.)

Open mid-Mar. to late Oct.

A large stone blast furnace is the only remnant of the 1830s town of Etowah and the Etowah Mining and Manufacturing Company, Mark Anthony Cooper's iron empire. Cooper sold the iron works, which supplied munitions to the Confederacy, to the Confederate government in 1863. Union cavalry destroyed the factory and the surrounding town on May 21, 1864.

When traveling to the Cooper's Iron Works on U.S. Highway 41, note the five stone pillars in the Etowah River approximately three miles south of Cartersville. After retreating from Cassville on May 20, 1864, Confederate troops destroyed the railroad bridge these pillars supported. However, the U.S. Army Corps of Engineers immediately began restoring this vital rail line, rebuilding the bridge in just four days. On the hill immediately to the north, the Federal earthworks constructed to defend the railroad are visible. The Confederates made no further attempts to destroy the bridge, which gave the Federal garrison idle time to swim, hunt, and play baseball.

The Cooper's Iron Works offers visitors a scenic picnic area on the river, along with hiking trails and a playground, all maintained by the Corps of Engineers.

Right: *Ruins of Cooper's Iron Works (Photo: Bob Price)*

Oak Hill Cemetery

319 N. Erwin St.
Cartersville, GA 30120
770-387-5604

Cemetery hours: Daily until dark
Office hours: Mon.–Fri.:
7:00 a.m.–3:30 p.m.

Among the Confederates buried in Oak Hill Cemetery is Major General Pierce M.B. Young, who would have graduated from West Point in 1861 had he not resigned his appointment to join the Confederate army. He served with Major General J.E.B. Stuart's cavalry in Virginia while Federal troops occupied his Cartersville home. Young became the first Georgian seated in Congress after the Civil War and was the youngest major general in either the Confederate or Union armies.

Also found in the cemetery is the grave of Private David B. Freeman, who was born in 1851 and served in the 6th Georgia Cavalry. Oak Hill Cemetery officials believe he was the youngest combatant in the Civil War. Other notables include evangelist Sam Jones and Civil War–era satirist and humorist Bill Arp.

Left to right: *The grave of Private David Freeman, thought to be the youngest soldier to serve in the Civil War (Photo: Rich Elwell); Rose Lawn (Photo: Bob Price)*

Rose Lawn (NRHP)

Rose Lawn, a beautifully restored Victorian mansion and nineteenth-century carriage house, currently houses the United Daughters of the Confederacy's Civil War collection. The house sits across the street from the antebellum First Baptist Church, which received four thousand dollars from the U.S. government in 1904 in restitution for damages inflicted by Federal soldiers in 1864.

224 West Cherokee Ave.
Cartersville, GA 30120
770-387-5162
www.roselawnmuseum.com

Tues.–Fri.: 10:00 a.m.–noon,
1:00 p.m.–5:00 p.m.

LAKE ALLATOONA VICINITY, Bartow County

The small pre-Civil War town of Allatoona, built along Allatoona Creek, was a gold mining area that reached its height in the 1840s and 1850s. In 1864 during Major General William T. Sherman's Atlanta Campaign the town served as a major Union supply depot with a garrison of around nine hundred men. A brief, but fierce, battle was fought there on October 5, 1864. The town of Allatoona was destroyed in the late 1940s when Lake Allatoona was formed. The town was never rebuilt.

Cartersville-Bartow County CVB
One Friendship Plaza, Ste. 1
Cartersville, GA 30120
770-387-1357/800-733-2280
www.notatlanta.org

Left: *War-era depiction of Allatoona (Courtesy of the UGA Hargrett Rare Book and Manuscript Library)*

Battle of Allatoona Pass

Cartersville-Bartow County CVB
770-387-1357/800-733-2280
www.notatlanta.org

Etowah Valley Historical Society
770-606-8862

Above: Allatoona Pass *by Don
Troiani, which can be seen
in the Civil War Gallery in the
Booth Western Art Museum
(Courtesy of Don Troiani,
www.historicalartprints.com)*

Confederate General Joseph E. Johnston established defensive positions in the rugged Allatoona Mountains surrounding the town of Allatoona. Major General William T. Sherman chose to avoid this area on his way to Atlanta by flanking to the southwest through Dallas. Johnston then had to abandon Allatoona, while Sherman left a strong garrison there to protect the railroad and extensive storehouses.

In October 1864, after Atlanta fell to Sherman in early September, General John B. Hood attempted to draw Union armies out of Atlanta by driving north. Hood ordered Major General Samuel G. French and 3,276 men to destroy the Etowah bridge to gain control of the Western and Atlantic Railroad at Allatoona Pass and capture the Union rations stored in the Allatoona Depot. On October 5, 1864, 2,025 Union defenders at Allatoona fought desperately to repulse repeated attacks, counting on a promise of reinforcements from Sherman. Both sides experienced frightful losses. The heroic Federal defense inspired the revival hymn *Hold the Fort, for I Am Coming.* Of the 5,301 men engaged in the four-hour battle, much of it fought hand-to-hand, 1,603 were killed or died of wounds, making it one of the bloodiest half-days of the Civil War.

Several historical markers are located at the intersection of Old Alabama Road and the Western and Atlantic Railroad. The still-visible Star Fort sits partly on private property and partly on land owned by the state of Georgia. Markers are also located at the Allatoona Dam Overlook and at Allatoona Creek at Georgia Highway 293 south of Emerson. The Allatoona battlefield is currently under management of the Red Top Mountain State Park (770-975-0055).

From I-75/Exit 283 (Emerson/Allatoona Road), go east on Old Allatoona Rd. In 0.5 miles the road curves left and crosses railroad tracks. Continue on for 0.1 miles (a total of 0.6 miles). The parking lot is on the left beneath the levee that creates Lake Allatoona.

Clayton House

The c. 1838 Clayton House served as a Union command post during the Battle of Allatoona Pass on October 5, 1864, and then as a field hospital for both sides after the battle. Accounts tell of amputated limbs being tossed from the front balcony into a wagon collecting them for disposal. Blood stains on the floor and bullet holes in the walls are still visible. A marker on the lawn honors twenty-one unidentified soldiers buried in the backyard after the battle.

The house, now known as the Clayton-Mooney House, is privately owned and not open to the public except for tours during the annual Civil War encampment at Allatoona in October.

620 Old Allatoona Rd. SE
Cartersville, GA 30121
770-387-1357

Left: *War-era view south through Allatoona Pass (Courtesy of the Library of Congress).*
Above: *Clayton House (Photo: Bob Price)*

U.S. Army Corps of Engineers Visitors Center

The museum housed in the U.S. Army Corps of Engineers Visitors Center contains Civil War relics, photos, and memorabilia about the role Cooper's Iron Works played in the Confederacy, as well as a display about the Battle of Allatoona Pass that was fought on October 5, 1864.

End of GA Spur 20 (GA 294) at the Allatoona Dam
678-721-6700
http://allatoona.sam.usace
.army.mil

Mon.–Sun.: 8:00 a.m.–4:30 p.m.

DALLAS, Paulding County

Paulding County Chamber of
Commerce
455 Jimmy Campbell Pkwy.
Dallas, GA 30132
770-445-6016
www.thepcoc.org

On May 22, 1864, three Union armies under Major General William T. Sherman moved out of Cassville and Kingston to the west. Major General Joseph Wheeler's cavalry scouts easily detected such a massive movement, which extended nearly twenty miles wide. Learning of the development, General Joseph E. Johnston once again correctly anticipated the strongest defensive position and established a line running four miles from Dallas to one mile east of New Hope and passing through a small mill community called Pickett's Mill.

The next ten days of sustained fighting in the tangled, dense wilderness and under constant rain were so intense that veterans on both sides labeled the area the "Hell Hole." The battles at New Hope Church on May 25–26, Pickett's Mill on May 27, and Dallas on May 27–28 resulted in more than twenty-six hundred Union troops killed, wounded, captured, or missing and an estimated eighteen hundred Confederates killed or wounded. Due to the terrain and weather, maneuvering was extremely difficult and the fighting so severe that the ratio of Federal troops killed to wounded was the highest of the Atlanta Campaign. These disastrous engagements so upset Sherman that he never mentioned them in his official reports or memoirs.

Left: *Pickett's Mill Visitors Center (Photo: Barry Brown)*

New Hope Church Monument and Battle Site

Dallas-Acworth Rd. and Bobo Rd.
Dallas, GA 30132
770-443-7850

On May 25, 1864, Union Major General Joseph Hooker's XX Corps advanced toward New Hope. The massed Union formations were exposed to a continuous fire from Confederate Major General Alexander P. Stewart's division of about 4,500 men and repulsed with great losses. Fighting continued the next day near the New Hope Church and persisted incessantly for three more days. A Union general wrote his wife, "We have been here now five days and have not advanced an inch." Nearly five acres of the area described by the soldiers as the Hell Hole have been preserved through efforts of the Georgia Civil War Commission. The Pickett's Mill State Historic Site maintains the New Hope Church Monument and Battle Site.

Left: *The New Hope Church Cemetery where Confederate troops fought from behind gravestones (Photo: Bob Price)*

Atlanta Campaign Pavilion #5

Dallas-Acworth Rd. and Bobo Rd.
Dallas, GA

Adjacent to the present brick New Hope Baptist Church on Dallas–Acworth Road is the last of the five Atlanta Campaign Pavilions, which houses a monument, marker, and relief map describing the events that took place in the area.

Left: *The peaceful wooded setting leaves little hint of the furious fighting that occurred here on May 27, 1864. (Photo: Barry Brown)*

Pickett's Mill State Historic Site (NRHP)

On May 27, 1864, a fierce battle occurred at Pickett's Mill that pitted fourteen thousand Federal troops under Major General Oliver Otis Howard against Irish-born Major General Patrick R. Cleburne's division, considered by many to be one of the South's finest military commanders. The intense battle was a clear-cut Confederate victory, with Union losses estimated at 1,600 and Cleburne's at 450. However, the battle only checked the Federal advance and prevented the turning of the Confederate right flank. It did not alter the outcome of the Atlanta Campaign.

Pickett's Mill is widely celebrated as one of the best-preserved battlefields in the nation. The state of Georgia has sensitively preserved the 765-acre site, which has remained largely unchanged since the Civil War. Visitors walk on roads used by both armies, see earthworks, and hike the same ravines in which hundreds of soldiers died. Well-marked trails are for walking only; running and bicycling are prohibited. Living-history programs demonstrating Civil War weapons, camp life, and military drills are held frequently. A visitors center offers exhibits and a film describing the battle.

4432 Mt. Tabor Church Rd.
Dallas, GA 30132
770-443-7850
www.gastateparks.org

Tues.–Sat.: 9:00 a.m.–5:00 p.m.
Sun.: Noon–5:00 p.m.

WHITESBURG, Carroll County

Located on land once owned by Coweta Indian Chief William McIntosh, Whitesburg was laid out in 1874 when the Savannah, Griffin, and North Alabama Railroad came through. The town is named for railroad president A.J. White.

Carrollton Area CVB
102 North Lakeshore Dr.
Carrollton, GA 30117
www.visitcarrollton.com

Moore's Bridge Park and Horace King Historic Site

Whitesburg, GA

Park not yet open to the public

Below: *The Moore House constructed by master builder Horace King (Photo: Janet Cochran)*

For more than a century, the Moore's Bridge crossing of the Chattahoochee River was the gateway to Carroll County from Coweta County. Master builder Horace King, a free black and noted craftsman of covered bridges throughout the Southeast from the 1830s to the 1880s, built Moore's Bridge as part of a business partnership with white businessmen James Moore and Charles Mabry. In 1864, King and his family lived on the east bank and collected a toll from travelers crossing the bridge.

On July 13, 1864, a Federal cavalry force under Major General George Stoneman looking for a crossing over the Chattahoochee River captured the bridge and its defending force of about twenty skinny-dipping Confederates. The next day Stoneman was driven from the bridge by a force from Brigadier General Frank Armstrong's Confederate cavalry, but not before the Federals had burned the bridge.

In January 2009, Carroll County acquired 485 acres, including the site of Horace King's bridge, the Moore House, and the battle site. The property includes 1.4 miles of frontage along the Chattahoochee River. Carroll County plans to build a replica of the bridge and turn the site into a park. It is not currently open to the public.

NORTHEAST GEORGIA MOUNTAINS

The Northeast Georgia Mountains region includes the major city of Gainesville, home to Confederate General James Longstreet. His home-site and grave and the hotel he operated after the Civil War are the primary attractions.

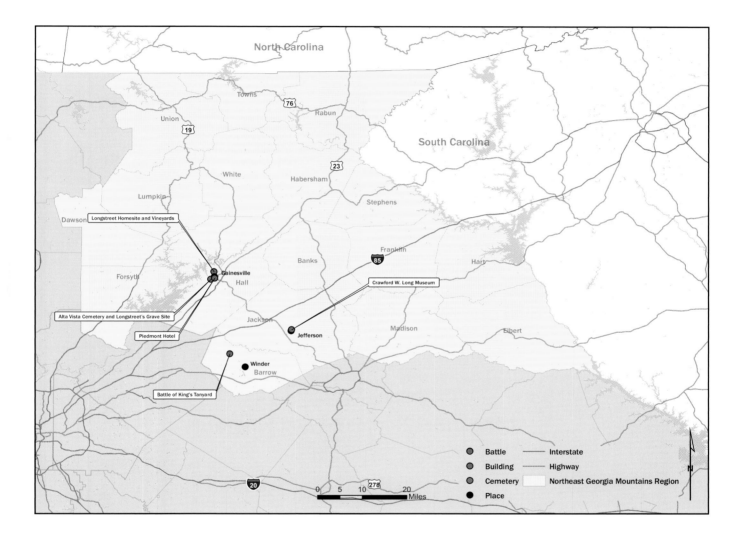

North Carolina

Towns
76
Rabun

Union
19

White

South Carolina

Lumpkin

Habersham

Dawson

Stephens

Longstreet Homesite and Vineyards

Franklin
85

Forsyth

Banks

Hart

Gainesville

Crawford W. Long Museum

Hall

Alta Vista Cemetery and Longstreet's Grave Site

Jackson

Madison

Elbert

Piedmont Hotel

Jefferson

Winder
Barrow

Battle of King's Tanyard

20

0   5   10   278   20
Miles

● Battle
● Building
● Cemetery
● Place

— Interstate
— Highway
☐ Northeast Georgia Mountains Region

N

GAINESVILLE, Hall County

Gainesville-Hall County CVB
117 Jesse Jewell Pkwy., Ste. 105
Gainesville, GA 30501
770-536-5209/888-536-0005
www.hallcounty.org/agencies/
ghcvb.asp

Right: *James Longstreet
(Courtesy of the National
Archives)*

Gainesville was home to one of the most famous generals of the Confederacy, Lt. General James Longstreet. A historical marker at the Gainesville Courthouse Square notes that Longstreet grew up in Augusta, Georgia, graduated from West Point in 1842, and served in the Mexican-American War. At the outbreak of the Civil War, he was a major in the U.S. Army but resigned to serve the Confederate cause.

Longstreet's Homesite and Vineyards and the Piedmont Hotel he operated after the war are open to visitors. His grave site is a significant feature in Gainesville's Alta Vista Cemetery.

Alta Vista Cemetery and Longstreet's Grave Site

1076 Jesse Jewell Pkwy.
Gainesville, GA 30501
770-535-6883

Mon.-Sun.: Daylight hours

Right: *Longstreet marker in
Alta Vista Cemetery (Photo:
Bob Price)*

Both an American flag and a Confederate flag mark the grave site of Confederate Lt. General James Longstreet. Also buried at Alta Vista Cemetery are two Georgia governors who served as Confederate officers: James Milton Smith was a colonel in the 13th Georgia Infantry, a Confederate congressman, and Georgia governor in 1872–1877; Allen Daniel Candler was a lieutenant colonel in the 4th Georgia Reserves, Georgia governor in 1898–1902, and the compiler of Georgia's Confederate records.

Longstreet Homesite and Vineyards

At the corner of Park Hill Dr. and
Longstreet Cir.
Gainesville, GA 30501

Right: *A contemporary statue
of Longstreet on display at the
Longstreet Homesite (Photo:
Bob Price)*

In November 1862, General Robert E. Lee reorganized the Army of Northern Virginia, placing Lt. General James Longstreet in command of the I Corps and Lt. General Thomas J. Jackson in command of the II Corps. Longstreet won Lee's admiration and praise for his performance at the battles of Second Manassas, Antietam, and Fredericksburg; Lee fondly referred to Longstreet as his "Old War Horse."

After the war, Longstreet settled in Gainesville and joined the Republican Party, one of only a few Confederate leaders to have done so. He served as minister to Turkey under President Rutherford B. Hayes and later became a U.S. marshal for Georgia.

The granite front steps and a few terraces are all that remain of the farm Lt. General James Longstreet built in 1875. A modern-day statue of the general stands on the Longstreet Homesite, along with an older monument erected by the United Daughters of the Confederacy.

Piedmont Hotel

Confederate Lt. General James Longstreet owned and operated the Piedmont Hotel from 1875 until his death in 1904. The first floor is all that remains of the building. Currently, a renovation of the lower north wing is nearing completion. A portion of this section will serve as a museum.

Maple St. between High St. and
Martin Luther King Jr. Blvd.
Gainesville, GA 30501
www.longstreet.org/piedmont.html

Left: *Piedmont Hotel (Photo: Longstreet Society)*

JEFFERSON, Jackson County

The town known today as Jefferson was established in 1805 on the site of a previous Indian settlement known as Thomocoggan. On November 24, 1806, it was incorporated and designated the county seat. The community's name was changed to Jefferson on June 30, 1824, in honor of Thomas Jefferson.

Jackson County Area Chamber of
Commerce
270 Athens St.
Jefferson, GA 30549
706-387-0300
www.jacksoncountyga.org

Crawford W. Long Museum

The Crawford W. Long Museum honors the physician Crawford W. Long, who attended the University of Georgia, where he shared a room with Alexander H. Stephens, the future vice president of the Confederacy. Long is credited as the first physician to use ether for surgical purposes. During the Civil War, he served as a Confederate surgeon and in the Athens Home Guard. Statues of Long and Stephens can be found in Statuary Hall in the U.S. Capitol, where two notables from every state are similarly honored.

The museum displays Long's medical instruments (including the amputation kit he used during the war), furniture, and personal papers as well as a replica 1840s doctor's office and a medicinal herb garden.

28 College St.
Jefferson, GA 30549
706-367-5307
www.crawfordlong.org

Tues.–Sat.: 10:00 a.m.–4:00 p.m.

Left: *Crawford W. Long Museum (Photo: Bob Price)*

WINDER, Barrow County

Barrow County Chamber of
Commerce
#6 Porter St.
Historic District Depot
Winder, GA 30680
770-867-6366

Barrow County was formed in 1914 from portions of Jackson, Gwinnett, and Walton counties. During the Civil War, Winder, the future Barrow county seat, was known as Jug Tavern.

Battle of King's Tanyard

On GA 211 about 5 miles north-west of Winder

Below: *Grave of a Kentucky cavalryman who died in the Battle of King's Tanyard (Photo: Bob Price)*

The Battle of King's Tanyard occurred on August 3, 1864, following Federal Major General George Stoneman's defeat two days earlier at the Battle of Sunshine Church. Portions of two brigades under Colonel Horace Capron and Lt. Colonel Silas Adams escaped capture at the battle and attempted, by different routes, to reach Union lines above Atlanta.

The brigades split up after encountering Confederate resistance at Athens, with Capron's force heading west toward Jug Tavern (now Winder), where they stopped to rest and water horses for a few hours on the night of August 2. While traveling west from Athens, Capron's column was followed by a large number of slaves who had left the surrounding farms hoping for protection. However, the worn-out cavalry-men were not in any condition for self-defense, much less to serve as protectors.

At early dawn on August 3, Confederates from Colonel C.P. Breckinridge's Kentucky Brigade overran Capron's sleeping men, stampeding them and the black refugees camped nearby. Caught by surprise, the Federals were unable to mount a meaningful resistance, and 430 men were killed or captured. A handful of Federals, including Capron, were able to escape on foot, arriving in Marietta several days later.

The Battle of King's Tanyard was effectively the end of the disastrous Stoneman's Raid. Major General William T. Sherman, in a report sent to Washington, under-stated the extent of the cavalry's failure when he wired, "On the whole the cavalry raid was not deemed a success."

ATLANTA METRO

Although many of the buildings from Civil War Atlanta burned and most of what remained was eventually supplanted by the city's growth and expansion, a number of Civil War sites are still accessible by car and by public transportation. In addition to being the setting for much of *Gone with the Wind*, Atlanta boasts one of the largest oil paintings in the world (the Cyclorama depiction of the Battle of Atlanta) and the world's largest bas-relief sculpture (Confederate leaders carved on the face of Stone Mountain, the world's largest exposed granite outcropping). Atlanta also houses the largest Civil War collection and exhibition in the Southeast (at the Atlanta History Center). And in places around the Atlanta metro area—Roswell, Marietta, Decatur, and Jonesboro—and inside the Atlanta city limits—Buckhead, East Atlanta, and West End—many Civil War sites still remain.

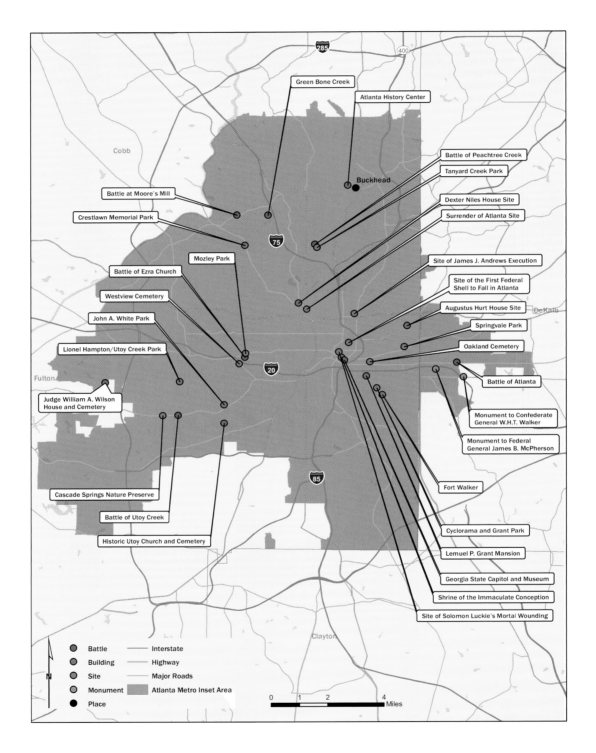

Green Bone Creek

Atlanta History Center

Battle of Peachtree Creek

Tanyard Creek Park

Battle at Moore's Mill

Dexter Niles House Site

Crestlawn Memorial Park

Surrender of Atlanta Site

Buckhead

Mozley Park

Site of James J. Andrews Execution

Battle of Ezra Church

Site of the First Federal
Shell to Fall in Atlanta

Westview Cemetery

Augustus Hurt House Site

DeKalb

John A. White Park

Springvale Park

Lionel Hampton/Utoy Creek Park

Oakland Cemetery

Fulton

Battle of Atlanta

Judge William A. Wilson
House and Cemetery

Monument to Confederate
General W.H.T. Walker

Monument to Federal
General James B. McPherson

Fort Walker

Cascade Springs Nature Preserve

Cyclorama and Grant Park

Battle of Utoy Creek

Lemuel P. Grant Mansion

Historic Utoy Church and Cemetery

Georgia State Capitol and Museum

Shrine of the Immaculate Conception

Site of Solomon Luckie's Mortal Wounding

Clayton

● Battle	—— Interstate	
● Building	—— Highway	
● Site	—— Major Roads	
● Monument	Atlanta Metro Inset Area	
● Place		

N

0   1   2   4
Miles

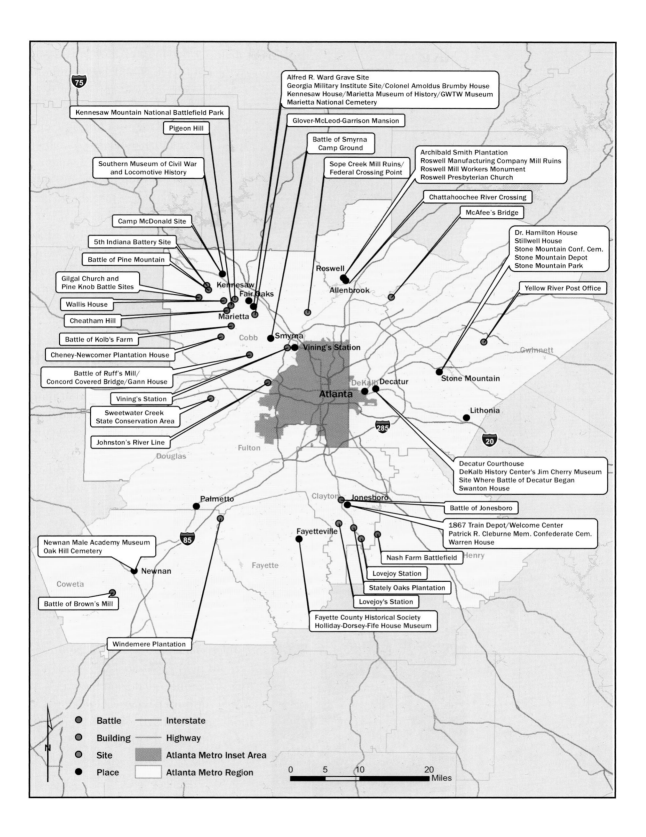

Alfred R. Ward Grave Site
Georgia Military Institute Site/Colonel Amoldus Brumby House
Kennesaw House/Marietta Museum of History/GWTW Museum
Marietta National Cemetery

Kennesaw Mountain National Battlefield Park

Pigeon Hill

Glover-McLeod-Garrison Mansion

Battle of Smyrna
Camp Ground

Southern Museum of Civil War
and Locomotive History

Sope Creek Mill Ruins/
Federal Crossing Point

Archibald Smith Plantation
Roswell Manufacturing Company Mill Ruins
Roswell Mill Workers Monument
Roswell Presbyterian Church

Chattahoochee River Crossing

McAfee's Bridge

Camp McDonald Site

5th Indiana Battery Site

Battle of Pine Mountain

Gilgal Church and
Pine Knob Battle Sites

Wallis House

Cheatham Hill

Battle of Kolb's Farm

Cheney-Newcomer Plantation House

Battle of Ruff's Mill/
Concord Covered Bridge/Gann House

Vining's Station

Sweetwater Creek
State Conservation Area

Johnston's River Line

Kennesaw
Fair Oaks
Marietta
Cobb
Smyrna
Vining's Station

Roswell
Allenbrook

Dr. Hamilton House
Stillwell House
Stone Mountain Conf. Cem.
Stone Mountain Depot
Stone Mountain Park

Yellow River Post Office

Gwinnett

Stone Mountain

DeKalb Decatur

Atlanta

Lithonia

Decatur Courthouse
DeKalb History Center's Jim Cherry Museum
Site Where Battle of Decatur Began
Swanton House

Newnan Male Academy Museum
Oak Hill Cemetery

Palmetto

Clayton Jonesboro

Fayetteville

Battle of Jonesboro

1867 Train Depot/Welcome Center
Patrick R. Cleburne Mem. Confederate Cem.
Warren House

Nash Farm Battlefield

Lovejoy Station

Stately Oaks Plantation

Lovejoy's Station

Henry

Newnan

Coweta

Battle of Brown's Mill

Fayette

Fulton

Douglas

Windemere Plantation

Fayette County Historical Society
Holliday-Dorsey-Fife House Museum

- Battle — Interstate
- Building — Highway
- Site — Atlanta Metro Inset Area
- Place — Atlanta Metro Region

N

0   5   10   20
Miles

KENNESAW AND VICINITY, Cobb County

Cobb County CVB
Galleria Specialty Mall
1 Galleria Pkwy.
Atlanta, GA 30339
678-303-2626/800-451-3480
www.cobbcvb.com

By June 1864, Major General William T. Sherman's advance toward Atlanta had forced General Joseph E. Johnston's army to the vicinity of Kennesaw Mountain. Sherman's cavalry managed to locate Johnston's army, which was entrenched along a ten-mile line from Brushy Mountain past Pine Mountain to Lost Mountain, positioning to protect Marietta and the railroad. On the morning of June 14, Confederate generals Johnston, Leonidas Polk, and William Hardee surveyed the threat to their positions from atop Pine Mountain. Less than a mile away an Indiana artillery battery fired on the observers. Lt. General Polk did not immediately seek cover. The third artillery shell fired struck Polk in the chest, killing him instantly. Polk, who was also an Episcopal bishop, was widely admired in the South and known by his men as the "Fighting Bishop." The Confederates abandoned Pine Mountain later that day.

Federal assaults on the Lost–Pine–Brushy Mountain Line continued on June 15. A series of Federal attacks by the three divisions of Major General Joseph Hooker's XX Corps at Pine Knob (two miles south of Pine Mountain) and at Gilgal Church were repulsed by Major General Patrick R. Cleburne's men. At Pine Knob, the more intense of the two battle sites, Hooker's two divisions suffered more than five hundred casualties. Fighting along this line continued with Major General James B. McPherson's men overwhelming and capturing a three-hundred-strong Alabama regiment at Noonday Creek at the foot of Brushy Mountain.

On the night of June 16, the Confederates withdrew from the Lost Mountain–Pine Mountain sector of the battle line and established a new line three miles east along Mud Creek. Lt. General Hardee's corps now faced west, forming a connection with Polk's former corps, now commanded by Major General William Wing Loring. They were positioned near Latimore's Farm (on New Salem Road) extending south to Powder Springs Road (near Kolb's Farm), thus covering Marietta and the railroad from a west-

Right: *Little Kennesaw Mountain as seem from Big Kennesaw Mountain (Photo: Barry Brown)*

ern approach. The Mud Creek Line was abandoned the night of June 18 due to Federal gains at the Latimore House. The new position was now the main Confederate battle line at Kennesaw Mountain, an arc anchored on Big Kennesaw and Little Kennesaw mountains just twenty miles north of Atlanta.

Both armies maneuvered for several days and then clashed on June 22 near Kolb's Farm on Powder Springs Road. Confederate Lt. General John B. Hood's forces made a costly attack against Federal positions but were caught in crossing artillery fire on open ground and suffered heavy casualties. The battle checked Sherman's effort to outflank the Kennesaw Mountain position.

Sherman's reports indicated that the muddy stalemate could be broken with a frontal assault to destroy Johnston's army at Kennesaw Mountain. With a furious cannonade by two hundred guns and an infantry advance at Pigeon Hill near Burnt Hickory Road, Sherman launched his attack on June 27, thus beginning the Battle of Kennesaw Mountain. During the next three hours, Federal attacks across difficult terrain and against well-entrenched Confederate defenders often involved brutal hand-to-hand combat, especially at Cheatham Hill and the "Dead Angle." The Confederates managed to repulse them all. Union casualties totaled three thousand, while Confederates lost around eight hundred. Once again, Johnston's earthworks had delayed the enemy, but Sherman's flanking movement sent Johnston's army to new positions closer to Atlanta. The late Civil War historian Shelby Foote coined this masterpiece of offensive and defensive maneuvering the "Red Clay Minuet." In his memoirs, Sherman credited his skilled opponent: "No officer or soldier who ever served under me will question the generalship of Joseph E. Johnston. His retreats were timely, in good order, and he left nothing behind."

Above: *Major General Joseph Hooker (Courtesy of the National Archives)*

Gilgal Church (NRHP) and Pine Knob Battle Sites

Gilgal Church was dismantled by Confederates in early June 1864 for use in their entrenchments. Though separated by about half a mile, the battles at Gilgal Church and Pine Knob on June 15, 1864, were intended to be components of the same battle.

Major General Joseph Hooker's Federal XX Corps was the attacking force: Brigadier General John W. Geary's and Brigadier General Alpheus Williams' divisions struck at Pine Knob, and Brigadier General Daniel Butterfield's division struck at Gilgal Church. In a poorly coordinated attack, Geary's and Williams' divisions suffered more than five hundred casualties, while Butterfield's casualties numbered less than one hundred. Hooker's three divisions united their flanks on the night of June 15. The battles of Gilgal Church and Pine Knob were just two of almost daily major clashes between Confederate and Federal forces that occurred between June 10 and July 3, 1864.

Original Union entrenchments can be seen at each site, and pull-off areas are available. At the Gilgal Church site, Confederate entrenchments are still visible, as well as a reconstruction of a Confederate trench modeled from photographs taken in 1864 by George Barnard, Major General William T. Sherman's photographer, that show similar earthworks from the Atlanta area.

In 2007, Cobb County placed a historical marker about the Battle of Pine Knob on the west side of Hamilton Road at the intersection of Kennesaw Due West Road. The marker reads: "The 60th New York Regiment's battle line can be seen nearby.

This shallow trench was dug late in the fight under hostile fire in darkness, with bayonets and canteens." Surrounded by Confederates on three sides, this Union regiment was especially hard hit at the end of battle.

Above, left to right: *An approximate replica of a Civil War entrenchment built on an existing trench line at the Gilgal Church battlefield (Photo: Bob Price); a photo of the earthworks around Burnt Hickory Road taken in 1864 by George Barnard*

Kennesaw Mountain National Battlefield Park (NRHP)

900 Kennesaw Mountain Dr.
Kennesaw, GA 30152
770-427-4686
www.nps.gov/kemo

Daily: 8:30 a.m.–5:00 p.m.
(extended summer hours)

Although a tactical defeat for Major General William T. Sherman, the Battle of Kennesaw Mountain was a decisive event in the Atlanta Campaign of 1864. Sherman's army was able to turn the flank of General Joseph E. Johnston's army and march closer to Atlanta.

The park's visitors center offers exhibits, an award-winning film, a bookstore, and knowledgeable park rangers and guides. A self-guided auto tour stops at the major sites—Big Kennesaw, Pigeon Hill, Cheatham Hill, and Kolb's Farm—with parking available at each. At Cheatham Hill there are gun emplacements, well-defined earthworks, and a large monument to the Illinois soldiers of Brigadier General Edward M. McCook's brigade, which lost 408 men killed in the June 27 assault.

A network of hiking trails traces a sixteen-mile loop from the visitor center to Kolb's Farm and back; the surroundings today appear much as the soldiers experienced them. A variety of interpretive programs are also available on summer weekends, including artillery firing.

Adjacent to the Kennesaw Mountain National Battlefield Park on Burnt Hickory Road (near the western boundary of the park) is the Hardage House. Confederate Lt. General Leonidas Polk used the house as his headquarters and conducted church services there just before his death. The original house was replaced by a c. 1900 structure still owned by Hardage descendents. A Georgia state historical marker denotes the site.

Left: *Kolb's Farm house*
(Photo: Phillip Lovell)

Battle of Kolb's Farm

On June 20, 1864, Federal General Joseph Hooker's corps moved to the southeast in an extension of the Federal line. The men formed a strong defensive position with eight batteries of massed artillery along the ridgeline near the corner of Powder Springs Road and Macland Road about 250 yards from the farmhouse of local pioneer Peter Valentine Kolb. This movement, intended to flank the Confederate's out of the Kennesaw line and cut the railroad, required quick action by General Joseph E. Johnston to counter it and avoid another strategic retreat.

On June 22, 1864, Johnston sent Lt. General John B. Hood's corps to the Confederate's extreme right, where Hood deployed three divisions across Powder Springs Road at Kolb's Farm. With little reconnaissance, an incomplete understanding of the terrain at his front, and no report of his intentions sent up the chain of command, Hood ordered an all-out assault on the Federal line. The attack soon faltered as Major General Carter L. Stevenson's division, massed tightly across open ground, was severely cut up by Federal artillery, while Major General Thomas C. Hindman's division became bogged down in thick brush and swampy terrain and ground to a halt. Hood's assault cost his corps nearly one thousand casualities. When he did send a dispatch regarding the battle, he described the combat to have been a defensive fight, costly to the Federals, though their loss was less than three hundred and they never attacked. Hooker made a false report to his superiors as well, passing on the exaggerated claim to have beaten back an assault by three corps of the Confederate army, a force equal to Johnston's entire command.

Today the Kolb's Farm house and cemetery are part of the Kennesaw National Battlefield Park, though most of the surrounding battlefield has been obliterated by suburban sprawl. The house is not open to the public, but a number of interpretive markers describing the troop movements and fighting on June 22, 1864, can be seen in the front yard. Limited parking is available.

Cheatham Hill Rd. and Powder Springs Rd.
Kennesaw, GA

Cheatham Hill and Pigeon Hill

Kennesaw Mountain National
Battlefield Park
900 Kennesaw Mountain Dr.
Kennesaw, GA 30152
770-427-4686
www.nps.gov/kemo

Major General William T. Sherman, impatient at the stalemate at the Kennesaw Mountain Line and facing increased pressure from his superiors in Washington to gain his objective of Atlanta, chose to commit a portion of his force to a risky frontal assault on the well entrenched Confederates. On June 25, 1864, Sherman issued an order directing that a general assault be made at eight o'clock in the morning on June 27.

The plan for the attack consisted of a feint to be made on the far left of the Federal line in the present area of the Kennesaw Mountain National Battlefield Park Visitors Center. This was done to keep the Confederates from shifting forces to the areas of intended intense Federal pressure. The main assaults would fall on the Confederates defending a spur of Kennesaw Mountain near Burnt Hickory Road and the center of the Confederate line known as Pigeon Hill, as well as on the far left of the Confederate line at a salient several miles to the south that would become known as Cheatham Hill.

Following an artillery barrage, the assaults began at nine o'clock in the morning on June 27. Troops under Major General John A. Logan advanced up Burnt Hickory Road and up the treacherously steep slopes of Pigeon Hill, trying to dislodge Confederates from Major General Samuel G. French's division dug in along the boulder-strewn apex. The Confederates easily threw back the Federal attackers, with many forced to remain behind, pinned down in the woods and unable to retreat back to their line until dark.

Units under Major General George H. Thomas also began their nine o'clock assault on Confederate lines positioned at a salient 2.5 miles south of Pigeon Hill. Five Federal brigades advanced in tight formation with only ten yards between regimental fronts with the intention of overrunning the Confederate position. Coming on like the waves of the ocean washing over a sandy shore, the Federals placed more men in front of Confederate guns than could be shot. However, the tactics failed and the Federals were repulsed at all points with heavy losses. Approximately three thousand Federals were killed or wounded on that morning while Confederate losses were around eight hundred. Federal Brigadier General Charles Harker and Colonel Daniel McCook were among the dead and mortally wounded.

Today, Pigeon Hill and Cheatham Hill are units of the Kennesaw National Battlefield Park. The Pigeon Hill trail can be accessed from the intersection of Burnt Hickory Road and Old Mountain Road. The steep walk to the top passes by trenches and rifle pits that are still clearly visible. While making the walk, the enormity of the task given to the Federals assaulting the position is evident. Referred to by both sides as the "Dead Angle," this area remains much the same as it was during the war. The large Illinois Monument marks the site of some of the most intense combat of the war.

Left: *Monument to Illinois troops at Cheatham Hill (Photo: Phillip Lovell)*

Pine Mountain

On June 13–14, 1864, approximately two thousand Confederate soldiers of Major General William B. Bate's division occupied Pine Mountain, where the action consisted primarily of artillery exchanges. Two sections (four guns) of the famed Washington Artillery of New Orleans made up the Confederate artillery. Today, the artillery and infantry fortifications are still clearly visible. From the Georgia historical marker at the roadside, there is a narrow foot trail leading to the crest of the mountain to the site of Confederate Lt. General Leonidas Polk's death on June 14, 1864, by a Federal artillery shell. A twenty-foot-high stone obelisk marks the spot. However, the present stone marker is on private property accessible to individuals and small groups only. Large groups should first phone, 770-422-2300.

From the Kennesaw Mountain National Battlefield Park Visitors Center, go west on Stilesboro Rd. approximately 4.5 miles to Beaumont Dr.; turn left and proceed approximately 0.7 miles to the marker on right side of the road

Above: *Generals Johnston, Hardee, and Polk on top of Pine Mountain on June 14, 1864, shortly before Captain Peter Simonson's 5th Indiana Battery fired its fatal shot. Painting by Wilbur Kurtz (Courtesy of Dr. Philip Secrist).* Right: *Monument at the site of the death of General Polk on top of Pine Mountain (Photo: Rich Elwell)*

5th Indiana Battery Site

Mack Dobbs Rd. and Stilesboro
Rd. (a short distance into the
woods off Mack Dobbs Rd.)
Kennesaw, GA

The 5th Indiana Artillery was a six-gun battery commanded by Captain Peter Si-monson as part of Major General David S. Stanley's division, Major General Oliver Otis Howard's corps, of Major General George H. Thomas' Army of the Cumber-land. On June 14, 1864, Simonson's battery was involved in an artillery duel with Confederate artillery positioned a mile away on Pine Mountain. That same day Confederate General Joseph E. Johnston had asked his senior commanders, generals William Hardee and Leonidas Polk, to meet with him on the top of Pine Mountain. Simonson's 5th Indiana Battery spotted the three officers silhouetted on the crest of the mountain and fired three rounds in quick succession; the third round struck Polk, killing him instantly.

The Indiana battery site is clearly visible. Cobb County plans to erect a historical marker to interpret the site.

Southern Museum of Civil War and Locomotive History (NRHP)

2829 Cherokee St.
Kennesaw, GA 30144
770-427-2117
www.southernmuseum.org

Mon.–Sat.: 9:30 a.m.–5:00 p.m.
Sun.: Noon–5:00 p.m.

The famous Civil War locomotive the *General*, which figured prominently in the Great Locomotive Chase of April 1862, is housed in the 40,000-square-foot South-ern Museum of Civil War and Locomotive History complex. Other permanent exhibits include a collection of Civil War uniforms, flags, and rare weaponry. The museum also examines the vital role railroads played in troop movement and logis-tics support during the war. It houses a re-creation of the Glover Machine Works, a postwar locomotive factory that helped rebuild the South.

The museum has a gift shop, bookstore, archival library open to researchers by appointment, and theater, where a twenty-five-minute film about the Great Lo-comotive Chase is shown every thirty minutes. It also hosts many special events throughout the year, including traveling exhibitions from the Smithsonian.

Right: *The Confederate
locomotive the* General *at Big
Shanty shortly before being
hijacked by Andrews' Raiders. Camp McDonald is to
the right and the Lacy Hotel
to the left, where the Southern Museum of Civil War and
Locomotive History is now
located. Painting by Wilber
Kurtz (Courtesy of the Atlanta
History Center)*

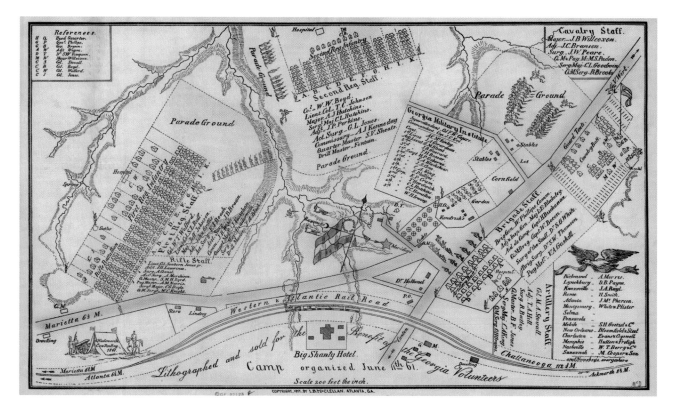

Camp McDonald Site (NRHP)

Wartime Governor Joseph E. Brown established Camp McDonald, a Confederate camp for training Georgia volunteers, in the town of Big Shanty (now Kennesaw) on the western side of the Western and Atlantic Railroad. It was named in honor of former Georgia Governor Charles C. McDonald. The sixty-acre camp, constructed on the site of an old railroad workers' camp, had a water supply fed by an excellent spring. To maintain order and control desertion, Governor Brown ordered the territory "within a circle of two miles," essentially the entire town, to be "under martial law, solely and entirely under military jurisdiction." Camp McDonald was commanded by Brigadier General William Phillips of the Georgia militia and used by instructors from the nearby Georgia Military Institute.

A grand review of the initial thirty-three companies of troops from Camp McDonald was held for Governor Brown on July 31, 1861, shortly before the first group was sent to the war's early campaigns in West Virginia. Legendary units, such as Phillips Legion, were trained at Camp McDonald. By March 1862, the camp was reactivated and again filled with volunteers, some joining the ranks to avoid the Confederate conscription law that would take effect April 16, 1862. Camp McDonald is best known as the site of the theft of the locomotive the *General*, the beginning point for Andrews' Raiders in the Great Locomotive Chase.

There are no visible remains of Camp McDonald today, as it was made up of temporary structures, tents, and parade grounds. A state historical marker at the railroad indicates the location of the camp.

Main St. adjacent to the CSX
Railroad
Kennesaw, GA

Above: *A pictorial map showing the parade grounds, tents, buildings, hospitals, streets, relief by hachures, and the names of principal officers of Camp McDonald (Courtesy of the Library of Congress)*

Wallis House

Burnt Hickory Rd. south of
Barrett Pkwy.
Kennesaw, GA 30064

In the early 1850s, Josiah Wallis built a hall-parlor-style house on his 400-acre farm, which fronted Kennesaw Mountain to the south. When war came to the area in June 1864, the house was used as a Confederate hospital during the fighting on the Mud Creek Line and at Latimore's Farm. The Confederates tore out the walls in the main house and used the outbuildings for the wounded. The dead were buried in a peach orchard that was directly across Burnt Hickory Road.

When the Confederate army repositioned to the Kennesaw Line, Federal Major General Oliver Otis Howard chose the Wallis House for his headquarters. Major General William T. Sherman heard the fighting at nearby Kolb's Farm on June 22, 1864, while visiting Howard at the Wallis House. A large oak tree on the hill behind the house was used as a signal station by both armies.

Below: A view of Marietta Square that appeared in Harper's Weekly *on August 6, 1864 (Courtesy of the Library of Congress)*

Today, the house, outbuildings, and less than two acres of remaining land have been purchased by the effort of the Georgia Civil War Commission and Cobb County. Plans for the house include giving the property to the National Park Service as an addition to the Kennesaw National Battlefield Park for the sesquicentennial of the Civil War in 2011. Currently, the Wallis House is not open to the public.

MARIETTA, Cobb County

Marietta Welcome Center and
Visitors Bureau
#4 Depot St.
Marietta, GA 30060
770-429-1115/800-835-0445
www.mariettaga.gov

Cobb County, named after U.S. Senator Thomas Willis Cobb, was formed in 1832 from land ceded by the Creek Nation in the Treaty of Indian Springs eleven years earlier. Marietta became the county seat on December 19, 1834. The town already had a sizable population due to its popularity as a summer retreat for wealthy coastal planters. They came to the relatively cooler climate of this north Georgia piedmont town seeking refuge from the Deep South summers, which were wrought with heat, humidity, and disease.

The arrival of the Western and Atlantic Railroad brought increased economic viability to Marietta along with a proportionate increase in construction activity. New hotels, restaurants, and homes were erected around the town square and courthouse to accommodate the increasing numbers of travelers arriving in Marietta. During the 1850s, the community was damaged several times by fire but always rose from the ashes stronger and more vibrant.

The Civil War's first intrusion into Marietta occurred in April 1862 when Andrews' Raiders finalized plans for their sabotage mission along the Western and Atlantic Railroad here. Most of the raiders spent the night preceding the Great Locomotive Chase at the Fletcher House Hotel, now the Kennesaw House. As the war progressed, Marietta become a hospital center caring for wounded soldiers from the fighting in north Georgia.

After the Confederate retreat to the south, Marietta endured a five-month occupation by Union forces that ended in November 1864 when cavalry under Brigadier General Judson Kilpatrick set the town square on fire prior to departing. The damage was extensive but not complete as the fire spread slowly and was quickly extinguished. The Masonic Building was one of the few buildings left purposely unscathed. Repair and rebuilding began soon after the war. The town's many beautiful antebellum homes and mansions survived the occupation generally intact and today can be enjoyed by taking a leisurely stroll or by following one of the city's prepared walking or driving tours.

Kennesaw House/Marietta Museum of History/ Gone with the Wind Museum

The Kennesaw House was originally built c. 1845 by future Marietta Mayor John H. Glover and was used as a restaurant to feed the railroad passengers arriving at the adjacent Marietta Depot. Purchased by the Fletcher family in 1855, the building was converted to an inn known as the Fletcher House Hotel. It was considered one of the finest in the state. The majority of Andrews' Raiders, the Federal spies who participated in the Great Locomotive Chase on April 12, 1862, spent the night of April 11 at the Fletcher House. Afterward, the building served as a hospital and, for the night of July 3, 1864, as the headquarters for Major General William T. Sherman. Partially burned by departing Federals in November 1864, the building lost a balcony and the top floor but was rebuilt and reopened by Dix Fletcher in 1867. In 1898 the building came under the auspices of the United Daughters of the Confederacy.

1 Depot St.
Marietta, GA 30060
770-425-5566
www.mariettahistory.org

Below: *Kennesaw House, home to the Marietta Museum of History, with the Marietta Depot on the far left (Photo: Bob Price)*

Today, the second floor of the Kennesaw House is home to the Marietta Museum of History, one of Marietta's treasures. Its three galleries are overflowing with a wide variety of artifacts covering the varied history of the town. The Civil War gallery features replica uniforms, as well as authentic weapons and ammunition with displays covering Andrews' Raiders and the Great Locomotive Chase. The museum is also home to an outstanding privately owned collection of *Gone with the Wind* movie and book memorabilia. Other galleries focus on Native Americans, the gold rush, influential Marietta citizens, and the Bell Bomber plant, which is now known as the Lockheed Martin plant.

Marietta Depot

4 Depot St.
Marietta, GA 30060
770-429-1115
www.mariettasquare.com

Mon.-Sat.: 9:00 a.m.-3:00 p.m.
Sun.: 1:00 p.m.-4:00 p.m.

Before leaving Marietta in November 1864, Federal forces burned the original Marietta Depot that served the Western and Atlantic Railroad. The present building was constructed in 1898; however, the depot is still a required stop as it houses the Marietta Welcome Center. Here visitors can obtain state and local tour information, an all-day parking pass, maps, and brochures and find public restrooms.

Marietta City Cemetery/Marietta Confederate Cemetery

381 Powder Springs St.
Marietta, GA 30060

Daily: Dawn to dusk

Below: *The Georgia Military Institute's cannon and the United Daughters of the Confederacy's monument guard the Marietta Confederate Cemetery. (Photo: Bob Price)*

The first Confederates to be buried in the Marietta Confederate Cemetery, which is adjacent to Marietta City Cemetery, were twenty soldiers killed in a railroad accident north of town in September 1863. After this accident, the land for the cemetery was donated by the mayor's wife, Jane Porter Glover, from a quiet and secluded corner of her Brushy Park Plantation. During the Atlanta Campaign, and especially while the fighting was raging at nearby Kennesaw Mountain, Marietta became a hospital center, requiring the cemetery to be enlarged to accommodate a large number of new burials.

In 1866 the state allocated thirty-five hundred dollars for a reburial project that gathered Confederate dead from temporary graves along the paths of the mountain campaign in north Georgia and reinterred them in the Marietta Confederate Cemetery. Administered by Mary J. Green, who had overseen similar work at the Resaca Confederate Cemetery, the initiative resulted in an additional three thousand burials, the majority unknown.

The cemetery is separated into sections for each Confederate state with markers listing the number interred from each. Men who later died at the Confederate Soldier's Home in Atlanta were also buried here, including Bill Yopp, a black drummer of the 14th Georgia Regiment Volunteer Infantry who went to war with his owner, Captain Thomas M. Yopp. The last Confederate interred here was in 1989 when the remains of a soldier found during construction of a residential development were moved here and buried with honors.

The Marietta City Cemetery includes a slave lot, an unusual feature for a predominantly white Georgia cemetery of the era. It contains nineteen slaves and freedmen from Marietta, only four of whom have been positively identified. The slave lot shares a border with the Confederate Cemetery.

A small six-pound bronze cannon, originally from the Georgia Military Institute, is on display in the Confederate Cemetery as well as a twenty-five-foot obelisk monument to Cobb County's Confederate veterans. Confederate Brigadier General Clement Anselm Evans dedicated the monument with much fanfare and many members of the Georgia legislature present at a ceremony on July 7, 1908. The Marietta Confederate Cemetery was the first place that the St. Andrew's cross design of the Confederate flag, banned in the former Confederacy by the Federal government after the war, was again allowed to fly.

Confederate Colonel and Brigadier General of the Georgia State Troops William Phillips of Phillips Legion, who had combat experience in Virginia and later ran the Marietta Paper Mill on Sope Creek, is buried in the cemetery, but not in the Confederate section.

Right: *Black Confederate drummer Bill Yopp is buried at the Marietta Confederate Cemetery. (Photo: Bob Price)*

Marietta National Cemetery

Established in 1866, the twenty-four-acre Marietta National Cemetery contains seven thousand known and three thousand unknown Federal soldiers who were killed or died from wounds or disease while fighting in the Atlanta Campaign (buried in scattered places but moved here). The land's donor, Henry G. Cole, originally planned for both Federals and Confederates to be buried here as a symbol of national reconciliation. However, his plan never came to fruition as the sectional schism caused by the war was slow to heal. The National Cemetery Act of 1862 stipulated that Federals and Confederates were not to be buried together.

For decades after the war, former slaves would gather at the cemetery on National Memorial Day to honor the Federal dead and celebrate the end of slavery. Monuments from the various home states of the interred soldiers honor their ultimate sacrifice. Veterans who served in more recent conflicts from the Spanish-American War to the Vietnam conflict are also buried here.

500 Washington Ave.
Marietta, GA 30060
770-428-5631
www.cem.va.gov/CEM/cems/
nchp/marietta.asp

Daily: Dawn to dusk

Left: *The majority of the Federal soldiers who died during the Atlanta Campaign are buried in the Marietta National Cemetery. (Photo: Barry Brown)*

Fair Oaks

505 Kennesaw Ave.
Marietta, GA 30060
770-427-3494
www.mariettagardencenter.com

Built in 1852, Fair Oaks served as the headquarters for Confederate General Joseph E. Johnston in late June 1864 during the fighting around Kennesaw Mountain. Today this former residence houses the Marietta Educational Garden Center and is open to the public.

Georgia Military Institute Site/Colonel Arnoldus Brumby House

472 Powder Springs Rd.
Marietta, GA 30064

Founded in 1851, the Georgia Military Institute was the first military school in the state to follow the curriculum of the United States Military Academy at West Point. Sons from Georgia's best families learned military science and discipline here and conducted drills on the grounds. Early in the war, the cadets were used as instructors for Confederate volunteers—first at Camp Brown, located at Smyrna Campground, and later at the much larger Camp McDonald in Big Shanty. Due to the South's chronic manpower shortage, especially during the late stages of the war, the cadets became embroiled in the defense of Georgia; designated as the Battalion of the Georgia Military Institute Cadets, they were assigned to the Army of Tennessee.

Upon reaching Marietta, Federal forces occupied the school, using it as a hospital. When departing to begin the March to the Sea in November 1864, the Federals burned all of the school's seventeen-building complex.

However, the beautiful, well-preserved 1854 Greek Revival home of Colonel Arnoldus V. Brumby, the superintendent, is still standing. Used as a hospital during the Federal occupation, the home was spared, reportedly due to Brumby's association with Major General William T. Sherman while both were at West Point. The land the Georgia Military Institute once occupied is currently home to the Marietta Conference Center and Resort. The Arnoldus Brumby House can be rented for events but is not open to the public.

Left: *Depiction of the Georgia Military Institute (Courtesy of the UGA Hargrett Rare Book and Manuscript Library)*

Glover-McLeod-Garrison Mansion (NRHP)

250 Garrison Rd.
Marietta, GA 30060

This beautiful two-and-a-half-story temple-fronted Greek Revival mansion, was known as Bushy Park, as well as Rocking Chair Hill. Built in 1848 by Marietta's first mayor, John H. Glover, the house once presided over three thousand acres, which encompasses practically all the land between the present-day towns of Marietta and

Smyrna. Glover sold the house in 1852 to Francis McLeod, whose daughter lived there during the war with her husband, William King. He was the son of Roswell King, the industrialist and founder of Roswell, Georgia. During the Atlanta Campaign, a cavalry skirmish occurred near the home on July 3, 1864, while the family and servants hid in the cellar. After the fighting, the home served as a Union hospital and quarters. The room in the upstairs northwest corner was used as an operating room. Currently the home is not open to the public.

Alfred R. Waud Grave Site

Alfred R. Waud, arguably the most well known of the war-era battlefield illustrators, was laid to rest in the Saint James Episcopal Cemetery in Marietta rather than in his native England or his adopted home of New York. A prolific field artist during the war, he received his art schooling in London. Immigrating to the United States in 1850, Waud first worked as an illustrator on periodicals and books. When war broke out he joined the staff of the *New York Illustrated News*. His work was also prevalent in *Harper's Weekly* and *Frank Leslie's Illustrated Newspaper*. Waud was present at the battle of First Manassas and followed the Army of the Potomac for much of the war.

Saint James Episcopal Church
161 Church St. NW
Marietta, GA 30060
770-428-5841

Daily: Dawn to dusk

At Appomattox, he made his now legendary sketches of the surrender ceremony. After the war, Waud drew scenes of the American western frontier and of the postwar South. While on tour sketching battlefields in Georgia in 1891 he was stricken by a heart attack and buried in Marietta.

Right: *Alfred Waud (Courtesy of the Library of Congress)*

Cheney-Newcomer Plantation House

This 1856 Greek Revival home served as the headquarters of Federal General John Schofield on June 22–30, 1864, during the fighting at Kennesaw Mountain. The Cheney-Newcomer Plantation House was also used by the Federal Signal Corps and served as a hospital. In recent years, development has occurred on the land directly adjacent to the property, but the house remains in excellent condition. However, it is not currently open to the public.

Bankstone Dr. at
Power Springs Rd.
Marietta, GA

Right: *Cheney Plantation House (Photo: Barry Brown)*

Sope Creek Mill Ruins/Federal Crossing Point

Sope Creek Mill Ruins:
Mill Rd. at Sope Creek Crossing
Marietta, GA

Federal Crossing Point:
Confluence of Sope Creek and
the Chattahoochee River at
Columns Dr.
Marietta, GA

Below: *This portion of the original Ruff's Mill complex can
be seen from the road next to
the postwar covered bridge.*
(Photo: Bob Price)

Sope Creek, a picturesque rocky stream running southeast through Cobb County before flowing into the Chattahoochee River, has historic significance to the War Between the States. The extensive mill ruins in the north end of the Cochran Shoals Unit of the Chattahoochee River National Recreation Area are the remains of the once thriving Marietta Paper Mill Company. Managed by Confederate Colonel William Phillips during the war, the mill manufactured paper for newspapers and Confederate currency.

On the Federal left flank, cavalry under Brigadier General Kenner Garrard were searching for a Chattahoochee River crossing. They came upon the Sope Creek Mill complex and put it to the torch on July 5, 1864. Edward Denmeade's flour mill on the west bank of Sope Creek was also burned. The paper mill was rebuilt after the war and operated until the early twentieth century.

The first Federal crossing of the Chattahoochee River was made on July 8, 1864, at the mouth of Sope Creek. The site is accessible from Columns Drive and is not a part of the Chattahoochee River National Recreation Area. Elements of Major General John Schofield's corps were the first across, using twenty boats that were normally used to float pontoon bridges. The location was ideal because it was screened from detection by the high wooded bluffs on the south shore, allowing Schofield to easily secure a bridgehead on the south bank.

To enlarge the foothold, the Federal 1st Tennessee Cavalry under Colonel James Brownlow crossed the Chattahoochee at a stacked-rock dam above the mouth of Sope Creek at Cochran's Ford. Brownlow teamed up with an assault party that had crossed at Sope Creek earlier and surprised and captured a group of Confederate troops. The Confederates had a single artillery piece guarding this sector of the river. Before midnight, the Federals had two pontoon bridges in place, which allowed an entire division to cross, giving them a firm foothold on the south bank.

SMYRNA, Cobb County

Cobb County CVB
Galleria Specialty Mall
1 Galleria Pkwy.
Atlanta, GA 30339
678-303-2626/800-451-3480
www.cobbcvb.com

Smyrna contains two antebellum settlements: Smyrna Camp Ground and Ruff's Mill. The area on present-day Concord Road west of South Cobb Drive was known as Ruff's Mill Settlement from around 1855, when the Ruff family purchased the mill. The area in present-day downtown Smyrna on Atlanta Road was an Episcopal Methodist campground and in 1840 became known as Smyrna Camp Ground. The two settlements were later combined to form the present city of Smyrna.

Battle of Ruff's Mill/Concord Covered Bridge Historic District/Gann House (NRHP)

This site includes the ruins of Ruff's Mill, an antebellum gristmill; the miller's house; the Concord Covered Bridge; the Concord woolen mill; and the 1854 Gann House a quarter mile to the west. The first Federal assault on July 4, 1864, which occurred at the Smyrna Camp Ground near the railroad, was unsuccessful. However, the second attack a few miles to the west (approaching Old Concord Road) succeeded after softening Confederate resolve with a "furious shelling." Brigadier General John W. Fuller's brigade of Major General Grenville M. Dodge's XVI Corps drove in the Confederate skirmish line of Major General Carter L. Stevenson's division from the vicinity of Ruff's Mill to their main battle line near the present-day intersection of Old Concord Road at Gann Cemetery. Among the casualties during this action was future Ohio Governor Edward F. Noyes, who sustained a wound to his left foot, which was amputated later that month at a Chattanooga hospital.

The actual battle site has been developed with private homes and businesses. Of greater interest is a visit to the Concord Covered Bridge. It was built in 1848, burned by the Federal army on July 4, 1864, and rebuilt in 1872 using the original stone footings. The Federals also burned the woolen mill, which made cloth for Confederate uniforms. Though much of the area is private property and not open to the public, Ruff's Mill and the miller's house are visible from the east end of the covered bridge. However, public parking is not available. Cobb County has acquired ownership of the nearby ruins of the 1870s Concord Mill along Nickajack Creek, preserving the ruins and constructing walking trails where needed. The entire area is on the National Register of Historic Places. Access to the county portion of the site is by way of the nearby Silver Comet Trail and the Highway 120 East-West Connector.

West on Concord Rd. off South Cobb Dr., continue west until the road crosses the one-lane covered bridge
Smyrna, GA

Battle of Smyrna Camp Ground

Late, on the evening of July 2, and in the early morning of July 3, 1864, the Confederates abandoned the Kennesaw Mountain Line to a temporary position five miles to the south known as the Smyrna–Ruff's Mill Line. This line consisted of a double set of works that crossed Atlanta Road at Smyrna Camp Ground facing northwest and perpendicular to the Western and Atlantic Railroad. Major General William Wing Loring held the right, Lt. General William Hardee the center, with Lt. General John B. Hood the left. The ground on which the line was built lacked an abundance of natural topographical features to strengthen its defense and was not intended to be maintained as a long-term position. Major General William T. Sherman did not expect heavy resistance from the Confederates at the Smyrna–Ruffs Mill Line.

The Battle of Smyrna Camp Ground began on July 4, 1864, when elements of Major General Oliver Otis Howard's IV Corps attacked Major General Patrick R. Cleburne's division just east of the railroad (near the site of the present depot) and were handily repulsed. To avoid a Federal flanking movement around the Confeder-

Atlanta Rd. at the Smyrna Depot
Smyrna, GA

Below: *Fighting occured here on Independence Day 1864.* (Photo: Barry Brown)

ate left, that night General Joseph E. Johnston abandoned the position and withdrew to the more formidable line of prepared fortifications that fronted the Chattahoochee River, which became known as Johnston's River Line.

Johnston's River Line (NRHP)

Discovery Blvd. at Veterans
Memorial Blvd.
Smyrna, GA

Above: *General Johnston
(Courtesy of the National
Archives)*

Below: *An example of a typical
trench line from the Atlanta
Campaign (Photo: Barry Brown)*

Johnston's River Line was constructed with the labor of more than one thousand slaves impressed for the task by Confederate authorities from surrounding farms and plantations during the spring of 1864. An outstanding example of nineteenth-century military engineering, this set of breastworks, redoubts, and traverses was designed to be held by a force as small as a division, though much of the Army of Tennessee occupied this formidable position July 5–9, 1864.

Johnston's River Line was the last line of defense north of the Chattahoochee River. Major General William T. Sherman, who recognized a strong position when he saw one, chose not to commit his troops to an assault. Instead he entrenched the armies of Major General George H. Thomas and Major General James B. McPherson on a ridgeline parallel to the Confederates at the opposing side of the Nickajack Creek valley. With the majority of the Confederate army held up in the river line, Major General John Schofield's army was free to find a location to cross the river with little opposition.

The river line extended in a rough six-mile arc from the confluence of Nickajack Creek and the Chattahoochee River to the south, extending to the Vinings/Paces' Ferry area to the north. At its greatest distance from the river, the river line extends one mile from the Chattahoochee. It was anchored on the left by an eight-gun fort overlooking Nickajack Creek, currently owned by Cobb County, and to the north by another eight-gun battery, now on private property.

The engineer, Brigadier General Francis Asbury Shoup, had a unique vision for the river line in the form of an unusual log and earthen redoubt designed to be used by infantry that would become known as a "Shoupade." The Shoupades, thirty-six in all, were twelve feet thick at their base and fifteen feet in height and constructed from earth thrown over stacked logs. They were fairly evenly spaced at approximately eighty-yard intervals. Designed with an arrowhead shape positioned slightly advanced from the rest of the line, they created an interlocking field of fire that could sweep the entire plain at their front. A two-gun artillery redan was placed between each set of Shoupades at the reentrant angle, completing the design and allowing defenders to lay down a cover fire from both musketry and artillery that would be devastating to an attacking force. Sherman was not prepared to make another frontal assault on such a position, especially after the losses suffered during his June 27, 1864, attack at Kennesaw Mountain.

Though the Federals never directly assaulted the river line, a constant and steady fire between the opposing sides made the position a dangerous one to occupy. On the evening of July 9, 1864, the Confederates abandoned the river line and moved south to occupy Atlanta's outer ring of fortifications. The Federals crossed the river at the mouth of Sope Creek, making the river line untenable.

Cobb County owns more than one hundred acres on the far left end of the Confederate portion of the river line, which has been on the National Register of Historic Places since 1973. Plans to make a river line park have been discussed for years but have not yet come to fruition. Cobb County has recently purchased land containing Federal earthworks that opposed the river line in the Mableton vicinity with plans to use it as parkland as well.

Shoupade Park

Shoupade Park consists of the last remaining example of a Shoupade connected by an artillery redan to the adjacent Shoupade. This earthwork pattern that made up the Johnston's River Line has been destroyed over the years by farming and nearby development. Though a subdivision has been built in the area surrounding the park, the land with the earthworks was set aside by an agreement between the developer and Cobb County, preserving this unique piece of Cobb County's Civil War history.

Oakdale Rd. at Fort Dr.
Smyrna, GA

Right: *The new Shoupade Park (Photo: Charlie Crawford)*

VININGS, Cobb County

Vinings, which was originally know as Pace during the 1830s, was the home of Chattahoochee River ferry operator Hardy Pace. While the Western and Atlantic Railroad was being laid during the 1840s, Vinings became a storage site for construction materials and was named for a civil engineer who was involved with the railroad building project in the area. Vinings was occupied by Federal troops from July 1864 until the March to the Sea in November 1864. The Hardy Pace family cemetery is located on the crest of Vinings Mountain.

Cobb County CVB
Galleria Specialty Mall
1 Galleria Pkwy.
Atlanta, GA 30339
678-303-2626/800-451-3480
www.cobbcvb.com

Vining's Station

Paces Ferry Rd. at I-285
Vinings, GA 30339

Vining's Station, once a stop on the Western and Atlantic Railroad, was the home of Hardy Pace, an Atlanta-area pioneer and Chattahoochee River ferry operator. His home stood at 268 Paces Mill Road and was used during the war as both a hospital and the headquarters for Federal Major General Oliver Otis Howard on July 5–10, 1864. At the time of the war, Pace was an old man and died after he and his family fled to the central Georgia town of Milledgeville to avoid the military occupation of the area. The family returned to the area shortly after the war. The house presently occupying the site dates from the late nineteenth or early twentieth century and was not occupied by the Pace family.

The Confederates held Vining's Station, now know as Vinings, and the 1,170-foot Signal Mountain, or Vinings Mountain, until July 5, 1864, when they moved

to Johnston's River Line a short distance downstream on the Chattahoochee River. While the Confederate army approached Vining's Station, a Federal artillery shell severed Brigadier General Alfred Vaughan's leg while he was lighting his pipe by using a magnifying glass to focus the rays of the sun.

The summit of Mount Wilkinson, though not open to visitors, was the site of a Union signal station and the location where Major General William T. Sherman was first able to get a clear view of the city of Atlanta. He also had a bird's-eye view of the formidable Johnston's River Line, which he proclaimed was "one of the strongest pieces of field fortification I ever saw."

Left: Harper's Weekly *depiction of the Federal signal station atop Vinings Mountain. Sherman's first view of Atlanta was from this position. (Courtesy of the UGA Hargrett Rare Book and Manuscript Library)*

ROSWELL, Fulton County

Historic Roswell CVB
617 Atlanta St.
Roswell, GA 30075
770-640-3253/800-776-7935
www.cvb.roswell.ga.us

Roswell was the location of thriving woolen and cotton mills since its founding in 1839. Located in Cobb County during the war years, Roswell was incorporated into Fulton County in the 1930s. During the Civil War, the Roswell Gray fabric manufactured at the mills was used for Confederate uniforms, tents, and an array of military and civilian products that provided strategic support for the Southern war effort. The town's reputation as a New England–style manufacturing center was known throughout the country, making it a natural target. It came into Federal possession while Brigadier General Kenner Garrard's Union cavalry were seeking a Chattahoochee River crossing point above Atlanta.

On July 6, 1864, Garrard, during a northward movement around Johnston's River Line, skirmished with Confederate cavalry at the bridge over the Chattahoochee River. The outnumbered Confederate Home Guard, known as the Roswell Battalion, was forced south across the river by Federal cavalry. As the home guard fled, they set fire to the covered bridge to prevent the Federals from crossing. Garrard's cavalry quickly seized the crossing and soon captured the town. They discovered the Ivy Woolen Mill, a cloth manufacturing enterprise run largely by female employees, in full operation near the confluence of Vickery Creek and the Chattahoochee River. Further up Vickery Creek to the north, two cotton mills were producing cloth. The woolen mill's head weaver, French national Theophile Roche, raised the French flag over the mill in an attempt to present the factory as property of a neutral nation, thus technically making it exempt from destruction. When Major General William T. Sherman heard of this incident from Garrard's report, he wrote, "And I will see as to any man in America hoisting the French flag and then devoting his labor and capital against our Government and claiming the benefit of his neutral flag. Should you, under the impulse of anger, natural at contemplating such perfidy, hang the wretch, I approve of the act beforehand."

The mill buildings were burned and the approximately four hundred female employees and their dependents—along with a few men, all mill laborers—were sent by railroad from Marietta to Indiana. It was hoped they could no longer supply the Confederacy with their skilled labor at such a distance. In what was one of the forgotten tragedies of the

Below: *The mill dam on Vickery Creek powered the mill complex in this antebellum industrial center. (Photo: Phillip Lovell)*

war, many never returned to their native Georgia soil. A monument to the four hundred "Roswell Women" workers in Old Mill Park on Sloan Street was dedicated in July 2000.

Besides burning the mills, the Federal occupiers used Barrington Hall, Great Oaks, and other stately homes as headquarters for Union officers. The Roswell Presbyterian Church and the Old Bricks served dual purposes as hospitals and stables for cavalry horses. Vandalism, thievery, and destruction of private property were rampant throughout Roswell. After the war the only property of the Roswell Manufacturing Company that was not destroyed was the commissary.

Major General James B. McPherson's Army of the Tennessee later crossed the Chattahoochee River on pontoon bridges near Roswell. More than thirty-six thousand Federal troops occupied Roswell at one time or another throughout 1864. Fortunately, they spared the private homes, making Roswell one of the more interesting and historic locations in the state today.

Chattahoochee River Crossing

Roswell Rd. at the Chattahoochee River Roswell, GA

As Brigadier General Kenner Garrard's Federal cavalry arrived on the outskirts of Roswell, they encountered the Confederate defenders, mostly state line and local militia, who had burned the covered bridge over the river (the site of the modern Roswell Road bridge) on July 5, 1864. The Union cavalry were forced to find another crossing point, choosing the shallow ford located on the old Hightower Trail, which intersects with today's Azalea Drive at the River Park.

The Federal soldiers, armed with Spencer repeating carbines, dismounted and crossed the river on foot. They crouched down in the water to make for a smaller target while holding their carbines submerged. When the Federals rose to shoot at

Right: *The Federals fording the Chattahoochee River near Roswell (Courtesy of the Library of Congress)*

Confederate defenders on the south bank, water ran out the ends of the carbines' barrels, yet the weapons still fired. The amazed Confederates had never seen rifles able to function after being submerged. Being hopelessly outnumbered and severely outgunned, the Confederates were forced to give up their defensive positions and retreat from the Roswell area, leaving the town and south bank of the Chattahoochee River open for Union occupation.

Allenbrook (NRHP)

Allenbrook, a red-brick plantation-plain-style house was constructed in 1845 as a combination residence and office for Ivy Woolen Mill manager Theophile Roche. Upon hearing of the Union cavalry approach, Roche raised the French national flag over the mill in an attempt to claim French neutrality and save the enterprise from the torch. However, his efforts were futile as the ruse was recognized and the mill was burned to the ground. Roche was sent north as a refugee with the other deported mill workers.

Roswell Rd. 0.25 miles north of the Chattahoochee River
Roswell, GA

Still resenting his wartime experience, in 1882 Roche filed suit against the U.S. government claiming damages of $125,000 for false arrest and destruction of the Ivy Woolen Mill. When the French-American Claims Commission heard the suit on July 2, 1883, it was dismissed "for want of prosecution."

Right: Allenbrook (Photo: Phillip Lovell)

Roswell Town Square (NRHP)

The influence of town founder Roswell King's New England roots is evident throughout the square and the c. 1840–1856 buildings. A factory commissary located on the square, which is now a restaurant and bar, sold provisions to the workers.

Between South Atlanta St., Mimosa Blvd., Sloan St. and Mill St.
Roswell, GA

The square is also the place where Federal soldiers held Roswell's four hundred female mill workers and their dependents, forcing them to live in the open for several days under guard before putting them on a caravan of army wagons and escorting them to the railroad in Marietta, where they were transported north of the Ohio River into Indiana. The present site is a well-manicured grass plot with flower gardens and a centrally placed gazebo. Today, various shops and restaurants occupy the storefronts of the historic antebellum buildings.

Left: A few blocks off the Roswell town square is a monument to honor Roswell's mill workers who were deported to Indiana. (Photo: Bob Price)

Bulloch Hall (NRHP)

180 Bulloch Ave.
Roswell, GA 30075
404-992-1731
www.bullochhall.org

Mon.-Fri.: 10:00 a.m.-2:00 p.m.

The c. 1840 Bulloch Hall, one of the most significant Greek Revival homes in Georgia, was built by Major James Stephens Bulloch, grandfather of U.S. President Theodore Roosevelt. In 1853, the parents of the future president were married here. Margaret Mitchell was fascinated by the home and its history and wrote a feature article about the wedding for the *Atlanta Constitution*. Now it is a house museum featuring period rooms, a library, and a Civil War room with artifacts related to Roswell's occupation. During their occupation of the town, Federals used the house as a barracks.

Left to right: *Bulloch Hall (Photo: Bob Price); ruins of the Roswell Manufacturing Company's machine shop (Photo: Barry Brown)*

Roswell Manufacturing Company Mill Ruins (NRHP)

Entrance on Sloan St. across from
Founders Cemetery
Roswell, GA

The ruins of the 1839 Roswell Manufacturing Company are located on the hillside above Vickery Creek. Burned by Federal Brigadier General Kenner Garrard's cavalry on July 7, 1864, the mill was rebuilt after the war. Brick walls from the war-era buildings remain and can be viewed from the catwalk that descends the hill as part of the town's mill park. The dam and magnificent waterfall, as well as the brick machine shop and the sluiceway, are remnants from Roswell King's original cotton mill.

Roswell Presbyterian Church (NRHP)

755 Mimosa Blvd.
Roswell, GA 30075
770-993-6316
www.roswellpres.org

Roswell Presbyterian Church was founded in 1839. The building, one of the town's oldest, was first used as a sanctuary in 1840. Roswell's town limits were originally laid out to extend one mile in each direction from the church, which is located a few blocks north of the town square.

Left to right: *Roswell Presbyterian Church, Smith Plantation (Photos: Bob Price)*

During the Federal occupation of Roswell, the soldiers removed the church's pews and destroyed the pipe organ and hymnals. While regular Sunday services were temporarily suspended, the chaplain of the 72nd Indiana Mounted Infantry preached to a full house of Federal soldiers in a service on July 9, 1864.

Archibald Smith Plantation

The Smith family, like many of the original Roswell families, came to the area from the Georgia coast near Darien in 1838 along with thirty-six of their slaves. The Smith family prospered in Roswell and is an excellent example of the life-style of the well-to-do in antebellum Georgia. Their house and outbuildings surrounded by three hundred acres of land on the north end of Roswell were completed in 1845.

The two Smith sons enlisted in the Confederate army at the outbreak of the war. Their war-era letters were collected in *Death of a Confederate* edited by Dr. Lister Skinner and Arthur Skinner. During the Federal occupation of Roswell, the Smith family fled, returning after the war's end.

950 Forrest St.
Roswell, GA 30075
770-641-3978
www.archibaldsmithplantation.org

Mon.–Sat.: 10:00 a.m.–3:00 p.m.
Sun.: 1:00 p.m.–3:00 p.m.

McAfee's Bridge

The stacked stone bridge supports adjacent to the modern structure on Holcomb Bridge Road are of antebellum construction. The famous Chicago Board of Trade Battery and the 4th Ohio Cavalry were stationed at the bridge guarding the Federals' far left flank on July 18–19, 1864.

Holcomb Bridge Rd. at the
Chattahoochee River
Roswell, GA

BUCKHEAD, Fulton County

Atlanta CVB
233 Peachtree St. NE, Ste. 100
Atlanta, GA 30303
404-521-6600/800-285-2682
www.atlanta.net

Buckhead was originally known as Irbyville, a settlement that began in 1838 and included a general store and tavern owned by Henry Irby. The name was later changed to Buckhead after the head of a large buck deer was hung from a prominent location near the intersection of Roswell Road and Paces Ferry Road. Buckhead was incorporated as a town in 1908.

Prelude to the Battle of Peachtree Creek

Along Moores Mill Rd., Ridge-
wood Rd., Boulder Rd., and
Peachtree Battle Ave.
Atlanta, GA

In the week prior the Battle of Peachtree Creek, which was fought on July 20, 1864, one of the Federal objectives was to wrest strategic control from the Confederates of the western end of the valley of Peachtree Creek in order to fully open the way to Atlanta from the north. Confederate infantrymen posted along Peachtree Creek and Nancy Creek assumed the defense of the area from Major General Joseph Wheeler's cavalry, who were ordered to move to the east after burning the bridges over Peachtree Creek at the present-day Ridgewood, Moores Mill, and Howell Mill roads. The Confederate brigades of brigadier generals John Adams, Daniel Reynolds, and Claudius Sears were entrenched on the wooded ridges above the south bank of Peachtree Creek from its confluence with the Chattahoochee River to Howell's Mill three miles upstream. Federal Major General John M. Palmer's XIV Corps,

Right: *Late nineteenth-century photo of Atlanta landmark Moore's Mill. The mill was damaged but not destroyed during military operations along Peachtree Creek. (Courtesy of the Atlanta History Center)*

consisting of fourteen thousand men, advanced through this sector. Though greatly outnumbered, the Confederates put up a tenacious resistance along the line.

However, much of the military activity that occurred along Peachtree Creek during mid-July 1864 has been overshadowed by a concurrent event: the change in Confederate command on July 17 followed shortly by General John B. Hood's three desperate but failed offensives of late July. Because of these events, most histories written on the Atlanta Campaign overlook troop movements and combat along the western end of Peachtree Creek, essentially dooming these events to obscurity.

The sites where these actions occurred are all in close proximity to the Buckhead area in northwest Atlanta, where remnants of trench lines and rifle pits can still be found. Since most if not all of these sites are located on private property, they should only be viewed from the state historical markers and along the roadside. Since traffic in these areas is generally heavy, parking on a nearby side street and walking to the markers is recommended for safest viewing.

Below: *Atlanta History Center*
(Photo: Bob Price)

Atlanta History Center

The thirty-three-acre Atlanta History Center, in Buckhead, includes one of the Southeast's largest history museums and most comprehensive Civil War artifact collections. The award-winning, permanent exhibition Turning Point: The American Civil War, located in the 9,200-square-foot DuBose Gallery, features more than fifteen hundred Union and Confederate artifacts, enabling visitors to experience the Civil War through soldier and civilian eyes. Highlights include the Confederate flag that flew over Atlanta during its surrender, a Union supply wagon used by Major General William T. Sherman's army, Major General Patrick R. Cleburne's sword, rare Georgia-made Confederate arms and accoutrements, a Medal of Honor won by the United States Colored Troops in Virginia, and the logbooks of the CSS *Shenandoah*. Dioramas, videos, and interactive learning stations help further bring the war to life. A final section explores how the Civil War impacts Americans today.

The James G. Kenan Research Center at the Atlanta History Center offers public research space with open access to archival resources for the study of Atlanta, the Civil War, family genealogy, and regional history and culture. The 42,000-square-foot library possesses more than 15,000 cubic feet of records, including Civil War regimental histories, military manuals, letters, diaries, and manuscript and photograph collections.

Also on the Atlanta History Center campus are the 1928 Swan House, the 1860s Tullie Smith farm, and five historic gardens. The midtown campus, on Tenth and Peachtree Streets, includes the Margaret Mitchell House.

130 West Paces Ferry Rd.
Atlanta, GA 30305-1366
404-814-4000
www.atlantahistorycenter.com

Museum:
Mon.–Sat.: 9:00 a.m.–5:30 p.m.
Sun.: Noon–5:00 p.m.

Library and Archives:
Wed.–Sat.: 10:00 a.m.–5:00 p.m.

Battle at Moore's Mill

On July 18, 1864, the Confederates of Brigadier General John Adams' and Brigadier General Daniel Reynolds' brigades were entrenched on the high bluff south of Peachtree Creek. From this position they held off numerous assaults by Union troops from Brigadier General James D. Morgan's brigades. Reynolds' brigade, along with

Moores Mill Rd. at
Peachtree Creek
Atlanta, GA

the 15th Mississippi Regiment from Adams' brigade, initiated a successful counter-attack in which they captured sixty prisoners from the 52nd Ohio, including Colonel Charles Clancy. The 10th Michigan Regiment, occupying the two mill buildings and the surrounding ground on the north side of the creek, destroyed the flume and damaged the dam, thus emptying the millpond. After continued fighting the following day, the Confederates were forced off the bluff by a Union flanking movement that crossed Peachtree Creek between the confluence with Nancy Creek and the Chattahoochee River.

Although not a large engagement, its importance is often overlooked. With the Federal breakthrough and the collapse of Confederate resistance along Peachtree Creek, the stage was set for the Battle of Peachtree Creek. As the Confederates were being forced back into Atlanta's Outer Defense Line, the way was opened for Federal control of the Peachtree Creek valley.

The two historical markers on Moores Mill Road at the east end of the bridge over Peachtree Creek are located on the roadbed that led to Moore's Mill several hundred yards downstream.

Green Bone Creek

On Peachtree Battle Ave.
east of Bohler Rd. at
the bottom of the hill
Atlanta, GA

At the mouth of Green Bone Creek, a small tributary of Peachtree Creek, the first successful Federal crossing of Peachtree Creek occurred on July 19, 1864. While traversing a fallen log, Colonel Caleb J. Dilworth's brigade was assailed by elements of Brigadier General Daniel Reynolds' and Brigadier General John Adams' Confederate brigades, their pickets having detected the Federal movement earlier in the day. On what is now the Cross Creek Golf Course and along the I-75 corridor, the fighting raged as the Confederate assault came out of the wooded ridgeline toward Peachtree Creek and up the Green Bone Creek valley. The Confederates were repulsed and then driven from their works. Although a short but volatile fight, the Federal 3rd Brigade suffered heavily before effecting a lodgment on the south bank.

Crestlawn Memorial Park

2000 Marietta Blvd.
Atlanta, GA 30318
404-355-3380

Daily: Dawn to dusk

The high ridgeline running through Crestlawn Memorial Park known as Casey's Hill was named in honor of Atlanta pioneer John A. Casey, who lived on this hill near the site of the old Montgomery Church, a prewar landmark. Casey's Hill, which provides an outstanding view of the city, was chosen as the position for the far left of the Confederate Outer Defense Line. The original road from Atlanta to Marietta crossed this hill and via Montgomery's Ferry continued north to Marietta. A section of the original road is still visible today, as are a section of Confederate earthworks and a gun emplacement. This portion of the Outer Defense Line was occupied by elements of Confederate Major General Samuel G. French's division on July 18–21, 1864, before, during, and after the Battle of Peachtree Creek, when it was abandoned for a defensive line farther to the south.

Left: *Crestlawn Memorial Park: Casey's Hill, the site of the Confederate Outer Defense Line, allows for an outstanding panoramic view of the city.* (Photo: Barry Brown)

Battle of Peachtree Creek

Across the Clear Creek valley and along the Collier Road corridor from Peachtree Creek on the east to Defoor's Ferry Road on the west was the site of major conflict. It was the first of General John B. Hood's three offensive maneuvers in July 1864 in an effort to defend Atlanta. After taking command of the Confederate army in front of Atlanta on July 18, 1864, Hood wasted no time in attempting to defeat the Federal armies aligned against him. He first chose to commit two of his three corps against Major General George H. Thomas' Army of the Cumberland.

Hood's planned offensive against Thomas was for a massive assault en echelon by brigade front beginning to the east near the intersection of Peachtree Street and Collier Road and unfolding to the west. The time set for the attack was one o'clock in the afternoon, July 20, 1864, and was to be led by Lt. General William Hardee's corps followed by Lt. General Alexander P. Stewart's corps. Ideally the Confederates would strike as the Federals crossed Peachtree Creek and, catching them in a vulnerable position, would then drive their line several miles north into the angle formed by Peachtree Creek's confluence with the Chattahoochee River, thus forcing their surrender.

Hood's planned troop alignment as well as the one o'clock start time was complicated by events on Decatur Road, to the east. Major General James B. McPherson's Army of the Tennessee had advanced to a point within two and a half miles from the city center leaving a small cavalry force and about seven hundred state-line troops between him and the city. Hood was forced to move his entire line eastward to meet the threat. The Confederate realignment took several hours, and the assault began at four o'clock. It is debatable whether the

Along Peachtree Battle Ave., Peachtree St., Collier Rd., Howell Mill Rd., Northside Dr., and Brighton Rd.
Atlanta, GA

Below: *Monument to the Battle of Peachtree Creek located on a knoll in front of Piedmont Hospital* (Photo: Barry Brown)

delay was a help or hinderance to Hood's plan, but the massive attack was put in motion nonetheless.

The fighting started near today's Brighton Road on the east and extended to Peachtree Street and along Collier Road across Northside Drive and Howell Mill Road to I-75 on the west. In the resulting Battle of Peachtree Creek, Thomas' line was pressed to the extreme, and even broke temporarily, but managed to hold. The Confederates were forced to return to their Outer Defense Line after suffering a repulse with the cost of 1,900 casualties. The Federals were left in control of the field after sustaining 2,500 casualties and were able to continue their encirclement of the city, albeit with more caution. This costly sortie gained little for Hood, while it put Major General William T. Sherman on notice that Atlanta would be stubbornly defended and, despite his proximity, not be an easy goal to attain.

A number of state historical markers in the Collier Road, Northside Drive, and Peachtree/Brighton Road neighborhoods identify significant sites in the Battle of Peachtree Creek. A 1944 stone monument memorializing the courage of the American soldier is located on a small rise in front of Piedmont Hospital on Peachtree Street directly north of Collier Road. On Peachtree Street directly south of the Peachtree Battle Road intersection, where the road crosses the creek, Thomas directed the battle, including Federal artillery fire against a Confederate breakthrough. Other important sites are noted by markers along Collier Drive at the railroad crossing; the Bobby Jones Golf Course opposite Colonial Homes Drive; the Northside Drive entrance to the Bitsy Grant Tennis Center, where the Confederate assault succeeded in breaking the Federal line; and at the Mt. Zion Church at Howell Mill Road north of I-75.

Tanyard Creek Park

Collier Rd. at Redlands Rd. next to the bridge over Tanyard Creek Atlanta, GA www.friendsoftanyardcreekpark.org

The Tanyard Creek Park was dedicated in 1964 as a memorial commemorating the one hundredth anniversary of the Battle of Peachtree Creek. The park encompasses land that once held Andrew J. Collier's mill, originally located about a hundred yards downstream from the Collier Road bridge, and was the site of a Federal artillery battery involved in desperate and costly fighting during the battle. From this site the Federals used socks packed with minié balls as rounds of ammunition for their cannon, decimating the attacking Confederate columns as if with enormous shotgun blasts. Millstones and steel gears from the mill are displayed next to the Collier Road bridge over Tanyard Creek. Historical markers and stone tablets in front of the parking area off Collier Road give a list of the forces engaged in the fighting along with a chronological account of the battle.

Left: *Millstones from Collier's Mill, the site of intense fighting on July 20, 1864 (Photo: Bob Price)*

ATLANTA, Fulton County

First named Terminus and then Marthasville, the city underwent its final name change in 1845. The name Atlanta, a feminine of Atlantic, was likely inspired by the city's role as a major transportation hub and the endpoint of the Western and Atlantic Railroad. Atlanta was incorporated in 1848 with a population of twenty-one and an area extending one mile in all directions from the railroad terminus at the zero milepost.

A thriving community from the beginning due its importance as a railroad hub, Atlanta had a relatively small population of ten thousand by the time Georgia seceded from the Union on January 19, 1861. During the war, Atlanta's population more than doubled, becoming the second-most populated city in the Confederacy, eclipsed only by the capital, Richmond, Virginia (New Orleans was occupied by Federal troops after April 1862).

Railroads were the key to the war's logistics. Unfortunately for the Southern war effort, its railroad system became extremely overtaxed by the burdens of maintaining a wartime supply system. During the war, just one direct railroad line linked the Eastern and Western theaters of operation, tied together by a single link that ran through Atlanta. Due to this vital transportation link, Atlanta became an important center of industrial manufacturing for war materiel, as well as the location of many large hospitals that cared for the sick and wounded.

As the war entered its third year, the amount of territory under Southern control continued to shrink. The loss was attributable to the inability of the Confederacy to halt the ever-encroaching movement of Union forces across the thousand-mile front that made up the Western Theater. Many war industries, newspapers, hospitals, and refugees fled to Atlanta from these conquered areas, setting up shop in the Gate City.

By the second half of 1863, Atlanta had become a fortified military center. In anticipation of invasion, Captain Lemuel P. Grant, a Maine-born army engineer, was assigned the task of designing a ring of fortifications around the city. He oversaw the building of interconnected earthworks constructed at an approximately one-and-a-half mile circumference from the centrally located Five Point's intersection in downtown Atlanta using slave labor purchased from area farms and plantations.

With the opening of the military campaign season in the spring of 1864, Lt. General Ulysses S. Grant planned a double offensive against the eastern and western Confederate armies, exerting pressure through military envelopment as a terra firma version of Winfield Scott's Anaconda Plan from 1861. As the newly appointed head of all Federal armies, Grant placed his trusted lieutenant and friend, Major General William T. Sherman, in command of three armies. Sherman's assigned goals were to force the capitulation of Atlanta while destroying the Confederate Army of Tennessee.

Following a hard-fought campaign known as the Hundred Days Battle through northwest Georgia from Dalton to Atlanta, combat reached the city's gates by late July 1864. Unable to sever all the tenuous railroad lifelines, Sherman resorted to siege tactics, bombarding the city with as many as five thousand projectiles a day. When the last remaining railroad came under Federal control south of the city at Jonesboro, Atlanta capitulated on September 2, 1864. The battered though still formidable Confederate army, no longer constrained by having to defend territory, embarked on an offensive campaign. They marched off through north Georgia, toward Nashville and ultimate defeat.

The true impact of the fall of Atlanta went far deeper than the military advantages gained by the destruction of the city's war industry, or the cessation of vital food and armament shipments that maintained the Southern war effort, or the devastation to Southern morale. In the 1864 presidential referendum, northern Copperhead Demo-

Atlanta CVB
233 Peachtree St., NE, Ste. 100
Atlanta, GA 30303
404-521-6600/800-285-2682
www.atlanta.net

FULTON COUNTY JAIL   CITY HALL SOLOMON RES.   CREW RES. TRINITY CHURCH   NEAL RES.
GA·R·R· ENGINE HOUSE 2 ST·PHILIP'S CH·   CEN'L PRESB CH· 2ⁿᵈ BAPTIST CH·
MOUND HOUSE WASHINGTON HALL   CITY PARK   IMMACULATE CONCEPTION CH·   CITY MARKET
                                                   CAR SHED   AMERICAN HOTEL   ATLANTA IN 1864   CALABOOSE ENGINE HOUSE 1
LOYD ST·   MASONIC HALL TROUT HOUSE   M·&·W· FREIGHT DEPOT
                                                   ATHENÆUM   ATLANTA HOTEL   GA·R·R· BANK   CONCERT HALL INTELLIGENCER OFFICE   JACK'S BAKERY:C·S·A·   BRIDGE
PRYOR ST·   FIVE POINTS   NORCROSS' STORE   GEN MARCUS WRIGHTS HDQRS   WADLEY (FORSYTH) ST·   MARIETTA S
              PEACHTREE ST·   BRIDGE (BROAD) ST·   WALTON ST·   TALLULAH FIRE CO·
                                                                                    ST·LUKE'S CH·

Above: *Atlanta in 1864 (Wilbur Kurtz Collection, Courtesy of the Atlanta History Center and Beverly M. DuBose III)*

crats chose a "peace" candidate to run against President Abraham Lincoln on the platform that continuation of the war would bring death, debt, and destruction with no end in sight. The peace platform was vigorously championed by primary proponents Ohio Congressman Clement Vallandigham and former New York City Mayor Fernando Wood. It acquired great popular support. Their candidate was Lincoln's old nemesis, the twice-fired Army of the Potomac commander Major General George B. McClellan. Lincoln, having his feet held to the fire by Frederick Douglass on the issue of slavery, maintained the original war aims of unification of the nation and emancipation before any peace would be considered. An experienced and savvy politician, Lincoln was cognizant of shifting political winds, fully expecting to be "beaten and beaten badly" in the upcoming November presidential referendum. After having endured over three years of bloody warfare, the nation needed to maintain the will and determination required to "see the thing through." The Copperhead Democrats were depending on war weariness and a national lack of patience with "Lincoln's war" to put them in the White House. Lincoln required success on the battlefield to maintain the viability of his platform.

Somehow, somewhere in the Eastern or Western theaters, the stalemate had to be broken, as the future path of the nation lay in the balance. Victory in the Atlanta Campaign was the catalyst to changing public perception, giving hope of a definite and timely military victory to the people of the North. Atlanta's fall pushed the Lincoln administration to political victory, making him the first two-term president since Andrew Jackson and assuring that his war aims were carried out to a successful conclusion.

Battle of Atlanta

Dekalb Ave., Memorial Dr.,
Moreland Ave., Glenwood Ave.,
Degress Ave.
Atlanta, GA

After suffering defeat at the hands of Major General George H. Thomas' Army of the Cumberland at Peachtree Creek on July 20, 1864, General John B. Hood attempted another offensive flanking maneuver on July 22, this time on the city's east side. Hood's plan was to entice Major General James B. McPherson's Army of the Tennessee closer to the Atlanta inner fortifications by moving Confederate troops out of the outer fortifications, allowing them to be filled by Federals. While this maneuver was taking place, Lt. General William Hardee's corps was on a fifteen-mile march from the present intersection of Spring and Peachtree streets to assail the Federals on what he expected to be their unprotected left and rear. Simultaneously, Major General Joseph Wheeler's cavalry was to cut Major General William T. Sherman's supply line at Decatur while Major General Benjamin F. Cheatham's corps attacked the Federal front and center. It was a brilliant plan.

A major problem arose, however, with the miscalculation in timing that delayed Hardee's early-morning attack until the afternoon. In the meantime, McPherson realized that his flank was vulnerable, although at the time he had no idea that this unprotected flank was to be the target of the Confederate attack. McPherson deployed Major General Grenville M. Dodge's corps to fill the gap before Hardee's surprise attack took place, a move that changed the dynamic of Hood's entire plan.

Two of Hardee's divisions assaulted Dodge's corps, which was posted on the high ground at the present site of Alonzo Crim High School adjacent to Memorial Drive, but were repulsed all along the line. During this early phase of the Battle of Atlanta, while leading troops around the marshy wetlands of Terry's Mill Pond, Confederate Major General W. H. T. Walker was shot from his horse by a Federal picket and killed instantly.

Major General Patrick R. Cleburne's Confederates, after continuous costly charges, finally broke the Federal line but were unable to exploit the success on a prominence known as Bald Hill or Leggett's Hill. The Federals managed to drive off Cleburne with heavy artillery fire, inflicting an almost 40 percent casualty rate.

The attack on the Federal rear had stalled, but the forces attacking the left flank were having some success. McPherson was shot dead by Confederate skirmishers while riding to this part of the field. Cheatham, like Cleburne, had also broken through until Sherman himself, from his headquarters at the Augustus Hurt House on the hill at the site of the present Carter Presidential Library, ordered the fire of twenty guns massed at the breakthrough site. A counterattack led by Illinois politician and Lincoln appointee Major General John A. "Black Jack" Logan drove back Cheatham's men and ended the day of vicious fighting with the Federals in control of the field. This battle is portrayed in the Cyclorama painting at Grant Park.

Markers along Dekalb Avenue near the Inman Park and Candler Park MARTA stations identify the sites of the battle depicted in the painting. Most notable is the site of the Troup Hurt House near the intersection of Degress and Dekalb avenues, where Brigadier General Arthur Manigault's Confederate brigade is portrayed defending the five-gun Degress Battery that was captured from the Federals in a costly charge. The Federals, attempting to retake the position, are depicted shooting the Confederate battery horses to prevent the Confederates from moving the captured

Below: At the corner of Memorial Drive and Clay Street, Confederate troops struck the Federal line, opening the Battle of Atlanta.
(Photo: Barry Brown)

Above: *Federals of Mersey's Brigade retake Degress' Illinois battery of twenty-pound Parrott Rifles at the Battle of Atlanta, July 22, 1864. The Troup Hurt House is in the background. (Painting by Don Troiani, www .historicalartprints.com)*

guns. This breakthrough, though temporary, was one of the few Confederate successes of the day.

The Atlanta neighborhoods of Inman Park, Little Five Points, Kirkwood, and East Atlanta are today located over most of the area where the Battle of Atlanta was fought. In the late 1970s and early 1980s, much of the land where key portions of the battle raged was cleared in preparation for the construction of Freedom Parkway. However, the construction of I-20 in 1962 obliterated the Battle of Atlanta's most notable landmark, Bald Hill or Leggett's Hill, the site of some of the bloodiest fighting of the campaign.

To tour the battlefield of July 22, 1864, a good point to start is the Inman Park–Reynolds Town MARTA station. The battlefield in this area is well interpreted by state historical markers, including Springvale Park one block to the north and Degress Avenue a few blocks to the east. In the area north of Dekalb Avenue and adjacent to the MARTA station are three interpretative markers, placed by the Georgia Battlefields Association, that describe the Confederate breakthrough and Federal counterattack. The long-obliterated Bald Hill was located where Moreland Avenue crosses over Memorial Drive at the I-20 bridge.

Dexter Niles House Site

The Dexter Niles House was the site of General Joseph E. Johnston's final headquarters as commander of the Confederate Army of Tennessee. A convenient location for the commander, the house fronted the Western and Atlantic Railroad and the Atlanta-Marietta wagon road halfway between the Chattahoochee River and the then center of Atlanta. Here on the night of July 17, 1864, Johnston received a telegram from Confederate Inspector General Samuel Cooper relieving him of command. His removal was a result of Confederate President Jefferson Davis having lost confidence in Johnston's ability to turn back the Federal juggernaut encircling Atlanta. General John B. Hood, who had a reputation as an aggressive combat commander, took his place.

After reading the telegram relieving him, Johnston wrote out his famous "General Orders No. 4," announcing the transfer of command to Hood and expressing farewell to the army. His words were communicated to the troops the next day. From this point on, the tenor of the campaign would vastly change.

A state historical marker denotes the location where the home once stood. There is also a monument consisting of a pyramidal stack of round shot placed atop a concrete base with a plaque.

950 West Marietta St.
Atlanta, GA 30318

Above: *Monument at the site of the Dexter Niles House (Photo: Bob Price)*

Surrender of Atlanta Site

The only evidence to indicate that this busy intersection is the place where Atlanta Mayor James M. Calhoun surrendered the city of Atlanta to Federal Colonel John Coburn on September 2, 1864, is the state historical marker on the north corner.

Here, as in much of the city, nothing visible remains from the war. However, on a nearby street, Fort Hood Place, is the site of one of the larger Confederate fortifications that ringed the city. Also the Georgia Institute of Technology Aquatic Center, visible from the intersection, is built on the site of the Ponder House, the stark shell-pocked landmark from George Barnard's series of Atlanta Campaign photographs.

Northeast corner of Northside Dr.
and Marietta St.
Atlanta, GA

Left: *War-era view near the site of Mayor Calhoun's surrender of Atlanta showing Confederate fortifications in the foreground and the Ponder House in the background (Photo: George Barnard, courtesy of the LIbrary of Congress).*
Above: *General John B. Hood (Courtesy of the UGA Hargrett Rare Book and Manuscript Library)*

Site of James J. Andrews' Execution

In April 1862, James J. Andrews and nineteen of his handpicked Federal soldiers and civilians attempted an espionage mission deep in Southern territory. Their intention was to cut telegraph lines, sabotage railroad tracks, and destroy bridges on the Western and Atlantic Railroad between Big Shanty (Kennesaw), Georgia, and Chattanooga, Tennessee. They wanted to keep Confederate reinforcements from traveling up the line to stop the Federal force that was advancing from Huntsville, Alabama, to capture Chattanooga. This incident, known as Andrews' Raid, failed due to haphazard planning, bad weather, and the unexpected tenacity of Captain William A. Fuller and his men.

Originally imprisoned in Chattanooga, Andrews was tried, convicted, and sentenced to death. Seven other raiders received the same sentence and were shipped to Atlanta along with Andrews. Shortly after his arrival at the Fulton County Jail on June 7, 1862, Andrews was taken to the present-day intersection of Juniper and Third streets, executed by hanging, and buried nearby in an unmarked grave.

On April 11, 1887, Andrews' bones were exhumed and transferred to the National Cemetery in Chattanooga to lie beneath a memorial topped by a locomotive.

Site of the First Federal Shell to Fall in Atlanta

The first Federal shell fell on the east corner of the intersection of Ellis Street and Ivy Street (now Peachtree Center Avenue) on July 20, 1864, marking the beginning of Major General William T. Sherman's warfare against the civilian population of Atlanta. The shell killed a young girl who was crossing the intersection with her parents. At the height of the bombardment, the city would be struck by as many as five thousand projectiles a day, though only about fifty civilians were killed.

Right: *Residents preparing to leave Atlanta on orders of General Sherman (Courtesy of the UGA Hargrett Rare Book and Manuscript Library)*

Site of Solomon Luckie's Mortal Wounding

This gas streetlamp is one of fifty erected by the Atlanta Gas Light Company in 1856. It stands adjacent to where Atlanta barber Solomon "Sam" Luckie was standing while talking with a group of businessmen on July 22, 1864, when a Union shell struck the base of the lamp, wounding Luckie in the leg with a piece of shrapnel. He was carried to a local surgeon where his leg was amputated, but he died a few hours later.

Luckie, a freed black, owned the Barber and Bath salon in the nearby Atlanta Hotel. Luckie Street was later renamed in his honor. The gaslight was relit in a ceremony commemorating his memory during the 1939 movie premier of *Gone with the Wind*. It was then known as the "Eternal Flame of the Confederacy."

In Underground Atlanta at the gaslight at Lower Alabama St. and the MARTA Tunnel
Atlanta, GA

Shrine of the Immaculate Conception (NRHP)

The first Roman Catholic church in Atlanta was a rectangular wood-framed building constructed in 1848. Wartime priest Father Thomas O'Reilly's influence with Union Major General Henry Slocum saved the shell-damaged building along with several other local churches and the nearby city hall on November 15, 1864. Father O'Reilly supposedly warned General Slocum, "If you burn the Catholic Church, all Catholics in the ranks of the Union Army will mutiny." He then went on to include four other churches in the negotiation.

A monument to Father O'Reilly in front of Atlanta City Hall at the corner of Mitchell and Washington streets credits him with preventing the destruction of the following buildings in the vicinity: Atlanta City Hall, the Church of the Immaculate Conception, St. Philip's Episcopal Church, and the Central Presbyterian Church.

The present Victorian Gothic Revival church was constructed between 1869 and 1873 and is one of the oldest buildings in the city. Father O'Reilly is buried in a crypt in the basement. In 1954, the Church of the Immaculate Conception was rededicated as a shrine.

48 Martin Luther King Jr. Dr.
Atlanta, GA 30303
404-521-1866
www.archatl.com/parishes/
immaculateconception.html

Left: The burning of the railroad roundhouse at Atlanta on November 14, 1864 (Courtesy of the UGA Hargrett Rare Book and Manuscript Library)

Georgia State Capitol and Museum (NRHP)

431 Capitol Ave.
Atlanta, GA 30334
404-656-2844
404-651-6996 (museum)
www.georgiacapitolmuseum.org

Museum:
Mon.–Fri.: 8:00 a.m.–5:30 p.m.

The Georgia State Capitol sits on the site of Atlanta's wartime City Hall and Fulton County Courthouse building, built in 1853. During Major General William T. Sherman's occupation of the city, the 2nd Massachusetts Regiment, serving as the Federal Army's Provost Guard, encamped on the grounds. City Hall survived Sherman's conflagration and was later replaced by the current neoclassical stone capitol building, completed in 1889. Atlanta became the state capital in 1868, three years after the war, acquiring the distinction from the central-Georgia town of Milledgeville.

The capitol houses the Flags That Have Flown Over Georgia: History of the Georgia State Flag exhibit located on the bottom floor. Many of the Georgia Civil War regimental flags are included in this rotating collection. Former Museum Director Dorothy Olson worked for years collecting, reconstituting, and preserving the historic banners. The flags on display are not restricted to the War Between the States but span the colonial era to the Persian Gulf conflict, giving a martial overview of Georgia's history. A booklet telling the story of each flag in the collection is available at the museum with all proceeds going toward the acquisition and preservation of these delicate, finite relics.

The walls of the capitol are lined with portraits and the halls filled with monuments honoring Georgians of distinction and luminary Southerners Robert E. Lee, George Washington, and Andrew Jackson. Other wartime statesman and military notables include Alfred H. Colquitt, Robert A. Toombs, Hershel V. Johnson, and Alexander H. Stephens and a larger-than-life statue of Confederate congressman Benjamin Harvey Hill.

On the capitol's well-manicured grounds are statues of leaders from throughout Georgia's history, such as Tom Watson, a Populist leader, presidential candidate, senator, and author from the east-Georgia town of Thomson. An equestrian statue commemorates Confederate general, governor, and senator John B. Gordon, possibly the most influential Georgian of the nineteenth century. Wartime governor Joseph E. Brown and his wife, Elizabeth, are also memorialized on the grounds. In addition, a monument relevant to Reconstruction, aptly titled

Below, left to right: *Georgia's wartime governor, Joe Brown, and his wife are commemorated in front of the capitol (Photo: Marla Bexley-Brown); the camp of the 2nd Massachusetts Infantry on the grounds of the Atlanta City Hall (Courtesy of the Library of Congress)*

"Expelled Because of Color," commemorates the thirty-three black Republican state legislators who were removed from their positions after a vote by a coalition of white Democrats and Republicans in September 1868.

Augustus Hurt House Site

The Carter Presidential Center now occupies the hilltop site where the house of Atlanta pioneer Augustus Hurt once stood. The Confederate's Outer Defense Line, which was evacuated on July 21, 1864, was located on the hill's eastern slope. Erroneously referred to by the occupying Federals in their dispatches as the Howard House, the house and grounds were the headquarters for generals William T. Sherman, Oliver Otis Howard, and John Schofield during the fighting on July 22, 1864. It is also the site where Major General James B. McPherson's body was brought after being retrieved from the field by an ambulance. From this vantage point, Sherman ordered several batteries to be massed and direct their fire at that critical point in the line to drive back the attacking forces, thus helping to win the day for the Army of the Tennessee.

Carter Presidential Center
1 Copenhill Ave.
441 Freedom Pkwy.
Atlanta, GA 30307
404-865-7100
www.cartercenter.org

Mon–Sat.: 9:00 a.m.–4:45 p.m.
Sun.: Noon–4:45 p.m.

Left: *The Augustus Hurt House, which served as General Sherman's headquarters on July 22, 1864, during the Battle of Atlanta (Wilbur Kurtz Collection, courtesy of the Atlanta History Center).* Above: *Springvale Park Monument (Photo: Phillip Lovell)*

Springvale Park

This wooded ravine with its small stream was the site where Confederate Brigadier General Arthur Manigault's brigade, using the cover provided by the slope, prepared for a final assault on the Degress Battery at the Troup Hurt House on July 22, 1864. After the Confederates captured the position, the Federals counterattacked and succeeded in retaking it. A state historical marker and stone monument describe the fighting at this point.

Edgewood Ave. and Waverly Way
Atlanta, GA

Oakland Cemetery

248 Oakland Ave. SE
Atlanta, GA 30312
404-688-2107
 www.oaklandcemetery.com

Open daily until dusk

Established in 1850, Oakland Cemetery is Atlanta's most important historic cemetery, with close connections to the city's Civil War history. It is also an excellent example of the nineteenth-century Rural Cemetery Movement, when cemeteries served as urban gathering places. Interred within forty-eight acres are five Confederate generals, including John B. Gordon, Clement Anselm Evans, and Alfred Iverson Jr., as well as thirty-nine hundred known and three thousand unknown Confederate soldiers, many of whom died at hospitals in Atlanta between 1862 and 1864. Monuments were erected in memory of the Confederate dead, including a sixty-five-foot-tall stone obelisk following Robert E. Lee's death in 1870 and a statue of a dying lion. The lion statue was based on the famous monument in Lucerne, Switzerland, which was dedicated to the seven hundred Swiss guards killed during the French Revolution while defending Louis XVI.

Interred in family plots separate from the Confederate section are statesman Benjamin Harvey Hill, who before serving in the Confederate congress was active in the Whig and Know-Nothing parties; Brigadier General Lucius J. Gartrell, a "fire eating" advocate of states' rights; and North Carolina district commander General William S. Walker.

Seven of Andrews' Raiders, who were convicted of being spies for their participation in the Great Locomotive Chase of April 1862, were hanged outside the cemetery gates along Memorial Drive (then known as Fair Street) and were buried in Oakland. They were later reinterred at the Federal Cemetery in Chattanooga, Tennessee, in 1866. A bronze plaque on the inner wall of Oakland's Memorial Drive entrance honors their memory. Also buried here are three Confederate participants in this event: Captain William A. Fuller, Jeff Cain, and Anthony Murphy.

At one of the cemetery's highest points, near the bell tower, a state historical marker indicates the site of the James E. Williams House. From the house's second floor balcony, General John B. Hood and members of his staff watched the Confederate assault on the Federal XV Corps during the Battle of Atlanta on July 22, 1864.

Oakland Cemetery is a favorite spot for jogging and sightseeing. The grave site of Margaret Mitchell, author of *Gone with the Wind*, is the cemetery's most visited. Cemetery tours are regularly conducted on weekends and sometimes on weekdays. Parking in the cemetery and the surrounding area is available. Call or check the cemetery's website for specific inquiries.

Below: *The monument to the unknown Confederate dead at Oakland Cemetery (Photo: Bob Price)*

Cyclorama and Grant Park (NRHP)

800-C Cherokee Ave. SE
Atlanta, GA 30315
404-624-1071

Civil War Museum and Bookstore:
Mon.–Sun.: 9:20 a.m.–4:30 p.m.

Colonel Lemuel P. Grant, the Confederate's chief engineer of the Department of Georgia, who later became a wealthy Atlanta railroad entrepreneur, gifted land to the city of Atlanta for a park in 1882. Grant Park is the home of several major Atlanta attractions, including the award-winning Zoo Atlanta and the Cyclorama, one of the world's largest circular paintings with a diorama, which depicts major portions of the Battle of Atlanta on July 22, 1864.

The painting vividly portrays the Federal counterattack led by Major General John A. Logan. Another major focus of the painting is the intense fighting that occurred in the vicinity of the Troup Hurt House around the captured Federal Degress Battery.

The painting was created by a team of German artists with the American Panorama Company in Milwaukee, Wisconsin. The artists studied the topography of the battlefield and interviewed veterans to produce the most accurate representation possible. Famed *Harper's Weekly* illustrator Theodore Davis, an eyewitness to the battle, served as a consultant. The painting toured the country until 1892 when, in Atlanta, the exhibitors ran out of funds. In 1898 the painting was deeded to the city by lumber dealer George Gress and was moved to Grant Park. However, it was not given a permanent home until the present marble building was constructed in 1921.

Above: *Cyclorama (Photo courtesy of the Cyclorama)*

More changes were made to the Cyclorama in the 1930s under the auspices of President Roosevelt's WPA and local historian and artist Wilbur Kurtz, when a three-dimensional diorama, including plaster figures of soldiers, was added to give the painting a more realistic look and feel. After the 1939 premier of *Gone with the Wind*, one of the dead Federal soldiers in the foreground was given the face of the movie's male lead, Clark Gable.

In 1967 a violent thunderstorm heavily damaged the building and the painting. A detailed investigation uncovered further deterioration. Continuing problems forced the building to close in 1979 so that renovation to both the painting and the structure could be done. After a seven-million-dollar renovation, the Cyclorama reopened amid great fanfare in 1982. Tiered seating that revolves 360 degrees around the circular painting was added along with an updated narrative.

The Cyclorama experience begins with a thirteen-minute film explaining the campaign that led to the battle. The film features five thousand Civil War reenactors and is narrated by actor James Earl Jones. The *Texas*, the most famous of the three locomotives commandeered by conductor Captain William A. Fuller in pursuit of Andrews' Raiders during the Great Locomotive Chase, stands in the lobby.

The Civil War museum on the second floor features artifacts relating to the Atlanta Campaign and an interactive computer display that reports on the activity of every day of the four-year war.

Lemuel P. Grant Mansion

In 1857 Colonel Lemuel P. Grant built a two-story Italianate mansion on his large estate. A native of Maine and an engineer by training, Grant was the Confederate officer responsible for Atlanta's extensive protective fortifications. A railroad magnate, city builder, and philanthropist, he became one of Atlanta's leading citizens during the late nineteenth century. In 1882, he donated one hundred acres of his property to the city of Atlanta for a park that bears his name: Grant Park.

Atlanta Preservation Center
327 St. Paul Ave.
Atlanta, GA 30312
404-688-3353
www.preserveatlanta.com

The Grant Mansion is one of three surviving antebellum homes in the city and was also the birthplace of golfing great Robert Tyre "Bobby" Jones. At one time Margaret Mitchell, the author of *Gone with the Wind* and an advocate for the house, loaned money to a friend to buy the house. When her friend failed to maintain the home to the standards she expected, she filed a lawsuit against him.

The home has persevered through decades of neglect and several fires. The two-foot-thick walls of this once stately structure, which contained nine fireplaces and a ballroom, are only a shadow of its former glory. Currently only a portion of the first floor is intact. It is currently being used as the headquarters for the Atlanta Preservation Center, a nonprofit preservation organization that is working on a capital campaign to restore the house and establish an endowment for its future maintenance.

Above: *Lemuel P. Grant Mansion (Courtesy of the Atlanta Preservation Center).*

Below: *The last remnants of the fortifications that encircled the city (Photo: Barry Brown)*

Fort Walker

On Boulevard at the southeast
corner of Atlanta Ave.
Atlanta, GA

An example of a nineteenth-century artillery redoubt and one of the few remnants from the twelve miles of defensive lines that encircled Atlanta, Fort Walker is named for Confederate Major General W.H.T. Walker, who was killed in the fighting east of Atlanta on July 22, 1864. Fort Walker is at the far end of a salient that was added to Colonel Lemuel P. Grant's fortifications around the city after the initial phase of earthwork construction was completed. The reason engineers chose this location is easily seen from the rampart, where there is a clear, commanding view of the surrounding valley, as well as the city's tall buildings off to the west. The guns of the battery had the range to control movement in the valley below. Fort Walker is an example of one of the obstacles that discouraged Major General William T. Sherman from taking the city by direct assault.

The Confederate trench line that connected Fort Walker with the rest of Colonel Grant's fortified line has long since disappeared; however, there are still remnants of earthworks on some of the higher prominences in Grant Park. The best example can be found on the perimeter of the ball field, where a portion of the works is faintly discernable for several hundred feet.

Monument to Confederate General W.H.T. Walker

Wilkinson Rd. and Glenwood Ave.
at I-20
Atlanta, GA

An upturned artillery tube stands at the approximate location where Major General W.H.T. Walker was killed on July 22, 1864. Walker was a native son of Augusta, Georgia; a West Point graduate; and a veteran of the Mexican-American War. Early in the battle, while leading troops around Terry's Mill Pond, Walker was shot dead by a Federal picket. General Joseph E. Johnston once pronounced Walker, who was then assigned to the Western Theater, the only officer fit to lead a division. Walker received the nickname "Old Shot Pouch" due to battle wounds he suffered in the Mexican-American War that caused him painful health problems throughout his life. He was forty-seven years old at the time of his death. He is buried in Augusta.

Monument to Federal General James B. McPherson

This granite monument with an upturned cannon tube marks the location where Major General James B. McPherson, the young and promising commander of the Federal Army of the Tennessee, was killed on July 22, 1864. McPherson graduated at the top of his West Point class of 1853, the same class as his adversary General John B. Hood. McPherson was killed by troops from Major General Patrick R. Cleburne's division who first attempted to get the Federal army commander to submit to capture after he inadvertently crossed into enemy lines. After being ordered to surrender, McPherson tipped his hat to the Confederates and wheeled his horse around in an attempt to escape. A volley was fired that struck the young general in the back; a round passed through his lung as he fled. At thirty-six, McPherson was the only Federal army commander killed in combat during the war.

McPherson Ave. and
Monument Rd.
Atlanta, GA

Left: *The momument to Major General McPherson (Photo: Bob Price)*

Battle of Ezra Church

The Battle of Ezra Church, also known as the Battle of the Alms House, followed General John B. Hood's defeats in the Battle of Peachtree Creek on July 20, 1864, and the Battle of Atlanta on July 22, 1864. It was also the last of three major offensive actions that Hood carried out in the Atlanta area.

Both Northern and Southern armies underwent changes in high command after the Battle of Atlanta. On the Confederate side Lt. General William Hardee, whose corps was heavily engaged in both battles, tendered his resignation due to his unhappiness with Hood's appointment. However, he remained after being persuaded by Confederate President Jefferson Davis not to request reassignment at such a crucial point in the campaign. In addition, Lt. General Stephen D. Lee was transferred to Georgia from a cavalry command in the Department of Mississippi to replace Hood as corps commander; Major General Benjamin F. Cheatham was returned to his previous assignment as commander of his Tennessee division.

Major General William T. Sherman's command change involved appointing a replacement for the slain Major General James B. McPherson. Major General Joseph Hooker was the senior corps commander and the logical choice. However Sherman didn't hold a high opinion of Hooker or his abilities but did regard next-in-line Major General Oliver Otis Howard as capable. Howard was Hooker's nemesis and the man he blamed for the Army of the Potomac's disaster at Chancellorsville, Virginia. When Sherman placed Howard in command of the Army of the Tennessee, Hooker naturally took this as a slight and requested to be relieved as commander of the XX Corps, in essence to be taken out of the Atlanta Campaign. Sherman gladly acquiesced to the request. Major General Henry Slocum was brought in from Mississippi as the replacement commander of the XX Corps. Major General John A. Logan, a political appointee, not a career military man, had taken command of McPherson's army

Mozley Park
1585 Martin Luther King Jr. Blvd.
Atlanta, GA

Below: *Wartime sketch of Confederate casualties following the Battle of Ezra Church (Courtesy of the UGA Hargrett Rare Book and Manuscript Library)*

Above: *One of the historical markers at Mozley Park (Photo: Bob Price)*

after his death on July 22, 1864, and also resented being replaced by Howard. Logan correctly saw the appointment as an example of West Point graduates receiving favorable consideration over that given to generals without a professional military background.

Sherman put in motion the events that would lead to the Battle of Ezra Church when he decided to approach Atlanta on the west side to cut the Macon and Western Railroad and the Atlanta and West Point Railroad at their juncture at East Point. This railroad was Atlanta's last major remaining avenue of supply, and cutting it would force the Confederates to abandon the city.

On the evening of July 26, 1864, the Federal Army of the Tennessee began a covert march from east of the city to the west side while Federal cavalry moved in to occupy the vacated trenches and give the visual impression that the army was still there. The Federals, silent in their movement, were at first successful with their ruse, not alerting the Confederate pickets. However, by midday on July 27, 1864, Hood was aware of the reconnaissance-in-force and was making plans to counter Sherman's movement. When Howard encountered determined resistance from Confederate cavalry, he deduced that the movement was discovered and an infantry attack was imminent. He ordered a halt and set up a makeshift defensive line on a ridge in today's Mozley Park adjacent to a small Methodist meetinghouse known as Ezra Church. Sherman, who had been following the movement, gleefully awaited the Confederate attack exclaiming, "They'll only beat their brains out."

Hood ordered Lt. General Stephen D. Lee's corps to move along Lickskillet Road to check Howard's advance. Confederate Lt. General Alexander P. Stewart's corps was given orders to march on Lee's left and attack Howard from the rear. At 12:30 on the afternoon of July 28, Lee's corps formed in line of battle and repeatedly assaulted the fortified Federal line. The Confederates were cut to pieces with an unusually high percentage of casualties among the officers. Later in the afternoon a Federal counterattack drove Lee's troops back to their starting point.

Stewart, realizing Lee was in trouble, didn't make the planned march around the Federal flank but instead struck in the front, attacking over the same body-strewn ground from which Lee had recently withdrawn. Stewart, while near the alms house gate at the present-day Westview Cemetery, was wounded in the forehead by a spent bullet and was removed from the field, with command temporarily going to one of his division leaders, Major General Edward C. Walthall. Walthall, who had just led three separate attacks by his division on horseback, fully realized the futility of continuing a frontal assault and decided to put an end to the slaughter. The attack was called off at four o'clock, thus ending the battle.

In terms of casualties, this was a severely lopsided battle. Hood, who was not present on the battlefield, suffered his third defeat in a row and sustained losses of about three thousand men. The Federals, deployed on high ground fighting from behind barricades, lost about 650. The Union attempt to cut the railroad had been temporarily halted, but the price was higher than the Army of Tennessee or the South could afford to pay. General Hardee afterward said, "So great was the loss in men, organization and morale in that engagement, that no action of the campaign probably did so much to demoralize and dishearten the troops engaged in it."

Mozley Park

State historical markers at Mozley Park track troop movements and battle action during the Battle of Ezra Church on July 27, 1864. Much of the fighting occurred in the area now bounded by the park. The terrain over which the Confederates assaulted and the Federals defended is still relatively unchanged. Unfortunately, nothing remains of the Ezra Church, located near the center of the Federal line and from which pews were removed to make hasty fortifications.

1585 Martin Luther King Jr. Blvd.
Atlanta, GA

Westview Cemetery

At the time of the Battle of Ezra Church, the city's alms house, or poorhouse, was located near the entrance to Westview Cemetery, at the site of the present-day gatehouse, and served as a gathering place for war refugees. The alms house was near the center of the Confederate line of battle. In section 38 of the cemetery stands a monument to the battle, consisting of a bronze memorial plaque bordered by a low rectangular brick wall.

Fulton County Confederate veterans also erected a monument on a nearby prominence. One hundred veterans are interred in a circle around a tall marble statue of a Confederate soldier facing north in eternal vigil, along with a flagpole displaying the array of Confederate flags. The monument's north side contains two Confederate mortars.

A portion of a Confederate gun emplacement also remains in the rear section of the cemetery as well as the grave of a casualty of the battle, Confederate Lt. Edward Clingman. These sites are located directly off the cemetery's circular drive near section 70 toward the back. Fronted by a growth of small pines and covered by overgrown weeds and brush during the warmer months, the gun emplacement is most evident during the colder months, when the foliage is in a dormant state.

1680 Ralph David Abernathy Blvd.
Atlanta, GA 30310
404-755-6611

Battle of Utoy Creek

Shortly before the Battle of Ezra Church, a frustrated Major General William T. Sherman gave orders to begin shelling Atlanta in earnest with siege artillery. Impatient at having his armies bogged down in siege operations, he began to probe the Confederate lines looking for a vulnerable point. In addition, the Federals still planned to extend their right flank to cut the Macon and Western Railroad between East Point and Atlanta and were competing with the Confederates in a race to extend lines of entrenchment. To aid his objective, Sherman ordered Major General John Schofield's Army of the Ohio to move from the Federal left flank around to the right to a new position on the north bank of Utoy Creek. From this location on August 5, 1864, Schofield's force combined with elements of Major General John M. Palmer's XIV Corps to launch an offensive movement that succeeded in driving the Confederate forces before them until a halt was ordered for regrouping.

2800 block of Cascade Rd., Dodson Dr., Willis Mill Rd., and Veltre Cir., Woodland Ter.
Atlanta, GA

After the halt, a heated disagreement arose between Schofield and Palmer over seniority and command issues that resulted in Palmer's resignation. There was no further progress for that day. The delay gave Lt. General William Hardee's Confederates time to lengthen and strengthen their positions in preparation for the expected onslaught.

The route of the Union attack of August 6 traversed across the Sandtown Road and up a steep incline through rough terrain and well-prepared abaitis against positions defended by Kentucky's famed Orphan Brigade of Major General William B. Bate's division. The Federals could get no closer to the Confederate trenches than thirty yards before the fierce resistance forced them to fall back. Late in the afternoon, one of Schofield's divisions managed to flank Bate out of his position, but the Confederates fell back to a new line closer to the railroad. Due to this battle, Sherman stopped his attempts to outflank the Confederates on the right. "The enemy can build parapets faster than we can march," Sherman wrote.

Utoy Creek was a very lopsided battle, with Federal casualities reported as high as eight hundred (but probably closer to three hundred) and little to show for the sacrifice. Confederate casualities were about twenty-five, proof of the advantage gained by fighting from behind earthworks.

From the top: The Battle of Utoy Creek *(Painted by Marc Stewart, aviationart.homestead.com); Major General John Schofield (Courtesy of the Library of Congress)*

Historic Utoy Primitive Baptist Church

The 1828 Utoy Primitive Baptist Church, the oldest Baptist church in Fulton County, was used as a Confederate hospital during the latter part of the Atlanta Campaign. After the Battle of Atlanta on July 22, 1864, the colonel of the 30th Georgia Regiment, James S. Boynton, who later served as president of the Georgia senate and governor of Georgia in 1883, was a patient here. Today, the Utoy Church operates under the name the Temple of Christ Pentecostal, Inc.

At the northwestern corner of the churchyard cemetery are the eighteen graves of the Confederates killed in the fighting at Utoy Creek. There are also remnants of the Confederate entrenchments directly north of the graves at Venetian Drive and Cahaba Street. In this same cemetery are the graves of four Revolutionary War veterans as well as slaves who died of smallpox during an antebellum epidemic in the area.

From the intersection of Ralph David Abernathy Rd. and Cascade Rd. travel 1.6 miles west and turn left onto Centra Villa. Travel 0.5 miles and turn left onto Venetian Dr. Continue for 0.3 miles and turn left onto Cahaba St.
Atlanta, GA

Left: *Unknown Confederate casualties from the Battle of Utoy Creek, their different religions depicted on their headstones (Photos: Barry Brown)*

Lionel Hampton/Utoy Creek Park

The wooded 105-acre Lionel Hampton/Utoy Creek Park contains remnants of the line occupied by Major General John M. Palmer's XIV Corps. These trenches, which were dug in early August 1864 during the military operations in the vicinity, mark the Federal staging area for the Battle of Utoy Creek on August 6, 1864.

To reach the trench line, walk about 0.4 miles, cross over the bridge, and continue up the steep incline on the Willis Mill Road bike path. Proceed past the first park bench on the left until you reach the crest of the hill. Continue down from the crest several hundred feet past the "control bike speed" sign and enter the woods. Remnants of the Federal line are on both sides of the bike trail, to the left and to the right across the power right-of-way.

These trenches and the surrounding forest, one of the largest areas of undeveloped forested land within the city limits, were acquired and preserved by a joint effort of the Georgia Civil War Commission, the Arthur Blank Foundation, and city of Atlanta green space funding.

Take Cascade Rd. west to Benjamin Mays Dr. for approximately 0.4 miles until the Autobahn Park neighborhood sign. Turn right at Flamingo Rd. and proceed 1 mile to Lionel Hampton/Willis Mill Greenway Bike Trail
Atlanta, GA

Daily: Dawn to dusk

Cascade Springs Nature Preserve

2800 block of Cascade Rd.
Atlanta, GA

Mon.-Fri.: 9:00 a.m.-5:00 p.m.

Cascade Springs Nature Preserve, one of the least known yet best preserved small battlefield sites in the country, encompasses much of the core area of fighting from the Battle of Utoy Creek on August 5–7, 1864. The heavily wooded area of steep hills and deep ravines that make up this 137-acre park is within the city limits of Atlanta. The nature preserve contains a cascading waterfall for which the area is named. According to wartime letters, Confederate soldiers used this same waterfall for washing clothes and bathing. At the end of the park's entryway boardwalk is an early twentieth-century fieldstone springhouse that is one of the few intact remnants of the Cascade Springs Health Resort, once a well-known area attraction. An extensive section of Confederate trench lines remains in an excellent state of preservation, with numerous rifle pits and cannon emplacements in their prominent positions across high ground on the south-central portion of the property. An added feature of this park, though unmarked and difficult to find, is the remnant of a civilian bombproof shelter, common during the siege operations of August 1864. This rare vestige from the Atlanta Campaign is still discernable on the southern portion of the property.

The nature preserve is closed on nights and weekends, making it a difficult site to visit for travelers on a weekend schedule. For those searching for earthworks, it is best to visit the site during the fall or winter months, as foliage is so thick during the late spring and summer that the woods are almost impassable.

John A. White Park

Cascade Rd. at Cascade Cir.
Atlanta, GA

On the ridge at the highest point of John A. White Park, adjacent to the swimming pool and behind the covered picnic areas, are several hundred yards of Confederate earthworks. These earthworks were constructed in late July 1864 to protect Atlanta's two remaining railroads, which General John B. Hood depended on to maintain the supply line and control of the city.

Judge William A. Wilson House (NRHP)

501 Fairburn Rd.
Atlanta, GA

While moving to Jonesboro in late August 1864, the Federal Army of the Tennessee camped on the grounds of the William A. Wilson plantation. The XV Corps commander, Major General John A. Logan, used the home as his headquarters. The 1857 masonry Georgian house is one of only three antebellum structures remaining in the Atlanta city limits. It is on the National Register of Historic Places, and efforts are under negotiation to preserve and rehabilitate the deteriorated structure. Currently, the house is not open to the public but can be viewed from the roadside.

Above: The cascading springs from which the area gets its name. Right: Wilson House (Photos: Barry Brown)

DECATUR, DeKalb County

Decatur is the county seat of DeKalb County and the last major stop on the Georgia Railroad before Atlanta. Founded prior to Atlanta, Decatur's growth never matched that of its nearby neighbor. Unlike adjacent Fulton County, DeKalb residents voted against the Articles of Secession in 1861 when the matter came up for a referendum but fully supported the Southern cause when war was declared.

On July 22, 1864, while the Federal army was regrouping on the outskirts of Atlanta after the severe fighting at the Battle of Peachtree Creek on July 20, the soldiers were bracing for another assault. Following an all-night march across town, General John B. Hood again attacked in force on the east side of the city. At the same time, Confederate cavalry under Major General Joseph Wheeler attacked the wagon trains of Major General James B. McPherson's Army of the Tennessee, then parked in and around Decatur Cemetery. Much of the fighting consisted of a running battle through the streets of Decatur between mounted and dismounted Confederates and a Union brigade protecting the supply train under Colonel John W. Sprague. Sprague's troops, supported by the famous Chicago Board of Trade Battery, were forced from entrenchments around the present Agnes Scott College area and driven up North Decatur Road. They were eventually able to save much of their supply train after Wheeler was ordered to break off the engagement to support Lt. General William Hardee, who was heavily engaged in fighting off to the west. Although the Battle of Decatur lasted barely two hours, one hundred Confederates and 242 Union soldiers were killed or wounded. Union troops reentered Decatur on July 24.

Today, Decatur is an attractive, historic bedroom community of Atlanta. The downtown area offers unique shopping and historic sites. Decatur has a MARTA station behind the Old Courthouse and is easily accessible from Atlanta.

DeKalb County CVB
1957 Lake Side Pkwy, Ste. 510
Tucker, GA 30084
770-492-5000/800-999-6055
www.dcvb.org

Site Where the Battle of Decatur Began

An engraved stone, almost hidden by ivy in front of the main entrance to Agnes Scott College, marks the site where the Battle of Decatur began on July 22, 1864. The Agnes Lee Chapter of the United Daughters of the Confederacy erected the monument in 1921. The fighting occurred between Major General Joseph Wheeler's Confederate cavalry and Federal soldiers guarding the supply train under the command of Colonel (later Brigadier General) John W. Sprague. Sprague's forces fiercely contested nearly every foot of ground within the present city limits. Sprague's command, which was the extreme rear of the left wing of Major General William T. Sherman's army, was finally dislodged after nearly two hours of intense fighting. Wheeler successfully drove the Union forces northward out of Decatur.

Agnes Scott College
141 E. College Ave.
Decatur, GA 30030
www.agnesscott.edu

Left: Site where the Battle of Decatur began, near the present-day entrance to Agnes Scott College (Photo: Bob Price)

Decatur Cemetery (NRHP)

229 Bell St.
Decatur, GA 30030
www.decaturga.com

Open daily until dark

The oldest known publicly owned burial ground in metro Atlanta, the Decatur Cemetery is believed to predate the city's 1823 incorporation. Expanded many times, the cemetery's fifty-four acres contain more than twenty thousand grave sites. Monuments include a six-foot tablet erected in 1884 to honor Decatur's Confederate dead and a historic African American section in the 7.5-acre Old Cemetery.

Among the many community leaders buried in the Decatur Cemetery are Mary Ann Harris Gay, author of *Life in Dixie During the War*; George Washington Scott, founder of Agnes Scott College; and the Honorable Charles Murphy, a congressman who died before he could serve as a delegate to Georgia's secession convention. Of Murphy's untimely death, Jim Miles wrote in *Civil War Sites in Georgia*, "He had expressed the hope that he would not live to see Georgia leave the Union, and he did not."

Right: *Decatur Cemetery*
(Photo: Bob Price)

DeKalb History Center's Jim Cherry Museum (NRHP)

Old Courthouse on the Square
101 East Court Square
Decatur, GA 30030
404-373-1088
www.dekalbhistory.org

Mon.–Fri.: 9:00 a.m.–4:00 p.m.

The Jim Cherry Museum's focus on the history of DeKalb County includes the Civil War exhibit Johnny Reb and Billy Yank: The Life of the Common Soldier, with archaeological artifacts, naval relics, musical instruments, weapons, surgical and medical-related items, and uniforms, including a dress uniform worn by the Clinch Rifles, a militia unit in Augusta. An extensive archive, which contains muster rolls of DeKalb County militia units and regimental histories, is available to researchers.

The building that houses the museum is a beautiful example of Romanesque Revival architecture and was the former county courthouse, built in 1914 on the site of the wartime courthouse. An engraved stone in front of the building and a granite obelisk at the back honor DeKalb County's Confederate veterans. During construction of the MARTA rail line behind the museum, many artifacts from the July 22, 1864, Battle of Decatur were uncovered and are displayed in the museum.

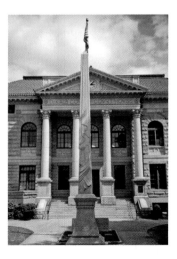

Right: *The Jim Cherry Museum*
(Photo: Bob Price)

Mary Gay House (NRHP)

Mary Ann Harris Gay, a local heroine who refused to evacuate her home when Union troops occupied Decatur, lived in this house from 1850 to 1914. She witnessed the Battle of Decatur on July 22, 1864, and later wrote about her experiences in *Life in Dixie During the War*. Margaret Mitchell is known to have used the book as a reference and inspiration for her novel *Gone with the Wind*. The Mary Gay house, which has been moved from its original site, is operated by the Junior League of DeKalb County, Inc.

716 West Trinity Pl.
Decatur, GA 30030
404-378-2162
www.decaturga.com

Open by appointment only

Left to right: *Mary Gay House, Swanton House*
(Photos: Bob Price)

Swanton House (NRHP)

The plantation-plain-style Swanton House, the oldest surviving building in Decatur, was built in 1825, with additions dating to 1852. During the Civil War, Mr. Swanton and his wife and daughter lived in Maine, leaving the home in the care of a widow Mrs. Johnson and her ten daughters. On July 19, 1864, Brigadier General Thomas W. Sweeny, the Union commander of the 2nd Division of Major General Granville M. Dodge's XVI Corps, used the Swanton House as his headquarters. Recollections through the years indicate that, as the Federal troops were arriving, a number of Decatur's women and children sought shelter in the basement of the Swanton House and, when discovered by Union soldiers, were not harmed. Minié balls from the fighting around Decatur are still embedded in the walls. The house is owned by the DeKalb History Center.

720 West Trinity Pl.
Decatur, GA 30030
404-373-1088
www.decaturga.com
www.dekalbhistory.org

Open by appointment only

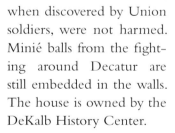

Left: *The interior of a bombproof shelter*
(Courtesy of the UGA Hargrett Rare Book and Manuscript Library)

STONE MOUNTAIN VILLAGE (NRHP), DeKalb County

DeKalb County CVB
1957 Lake Side Pkwy., Ste. 510
Tucker, GA 30084
770-492-5000/800-999-6055
www.dcvb.org

www.stonemountainvillage.com

The site that would become the village of Stone Mountain was incorporated in 1839 as the village of New Gibraltar, a vestige of civilization in the wilderness adjacent to the unusual geologic anomaly and early tourist attraction then known as Rock Mountain. In 1845 the town was moved a half mile west to its present location paralleling the new Georgia Railroad but still within walking distance of the giant granite monadnock.

Stone Mountain Village entered the war era like many other small towns in the South with the majority of its young men volunteering for Confederate service. The men from Stone Mountain and its district of DeKalb County formed Wright's Legion, 38th Georgia Regiment Volunteer Infantry. The local artillery battalions used the mountain as an occasional testing ground and firing range for breech-loading cannons forged in nearby Atlanta by arms manufacturer William Rushton. The mountain was used to gain range, trajectory, and accuracy by the untested artillerists, honing their skills by firing at a target hung from the face of the mountain.

The village saw military action during the latter stages of the Atlanta Campaign. Federal attempts to sever the Georgia Railroad brought Stone Mountain Village headlong into the conflict. The Federal cavalry who were assigned to break this important lifeline were met with stiff resistance from Confederate cavalry and mounted infantry.

On July 15, 1864, constant skirmishing broke out on the Stone Mountain Road north of the village between Union Brigadier General Kenner Garrard's troops and elements of dismounted Confederate cavalry. Three days later on July 18, Garrard ordered five regiments, a force of several thousand men, to tear up the tracks, burn the ties, and twist the heated iron to render it useless. The destruction began one mile west of the Stone Mountain Depot and included several culverts and a water tank. Garrard's report of the day's action sent to Major General James B. McPherson stated:

Below: Wilbur Kurtz painting depicting the fighting at Stone Mountain (Courtesy of Dr. George Coletti and the Stone Mountain Memorial Hall Museum)

In obedience of orders, I left my camp at 5:00 a.m. this morning to break the railroad between Stone Mountain and Decatur. At Browning's Court House [Tucker] I struck the rebel pickets, and skirmished for three miles to the railroad which I effectually destroyed for more than two miles, including several culverts and the water tank at Stone Mountain depot. The only force I had opposed to me, as well as I can learn, was one brigade. I sent a force into Stone Mountain, and found the rebels there about 5:00 p.m., but not in force. The depot was not burned.

Elements of Garrard's cavalry in the vicinity of Stone Mountain Village continued to encounter stiff resistance and fought a protracted engagement at the edge of town against Confederate troops from Colonel George G. Dibrell's mounted infantry brigade. Confederate rifleman took up sniper positions in the buildings and residences in the village's northern edge and maintained a constant fire that forced the Federals to bring up their artillery, driving Dibrell's men from their positions and through the town. While retreating, the Confederates burned two hundred bales of cotton along with quartermaster and commissary stores to keep them from falling into Federal hands.

The Federals returned to Stone Mountain on November 16, 1864, where the left wing of Major General William T. Sherman's army camped in this vicinity on the first night of the March to the Sea. Stone Mountain's historic African American neighborhood, Shermantown, was named in honor of the night that the general spent in the area, as many slaves followed the army to freedom.

Below: *Late nineteenth-century photo of the Stone Mountain Depot (Courtesy of the DeKalb History Center*

Stone Mountain Depot (NRHP)

The first Stone Mountain Depot, built by the Georgia Railroad Company at the time of the railroad's construction in the 1840s, was originally a wood-frame building. The stacked granite portion on the south side of the archway of the present building was constructed in 1857. Here the walls are composed of two-foot-thick rough-hewn granite blocks separated by red-clay-based mortar joints. The granite blocks were quarried from exposed ledges around the perimeter of Stone Mountain, giving them their rough and weathered appearance. The north end of the structure separated by the arch was built in 1914.

Stone Mountain City Hall
922 Main St.
Stone Mountain, GA 30083
www.stonemountainvillage.com

During late July 1864, the depot was central to much of the military activity that took place in the Stone Mountain vicinity. Elements of Brigadier General Kenner Garrard's Federal cavalry destroyed the Georgia Railroad for several miles around the depot. While retreating from the village, Confederate troops burned cotton bales and other supplies to keep them from falling into Union hands. The water tower was also destroyed. The 1857 depot would survive this engagement intact but would not survive the war.

On November 16, 1864, the first night of Major General William T. Sherman's March to the Sea, the Federal left wing camped in the area between Stone Mountain and Lithonia. The next day the 2nd Massachusetts Volunteer Infantry, acting as the rear guard of the army, stayed behind in the village and burned public property, including the depot. With its thick granite walls impervious to the flames, the fire only consumed the wooden roof and freight platform. These elements were replaced shortly after the war, and the building was again used as a depot.

Today the Stone Mountain Depot serves as both a police headquarters, which occupies the 1857 structure, and the Stone Mountain City Hall, located in the 1914 structure. The 1857 depot holds the distinction of being the only building in the Atlanta area to have survived burning by Federal troops and to still be in use today.

Dr. Hamilton House (NRHP)/Stillwell House (NRHP)/Wayside Inn

Below, from the top: Dr. Hamilton House (Photo: Barry Brown); early twentieth-century Wayside Inn (Courtesy of Dr. George Coletti)

Dr. Hamilton House
5329 Mimosa Dr.
Stone Mountain, GA 30083
770-465-6789

Stillwell House
992 Ridge Ave.
Stone Mountain, GA 30083
770-469-3459

Three Confederate hospitals were located in Stone Mountain Village during the Civil War, caring for sick and wounded from the fighting east of Atlanta. Two of the three hospitals, the Dr. Hamilton House and the Stillwell House, are standing today.

The Dr. Hamilton House currently functions as a restaurant, the Sycamore Grill, named in honor of the large, majestic 150-year-old sycamore tree that blankets the verandah on the east side of the building. Constructed in 1836, the Dr. Hamilton House predates the Georgia Railroad's arrival in town and is the oldest surviving structure in Stone Mountain. The village's first mayor, Andrew Johnston, built the house, placing it adjacent to the route later chosen for the railroad. As a result, a portion of its eastern section had to be removed to safely accommodate passing trains.

Constructed of brick using a horsehair, mud, and granite aggregate, the walls of the Hamilton House are two feet thick on the first floor. In 1840, the Georgia Railroad and Banking Company added the clapboard second-floor addition so that the building could be used to house railroad workers. A granite post in the front is the original marker for the Stone Mountain Village boundary, which was set at a distance of six hundred yards in all directions. By the time of the Civil War, when the house was designated for use as a Confederate hospital, the town's boundary had been increased to one thousand yards. When the Union army captured the town, the patients, mostly Confederate soldiers, were left undisturbed to continue their convalescence. At times, the hospital was so crowded that as many as twenty-six men were packed into the small upstairs hotel room number two. The men who died in this hospital were buried in the Confederate section of the Stone Mountain City Cemetery.

The 1850 clapboard Stillwell House is another surviving Stone Mountain home that was used as a Confederate hospital. Today it serves as a B&B and is known as the Village Inn Bed & Breakfast.

The Wayside Inn, the third Stone Mountain Confederate hospital, was located in the present Stone Mountain Park on the site where Confederate Hall now stands. The building was burned in 1925 and never rebuilt.

Stone Mountain Confederate Cemetery (NRHP)

During the war as many as 150 Confederate soldiers were buried in the c. 1850 Stone Mountain City Cemetery's Confederate section, most of whom died in the three local hospitals. Some of those interred in the cemetery were casualities from the fighting in and around Stone Mountain Village during July 1864. Confederate graves are located adjacent to East Ponce De Leon Avenue at the cemetery entrance and can be seen from the five-point intersection at the north end of Stone Mountain Village's Main Street.

North Main St., East Ponce de Leon Ave., and Silver Hill Rd. Stone Mountain, GA 30086

Daily: Dawn to dusk

Left: *The metal tag at the base of the headstone is an example of an attempt to obtain genealogical information on a Civil War ancestor. (Photo: Phillip Lovell)*

Stone Mountain Park

Stone Mountain Park, a park owned by the state and managed by the Stone Mountain Memorial Association since the land was acquired from the prominent Venable family in 1958, contains the world's largest exposed granite monadnock, rising 825 feet. The park's 3,200 acres include a lake and a memorial to the Confederacy carved on the mountain's face. Although the mountain was a war-era landmark of some importance, used by Confederate soldiers for artillery practice early in the conflict, it has few other direct historic connections to the war. Nonetheless, the park offers much of interest for the Civil War enthusiast.

The high-relief carving, larger than the heads of the presidents on Mount Rushmore, took fifty-seven years on and off and the skill of three master carvers to complete. Confederate heroes President Jefferson Davis, General Robert E. Lee, and Lt. General Thomas J. Jackson are depicted mounted on steeds, with hats reverently held in their right hand covering their heart. The monument was dedicated in 1970.

Memorial Hall houses a museum for the anthropologic history of the area that includes Native American artifacts. In addition, an outstanding Civil War exhibit highlights wartime military activity in the Stone Mountain area. Besides a large number of small arms, including a variety of pistols, muskets, rifles, carbines, swords, and knives, displays include uniforms and other military accoutrements. Of special interest is an original watercolor by famed Atlanta historian and artist Wilbur G. Kurtz that depicts the fighting in Stone Mountain Village. The Memorial Hall building is also the access point for the sky lift to the top of the mountain.

Another park building, Confederate Hall, sits at the base of the mountain adjacent to the walking trail to the summit. It contains exhibits on the geologic history of the area, has conference and classroom facilities, and offers regular showings of an excellent documentary on the Atlanta Campaign titled *Georgia in the Civil War*.

Hwy. 78
Stone Mountain, GA 30086
770-498-5702
www.stonemountainpark.com

Open 365 days a year

Below: *The Confederate monument at Stone Mountain (Photo: Cara Pastore, Georgia Dept. of Economic Development)*

LITHONIA, DeKalb County

DeKalb County CVB
1957 Lake Side Pkwy., Ste. 510
Tucker, GA 30084
770-492-5000/800-999-6055
www.dcvb.org

www.lithonia.org

On the morning of November 17, 1864, during the March to the Sea, Federal soldiers wrought destruction on Lithonia, a small east DeKalb County village. As in the nearby village of Stone Mountain, the Georgia Railroad track and depot were destroyed; however, in Lithonia a special vengeance was extracted. In retaliation for "bushwhacking," sabotage activities carried out by locals, much of the town was ransacked and burned, with Major General William T. Sherman on hand to oversee the destruction. An exception was the Masonic Lodge, an organization with many members from both sides. Federal guards were posted outside the building to ensure its protection. Sherman spent the night of November 16, 1864, in a Lithonia home that is no longer standing, and the next day the Federals marched twenty miles to Conyers.

Today Lithonia is still a small town with a railroad running through its center. Little if any evidence remains from the war besides the lay of the land surrounding the railroad and paralleling the main road between Stone Mountain and Lithonia where the massive Federal army encamped. While in and around Lithonia, Sherman's army first used specially designed tools to lift the steel track and place it on burning stacked ties to heat and then bend the track around a nearby tree or sapling, making them unusable. The practice became known as making "Sherman's neckties," a trademark of the army throughout the campaign.

Federal soldiers reported climbing nearby Arabia Mountain, now a National Heritage Area. From this vantage point they viewed plumes of smoke rising from various farms, businesses, and public properties in the distance all the way back to Atlanta, telltale signs of the army's destructive activities since the March to the Sea began two days earlier.

Right: *Making "Sherman's Neckties" (Courtesy of the UGA Hargrett Rare Book and Manuscript Library)*

LILBURN, Gwinnett County

No major engagements were fought in Lilburn during the Civil War. A skirmish occurred near Lilburn at the Yellow River near Five Forks Trickum Road with Major General William T. Sherman's troops foraging for supplies.

Gwinnett County CVB
6500 Sugarloaf Pkwy., Ste. 200
Duluth, GA 30097
770-623-3600/888-494-6638
www.gcvb.org

Yellow River Post Office Park (NRHP)

Built in the 1840s on the Hudson Farm, later the Nash Farm, this wood-framed building supported by fieldstone posts has served as a general store, post office, sharecropper's house, barn, and most recently a community center. The nearby slave quarters, also from the Hudson Farm, is one of the few surviving structures of its kind in Gwinnett County. Currently, these refurbished buildings, moved about sixty feet from their original location to make way for road widening, are known as the Yellow River Post Office Park and sit on the five remaining acres of the Hudson-Nash Farm.

In 1861, property owner Thomas Parks Hudson was one of three Gwinnett County delegates to the state convention in Milledgeville that adopted the Ordinance of Secession. The "Hudson Guards," Company H, 10th Georgia Regiment State Line Troops, held rifle practice in the ravine northeast of the store.

The books *In Care of Yellow River: The Complete Civil War Letters of Pvt. Eli Pinson Landers to His Mother* and *Weep Not for Me Dear Mother* immortalized the building. Lander's regiment fought in the Eastern Theater with General Robert E. Lee's Army of Northern Virginia, and his letters to his mother back home in the 6th Land District of Gwinnett County, the area now called Lilburn, passed through the Yellow River Post Office.

3490 Five Forks Trickum Rd.
Lilburn, GA 30047

Below: *Yellow River Post Office*
(Photo: Phillip Lovell)

JONESBORO, Clayton County

Jonesboro, originally know as Leaksville, was incorporated as a town in 1859. When the War Between the States broke out in 1861, local cavalry and infantry units were organized in Clayton County and drilled behind the courthouse in Jonesboro before departing for Virginia battlefields. In 1864 the war came to Jonesboro with a crucial battle fought there on August 31 and September 1 that resulted in the Confederacy's loss of Atlanta.

Clayton County CVB
104 N. Main St.
Jonesboro, GA 30236
770-478-4800/800-662-7879
www.visitscarlett.com

Battle of Jonesboro

Clayton County CBV
104 N. Main St.
Jonesboro, GA 30236
770-478-4800/800-662-7829
www.visitscarlett.com

In late August 1864, Major General William T. Sherman abandoned the bombardment of Atlanta, which had failed to dislodge or even discourage the Confederate defenders. He decided to take all but one corps of his army in a wide sweep to the west and south of Atlanta and strike at the two remaining railroads that supplied General John B. Hood's Confederate army, forcing it to evacuate Atlanta.

A large Federal force moved toward the town of Jonesboro, about eighteen miles south of Atlanta, to accomplish this objective. Hood sent two corps under Lt. General William Hardee to attack Sherman's force. Confederate attacks on the afternoon of August 31 were repulsed by stiff resistance from Union forces who had crossed the Flint River and were entrenched within rifle shot of Jonesboro. Southern losses were much heavier than those of the Union troops. That evening, Hood ordered Lt. General Stephen D. Lee's corps of Hardee's force to return to Atlanta. Already outnumbered by the Union forces at Jonesboro, the loss of Lee's corps left Hardee in a desperate situation.

The next day the Federals mounted a large-scale attack resulting in the capture of nearly a thousand Southern troops. Although Federal forces broke the Confederate lines in the vicinity of the Warren House, Confederates were able to restore the position and hold their fortifications until evening. In the dark of night, Hardee withdrew from Jonesboro down the railway to Lovejoy's Station.

Of the fighting at Jonesboro on September 1, one Union soldier wrote, "Today has been the heaviest fighting of any during the campaign. Could we only be blessed with 4 hours more of daylight we could make a cleen thing in wiping out the Rebel Army. But night has come and a darkness stops the battle for the night and favours the enemy with a chance to escape or fortify strongly."

The same evening Hardee retreated to Lovejoy, Hood evacuated Atlanta, and troops of the XX corps marched in to seize the city. On September 3, Sherman

Right: Federal forces destroying the Macon Railroad at Jonesboro (Courtesy of the Library of Congress)

wired Washington, "So Atlanta is ours and fairly won . . . in a day or so I will march to Atlanta and give my men some rest. Since May 5, we have been in one constant battle or skirmish, and need rest."

The fall of Atlanta helped seal the reelection of President Abraham Lincoln in November 1864 and left little doubt about the outcome of a Northern victory in the Civil War, ensuring both emancipation and the restoration of the Union.

Clayton County Courthouse (NRHP)

The Clayton County Courthouse, which was built in 1861, was burned during one of Brigadier General Judson Kilpatrick's raids in 1864 and rebuilt in 1869. Today the structure serves as the hall for the Jonesboro Lodge No. 87, Free and Accepted Masons.

144 N. McDonough St.
Jonesboro, GA 30326
770-477-8864

1867 Train Depot/Welcome Center

The 1867 Train Depot, constructed of Georgia granite, replaced the original wood depot, which stood near the Confederate Cemetery and was burned in 1864. The depot houses the Welcome Center and offices of the Clayton County Convention and Visitors Bureau. Stop here for directions for a twenty-five-stop driving tour of historic Jonesboro.

The depot is also home to the Road to Tara Museum, which contains the largest permanent display of *Gone with the Wind* memorabilia in the world, including rare photographs of the movie production, books and movie posters, and marquees from all over the world. The museum also contains artifacts from the Atlanta Campaign, including an example of a "Sherman's necktie" (a railroad rail that was heated and wrapped around a tree).

104 North Main St.
Jonesboro, GA 30326
770-478-4800
www.visitscarlett.com

Mon.–Fri.: 8:30 a.m.–5:30 p.m.
Sat.: 10:00 a.m.–4:00 p.m.

Right: *The postwar train depot, home to the welcome center (Photo: Bob Price)*

Johnson-Blalock House (NRHP)

James F. Johnson, a member of the Georgia legislature and a signer of the Georgia Secession Ordinance, built this house in 1859. In 1864, Confederates used Johnson's home to store their commissary supplies. The house also served as a hospital during and after the Battle of Jonesboro. The Blalock family has owned the house for five generations. This is a private home and is not open to the public.

155 N. Main St.
Jonesboro, GA 30326
770-477-8864

Patrick R. Cleburne Memorial Confederate Cemetery (NRHP)

Johnson St. and McDonough St.
Jonesboro, GA 30326

The Patrick R. Cleburne Memorial Confederate Cemetery holds the remains of between six hundred and one thousand unidentified Confederate soldiers who died during the Battle of Jonesboro. Originally buried where they fell, the remains were moved here in 1872 after this memorial was formed with a grant from the Georgia legislature. Named for Confederate Major General Patrick R. Cleburne, the cem-

etery is maintained by the United Daughters of the Confederacy. The unmarked headstones are laid out in the shape of the Confederate battle flag.

Right: *The Patrick R. Cleburne Memorial Confederate Cemetery (Photo: Rich Elwell)*

The Georgia Building Authority maintains the Patrick R. Cleburne Confederate Cemetery as well as five other Confederate cemeteries in Georgia. Call 404-656-3253 for information.

Warren House (NRHP)

102 West Mimosa Dr.
Jonesboro, GA 30326
770-471-5553

Guy L. Warren, one of Jonesboro's first town commissioners, built this house in 1860. During the Civil War, Confederate forces used it as a field hospital and head-

quarters until the 52nd Illinois Infantry took possession of it on September 2, 1864, using it for the same purposes. Union forces temporarily broke the Confederate line in the vicinity of the Warren House in heavy fighting. Today the house still bears the scars of battle; signatures of convalescing Union soldiers can be seen on the walls of the downstairs parlor.

Right: *Warren House (Photo: Bob Price)*

Stately Oaks Plantation

100 Carriage Ln.
Jonesboro, GA 30326
770-473-0197

Mon.–Sat.: 10:00 a.m.–4:00 p.m.

Built in 1839, the mansion originally stood on 404 acres four miles north of Jonesboro. During the Civil War, the plantation owner, Robert McCord, was away fight-

ing for the Confederacy while his wife and six children remained in the home. Union soldiers camped on the grounds during the Battle of Jonesboro but did not use the house out of respect for the family. The Greek Revival–style house is surrounded by outbuildings, including the original log kitchen.

Right: *Stately Oaks Plantation (Photo: Bob Price)*

HAMPTON, Henry County

Hampton was incorporated on December 20, 1872. It was previously known as Bear Creek Station. Depending on the source, Hampton was named in honor of either Lt. General Wade Hampton II of Civil War fame or his father, General Wade Hampton, from the American Revolution. Nash Farm Battlefield in Hampton is the site of the climax of the Battle of Lovejoy Station, where Federal Brigadier General Judson Kilpatrick was able to break through an encirclement of Confederate infantry.

Henry County Chamber and CVB
1709 Hwy. 20
Westridge Business Ctr.
McDonough, GA 30253
770-957-5786
www.henrycounty.com

Nash Farm Battlefield

During the late summer of 1864 several separate and distinct military actions involving cavalry and infantry occurred near the Thompson E. Nash house and farm in Henry County. The most notable engagement occurred in late August 1864 during Federal Brigadier General Judson Kilpatrick's cavalry raid against the Atlanta and West Point Railroad. On August 20, 1864, in a running battle that began at Lovejoy's Station, Kilpatrick's force was trapped and almost completely encircled near the Nash Farm. He was forced to stop after running headlong into Major General Patrick R. Cleburne's Confederate infantry in his front while Brigadier General W.H. Jackson's pursuing Confederate cavalry encompassed his rear. The Federals managed to punch their way through the front of the infantry near Babb's Mill and McDonough Road. In spite of their escape, the raid was not considered a success as little damage was inflicted and the railroad was back in operation within two days. This incident caused Sherman to reevaluate the effectiveness of using cavalry to destroy railroads.

The Nash Farm also saw action on September 3, 1864, after the fall of Atlanta. The Confederate corps of generals Alexander P. Stewart and Stephen D. Lee used the site as a staging area for their successful defense against attacks from Major General John Schofield's corps during the retreat from Jonesboro. Lee's corps remained in the Nash Farm area to encamp for several weeks.

Henry County recently acquired the site, including more than two hundred acres, for a Civil War park, saving it from the development and the urban sprawl that has eradicated so many of the Atlanta Campaign sites. Efforts are currently underway to develop a comprehensive preservation plan, raise the money to rehabilitate the Nash Farm house and restore outbuildings for use as a museum and visitors center, and to erect interpretative signage on the battlefield. A National Register of Historic Places nomination is pending.

4631 Jonesboro Rd.
Hampton, GA 30253
www.henrycountybattlefield.com

Below: *Brigadier General Judson Kilpatrick (Courtesy of the Library of Congress)*

SWEETWATER CREEK STATE CONSERVATION AREA,
Douglas County (NRHP)

From the Thornton Rd. exit off I-20, turn left and travel 0.4 miles to Blairsbridge Rd. Turn right and proceed for 2 miles and take a left on Mt. Vernon Rd.

Mount Vernon Rd.
Lithia Springs, GA 30057
770-732-5871
http://ngeorgia.com/parks/sweetwater.html

7:00 a.m. – 10:00 p.m.
Trails close at dark; other areas close at dark if not in use.

The mill ruins located within the heavily wooded 1,968-acre Sweetwater Creek State Conservation Area are an unusual example of antebellum industry in Georgia. The park also has a 215-acre lake fed by the rocky meandering Sweetwater Creek. Located in Douglas County west of Atlanta, the site once housed one of the largest textile mills in the South, including one of the tallest buildings in Georgia during that era. New Manchester Mill was constructed in 1849, along with many of the seventeen structures that made up the mill complex. The mill's water wheel, which powered the machinery, weighed an amazing fifty thousand pounds. Approximately five hundred people resided in the mill town on the ridge above Sweetwater Creek, including more than one hundred who worked at the mill. The mill's daily output was 750 yards of cloth, which was used for Confederate uniforms, blankets, and tents. Located approximately one mile upstream was a smaller gristmill and leather factory.

A Federal cavalry patrol from Major General George Stoneman's division under Colonel Silas Adams and Major Haviland Thompkins arrived at New Manchester on July 2, 1864. They stopped the mill and distributed the remaining cloth among the workers. On July 9, 1864, Federals burned the mill, the workers' homes, and the commissary. According to one account, the Federals fired a twelve-pound Napoleon artillery piece at the mill's dam to destroy it. Regardless, the dam was breached and the millrace flooded, causing water to fill the lower floor of the mill, ruining the machinery. The gristmill upstream was also destroyed.

New Manchester's mainly female workforce and their dependants were placed on a forced march to Marietta. They were held at the Georgia Military Institute until early on July 15, 1864. In Marietta they were joined by their counterparts, the "Roswell Women,"

Right: *The mill ruins at Sweetwater State Park (Photo: Andreas Yankopolus)*

and were transported via train to Nashville and later to areas north of the Ohio River. Unlike Roswell, the town of New Manchester ceased to exist as a living community after its destruction by Union forces.

PALMETTO, Coweta County

Shortly after the fall of Atlanta to General William T. Sherman, Confederate General John B. Hood gathered his forty thousand troops at Palmetto on September 19, 1864. While in Palmetto, Hood devised his ill-fated Tennessee Campaign, a northward attack on Sherman's supply lines. On September 25–26 Confederate President Jefferson Davis visited Hood at Palmetto, reviewing the troops and giving a speech before leaving for Richmond, Virginia. A monument, historical marker, and two cannons are located near the railroad tracks in downtown Palmetto.

Coweta County CVB
100 Walt Sanders Memorial Dr.
Newnan, GA 30265
770-254-2627/800-826-9382
www.coweta.ga.us

Windemere Plantation (NRHP)

The Windemere Plantation, an 1850s Greek-revival plantation home, contains period furnishings and boasts a secret hideaway where food was stored during the Civil War. According to legend, the Masonic emblem embedded in the stair banister saved the home from destruction when Union troops captured it.

The Windemere Plantation, which has also been known as the George R. Sims House and the Sims-Brown-Harrison House, is privately owned and not open to the public.

1851 Collinsworth Rd.
Palmetto, GA 30268

FAYETTEVILLE, Fayette County

Fayette County was the scene of a Union cavalry raid on July 29, 1864, when Brigadier General Edward M. McCook's thirty-six hundred troopers captured a Confederate supply train containing three hundred guards and teamsters and five hundred wagons. The Federals burned the wagons and slaughtered more than a thousand mules and horses. Three days later Confederate cavalryman Joe Wheeler freed the Confederate prisoners during the Battle of Brown's Mill near Newnan.

When McCook's cavalry entered the town of Fayetteville on their raid in July 1864, M.M. Tidwell, a local attorney and one of the signers of the Secession Order, believed the Union forces were intent on burning the county courthouse. To divert the raiders, Tidwell hung a Confederate flag in the window of his law office. He was then captured, placed on a mule, and paraded through the streets of Fayetteville; the courthouse was not burned.

Fayette County Chamber of Commerce
200 Courthouse Square
Fayetteville, GA 30214
770-461-9983
info@fayettechamber.org

Fayette County Historical Society

195 Lee St.
Fayetteville, GA 30214
770-716-6020

Tues.: 6:00 p.m. – 9:00 p.m.
Thurs.: 10:00 a.m. – 1:00 p.m.
Sat.: 9:00 a.m. – 1:00 p.m.

The Fayette County Historical Society maintains extensive research materials on individuals and families from Fayette County including photos of people, places, and buildings. Its Civil War holdings include the 128-volume *War of the Rebellion* and primary documents pertaining to Fayette County and Georgia. Fayette County raised six companies of infantry and two troops of cavalry for the Confederate cause. The county also raised state militia troops composed of those too old or too young for the regular forces.

Holliday-Dorsey-Fife House Museum (NRHP)

140 Lanier Ave. West
Fayetteville, GA 30214
770-716-5332
www.hdfhouse.com

Thurs. – Sat.: 10:00 a.m. – 5:00 p.m.

Built in 1855 by the Holliday family, the Holliday–Dorsey–Fife House derives its name from its three main owners: John Stiles Holliday, a prominent physician in Fayetteville and uncle of the infamous John Henry "Doc" Holliday; Solomon Dawson Dorsey, a colonel in the state militia who helped enlist volunteers for the Confederacy and whose son was the flag bearer for Company I, 10th Georgia Volunteers, "The Fayette Rifle Greys"; and Robert E. Lee Fife, who was born in 1865 and lived in the home until his death in 1956. Fife was a mayor of Fayetteville and a prominent merchant.

The museum has a room devoted to the Civil War collection of uniforms, muskets and swords, and archeological relics from the cavalry action that occurred in Fayette County. Photos of Confederate veterans adorn walls throughout the eight–room house.

Left: *The Holliday-Dorsey-Fife House (Photo: Jim Lockhart, Historic Preservation Division, Georgia Dept. of Natural Resources)*

PRESIDENTIAL PATHWAYS

In addition to the homes of presidents Franklin Delano Roosevelt and Jimmy Carter, the Presidential Pathways region is the location of Andersonville Prison, a notorious site during the Civil War and now a memorial to prisoners of war in all American wars. Less known are the extensive sites and relics of one of the Confederacy's major naval construction centers in Columbus. The National Civil War Naval Museum at Port Columbus houses Civil War vessels that have been salvaged and preserved and is a world-renowned repository on Civil War naval history and technology.

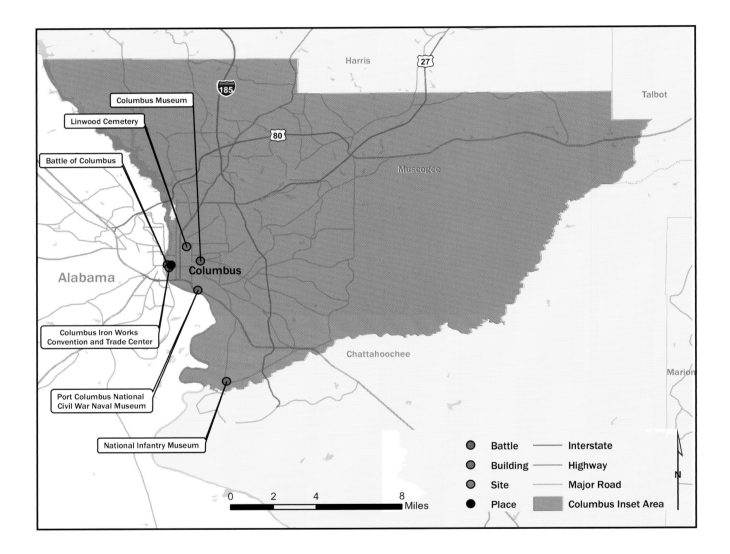

Harris

Talbot

`185`

Columbus Museum

Linwood Cemetery

`80`

Muscogee

Battle of Columbus

Alabama

Columbus

Columbus Iron Works
Convention and Trade Center

Chattahoochee

Marion

Port Columbus National
Civil War Naval Museum

National Infantry Museum

⬤ Battle	—— Interstate		
⬤ Building	—— Highway		
⬤ Site	—— Major Road		
⬤ Place	Columbus Inset Area		

0   2   4   8
Miles

N

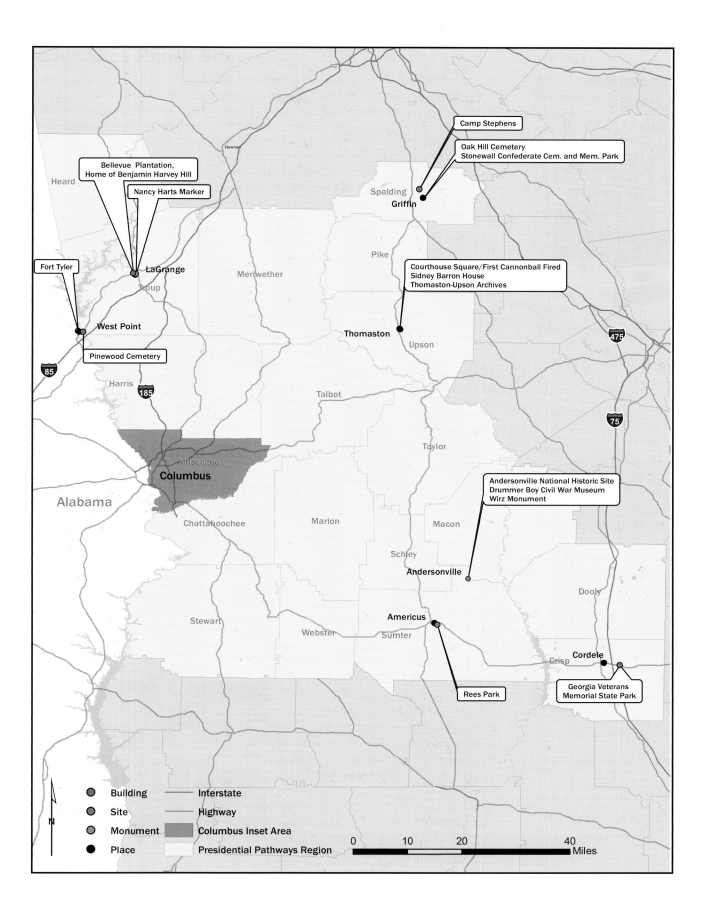

Camp Stephens

Oak Hill Cemetery
Stonewall Confederate Cem. and Mem. Park

Spalding

Griffin

Bellevue Plantation,
Home of Benjamin Harvey Hill

Nancy Harts Marker

Heard

Newnan

Pike

Courthouse Square/First Cannonball Fired
Sidney Barron House
Thomaston-Upson Archives

Fort Tyler

LaGrange

Troup

Meriwether

West Point

Pinewood Cemetery

475

85

Thomaston

Upson

Harris

185

Talbot

75

Muscogee

Columbus

Taylor

Alabama

Chattahoochee

Marion

Macon

Andersonville National Historic Site
Drummer Boy Civil War Museum
Wirz Monument

Schley

Stewart

Americus

Dooly

Andersonville

Webster

Sumter

Crisp

Cordele

Rees Park

Georgia Veterans
Memorial State Park

N

Building   Interstate

Site   Highway

Monument   Columbus Inset Area

Place   Presidential Pathways Region

0   10   20   40

Miles

NEWNAN, Coweta County

Coweta County CVB
100 Walt Sanders Memorial Dr.
Newnan, GA 30265
770-254-2627/800-826-9382
www.coweta.ga.us

Named in honor of Georgia Militia General Daniel Newnan, a hero from the War of 1812 and later a U.S. congressman, the town of Newnan was designated as the Coweta county seat in 1828. Newnan prospered from the cotton industry, allowing the leading citizens to invest in a railroad connection in 1851.

The Battle of Brown's Mill was fought three miles south of town in late July 1864, resulting in the defeat of Brigadier General Edward M. McCook's Federal forces, thus putting a stop to Major General William T. Sherman's plans of winning the Atlanta Campaign by cavalry action.

Battle of Brown's Mill

A monument commemorating the battle is located at the intersection of Millard Farmer Rd. and Corinth Rd.

On July 27, 1864, Federal Brigadier General Edward M. McCook departed his lines to carry out a raid in tandem with Major General George Stoneman. Their mission was to wreck the remaining Confederate railroads supplying Atlanta while keeping the enemy off balance and creating havoc behind Confederate lines. If the raid was successful, Stoneman then planned to continue on to Andersonville to liberate the thirty thousand Union prisoners held there.

McCook and his 2,400 troopers crossed the Chattahoochee River at Smith's Ferry and cut the Atlanta and West Point Railroad at Palmetto, capturing and burning one thousand wagons from a Confederate supply train at Fayetteville. They next traveled to the preset rendezvous point at Lovejoy on July 29, but Stoneman failed to appear, forcing McCook to retrace his steps toward the Chattahoochee River.

By this time McCook had Confederate cavalry pursuing him. Again at Lovejoy, McCook fought a sharp skirmish with the mounted forces of brigadier generals W.H. Jackson and Lawrence Ross that forced a retreat westward with Major General Joseph Wheeler and several hundred cavalry on his heels.

With the Confederates sniping at his rear guard, McCook's advance guard approached Newnan from the east, on what is now Broad Street, early on July 30, 1864, with his troops and horses in a state of exhaustion. They encountered a trainload of Confederate soldiers blocking the road on the outskirts of town. These troops, elements of Brigadier General P.D. Roddey's dismounted Alabama cavalry who had been traveling by train, were forced to stop in Newnan because of the

Right: This small monument surrounded by an iron fence marks a core area of the Battle of Brown's Mill. (Photo: Barry Brown)

damaged tracks at Palmetto. They were as surprised to see the Union cavalry as the Union cavalry was to see them.

Fighting erupted, causing McCook to begin a desperate search for a route that would bypass Newnan to the south and allow him to avoid the unwanted clash. While this was occurring, Wheeler's force rode into town and swiftly divided with the intention of striking the Federal marauders simultaneously in their front and rear.

Wheeler's men came into contact with McCook's about three miles southwest of Newnan at the intersection of today's Millard Farmer and Corinth roads. The Federal cavalry was driven off the roadbed and into the woods south of Millard Farmer Road. As the fighting seesawed back and forth through the heavy woods thick with underbrush, McCook's men were forced to dismount and fight on foot. McCook, believing they were surrounded, proclaimed, "Every man for himself."

As the Federals suffered heavy casualties, the Confederates received approximately fourteen hundred reinforcements who repeatedly charged McCook's line, driving it back. By late afternoon, after having lost two of its brigade commanders, McCook's force split up and cut their way out, only to be captured piecemeal over the next few days while attempting to reach safety behind Union lines.

The Battle of Brown's Mill was a major blow to Major General William T. Sherman's plans to use cavalry as a means of gaining major objectives in the Atlanta Campaign. McCook lost about one hundred killed and wounded and another thirteen hundred captured and sent to Confederate prisons, while the supplies continued to reach the Confederates in Atlanta by train. Wheeler suffered about half the casualties of McCook.

Coweta County is planning to preserve several hundred acres of the Brown's Mill Battlefield Site as a park. Currently, however, only a single monument surrounded by an iron fence commemorates this important cavalry engagement.

Newnan Male Academy Museum

Built in 1840, this former male seminary is now owned by the Newnan-Coweta Historical Society. It houses an excellent museum with a War Between the States exhibit that includes war-era flags, weapons, and surgical equipment, and period photographs. The museum also features a large selection of clothing from the nineteenth and early twentieth centuries.

30 Temple Ave.
Newnan, GA 30264
770-251-0270

Tues.–Sat.: 10:00 a.m.–noon,
1:00 p.m.–3:00 p.m.
Sun.: 2:00 p.m.–5:00 p.m.

Right: *Newnan Male Academy Museum*
(Photo: Bob Price)

Oak Hill Cemetery

More than 260 Confederate soldiers, many of whom died in hospitals in the Newnan area, are buried at Oak Hill Cemetery. Only two of the soldiers are unknown, and every state in the Confederacy is represented. Buried here is Confederate Medal of Honor recipient William Thomas Overby. A Georgia native and a member of Confederate Partisan Ranger John S. Mosby's cavalry in Virginia, Overby was executed by Federals at Front Royal, Virginia, for his refusal to reveal information about Mosby's whereabouts. A memorial to him stands on the Newnan Courthouse Square.

Across the highway from
Stonewall Cemetery
Griffin, GA 30223

GRIFFIN, Spalding County

Griffin-Spalding Chamber of
Commerce
P.O. Box 73
Griffin, GA 30224
770-228-8200
www.cityofgriffin.com

During the Civil War, Griffin was a hospital town and a printing center where much of the Confederate money and most of the Confederate government's stamps were produced. Griffin was also the site where many Georgians mobilized for the war. Volunteers for the cavalry went to Camp Milner, now the Municipal Park, just north of Griffin on McIntosh Road. Infantrymen went to Camp Stephens, named for Confederate Vice President Alexander H. Stephens, located on the Macon and Western Railroad near Griffin.

Spalding County provided nine companies, two from Griffin, to the Confederate cause, composed of infantry, cavalry, and artillery as well as a number of militia companies that served locally. The Spalding Grays, Company D, 2nd Battalion of Infantry, was the first unit from Griffin to join the Southern forces.

Griffin was where the famed Orphan Brigade of Kentucky became a cavalry unit and served under Confederate Major General Joseph Wheeler in action opposing Major General William T. Sherman. Early in the March to the Sea, as Sherman's right wing appeared to be closing on Griffin, 2,800 Georgia militia troops prepared to defend the town from entrenchments. Sherman eventually veered from his route and bypassed Griffin. However, on April 19, 1865, cavalry under Union Brigadier General James H. Wilson destroyed the railroad at Griffin and distributed the captured Confederate stores to local residents.

One of the first Confederate Memorial Days was held in Griffin in 1866, and one of the first monuments to Confederate dead was erected here in 1869.

Camp Stephens

On Stephens St. just off 9th St.
Griffin, GA
www.spaldingcounty.com/
history.htm

Right: *This stone, placed by
the United Daughters of the
Confederacy, marks the site of
Camp Stephens. (Photo: Bob
Price)*

Camp Stephens was the mobilization point for most of Georgia's infantry troops. The one-thousand-yard-long camp was located two miles north of Griffin a half mile east of the railroad. In the 1850s, Griffin resident Henry Holliday sold 136 acres to the developers of Camp Stephens. While stationed at Camp Stephens in March 1862, Private Asbury H. Jackson described the camp in a letter to his mother, stating that it housed about four thousand soldiers and more were arriving each day. Some of the original breastworks and trenches are still visible.

Stonewall Confederate Cemetery and Memorial Park

845 Memorial Dr.
Griffin, GA 30223
www.spaldingcounty.com/
history.htm

Stonewall Confederate Cemetery, which is part of the larger Oak Hill Cemetery, contains the graves of more than five hundred Confederate soldiers and one Union soldier. Among the Confederates are William A. Hughes, a recipient of the Confederate equivalent of the Medal of Honor, and a black soldier, Wiley Stewart. Many of these soldiers were patients at area hospitals, the locations of which are identified by historical markers. Others buried here died of wounds received during the battles of Atlanta and Jonesboro. A Georgia Historical Commission marker just outside the cemetery reads, in part, "Stonewall Cemetery is . . . given by Georgia Militia General Lewis Lawrence Griffin when he founded Griffin in 1840. . . . The principle monument, among the first to Confederate dead, was erected by the Ladies Memorial Association of Griffin in 1869."

Monuments to those killed in the Revolutionary War, both world wars, the Korean and Vietnam wars, as well as to the women who nursed soldiers in Griffin during the Civil War, are also located in the cemetery and the nearby Memorial Park.

Oak Hill Cemetery

Oak Hill Cemetery, adjacent to the Stonewall Confederate Cemetery, has over six thousand markers. Buried at Oak Hill is John McIntosh Kell, a Confederate naval hero who served on the famed CSS *Alabama*, which captured or sank more than sixty Federal ships before being sunk by the USS *Kearsarge* off the coast of France in June 1864.

797 Memorial Drive
Griffin, GA 30223
770-229-6410

Above: *Stonewall Confederate Cemetery.* Left: *The Oak Hill Cemetery grave of John M. Kell, second in command of the successful Confederate raider CSS* Alabama *(Photos: Bob Price)*

LAGRANGE, Troup County

During the Civil War, LaGrange was a railroad town along the Atlanta and West Point Railroad and the site of a number of Confederate hospitals. However, its most unique contribution was the Nancy Harts, a female military unit that saved the town from destruction. In addition to the Nancy Harts, eight companies were formed in LaGrange plus some militia and state guard units.

LaGrange-Troup County Chamber of Commerce
P.O. Box 636
LaGrange, GA 30241
706-884-8671
www.lagrangechamber.com

Bellevue Plantation, Home of Benjamin Harvey Hill (NRHP)

Bellevue was the home of Benjamin Harvey Hill, one of the greatest orators of his time and a powerful senator in the Confederate States Congress. Hill opposed secession but became one of the foremost champions of the Southern cause, frequently hosting Confederate President Jefferson Davis and other Confederate officials in his home. Hill was arrested at Bellevue in April 1865, along with Confederate Navy Secretary Stephen Mallory. After the war, Hill served several terms in the U.S. House

204 Ben Hill St.
LaGrange, GA 30240
706-884-1832

Tues.–Sat.: 10:00 a.m.–noon
Sun.: 2:00 p.m.–5:00 p.m.

of Representatives and Senate and during Reconstruction urged President Hayes to remove the Federal troops occupying the South.

Bellevue Plantation is regarded as one of the finest examples of Greek Revival architecture in the state of Georgia.

Left: Bellevue Plantation (Photo: Bob Price)

Nancy Harts Marker

A historical marker is located in the Courthouse Square along Ridley Ave.
LaGrange, GA

Organized in 1863 by Nancy Brown Morgan and named for Georgia Revolutionary War heroine Nancy Morgan Hart, the Nancy Hart Rifles was a militia unit comprised of women from LaGrange who practiced military drills in preparation to defend the town in the absence of its men. The women were mobilized on April 17, 1865, to resist a column of Union cavalry under Colonel Oscar H. LaGrange. After meeting with the ladies, the colonel, who hailed from Wisconsin, spared the town whose name he chanced to bear.

A marker commemorating the Nancy Harts stands in front of the courthouse and states in part, "Seeing the charmingly militant array formed to meet him, Colonel LaGrange complimented them upon their fearless spirit and fine martial air and, after a brief delay, marched on toward Macon leaving no scar other than the broken railroad to deface this gracious Georgia town."

Above: The Nancy Harts' Captain Nancy Brown Morgan
(Courtesy of the Troup County Historical Society)

WEST POINT, Troup County

www.cityofwestpointga.com

Greater Valley Area Chamber of Commerce
P.O. Box 205
Lanett, AL 36863
334-642-1411
www.greatervalleyarea.com

Shortly before the war's end, during March and April 1865, Union Brigadier General James H. Wilson and his thirteen thousand cavalry troops were dispersing the remaining Confederate pockets of resistance in Alabama and Georgia. Wilson, succeeding where many others had failed, defeated Confederate Lt. General Nathan Bedford Forrest in a battle at Selma, Alabama. Moving east, his next goal was Columbus, Georgia, and its mill operations on the Chattahoochee River. Running into unexpected resistance in Columbus, Wilson needed to cover his flanks and secure alternate crossing points south of the city. In order to do this, he dispatched 3,750 troops under Colonel Oscar H. LaGrange to the rail center of West Point, Georgia, on April 16, 1865.

Guarding the bridge at West Point was the Confederate earthwork that would become known as Fort Tyler, which was named in honor of its commander, the convalescing one-legged Confederate Brigadier General Robert C. Tyler. Placed strategically on a hill on the Alabama side of the river, the 35-square-yard earthwork was fronted by a deep ditch. A thirty-two-pound siege gun covered the bridge crossing, and two twelve-pound Parrott guns covered the other approaches. Tyler's irregular force consisted of convalescing wounded, civilians, and hospital workers, approximately 120 total.

Colonel LaGrange ordered an all-out assault on the bridge using both mounted and dismounted regiments. The defenders fired grapeshot, killing LaGrange's horse but not slowing the momentum of the charging force. The Federals successfully took control of the bridge and quickly repulsed a small group of Confederates who were attempting to set the bridge on fire. LaGrange then attacked the earthwork. When the attack stalled in the fort's ditch, LaGrange ordered his artillery to bombard Fort Tyler, knocking out the fort's three guns and resulting in the fort's capitulation.

The Confederates lost 18 dead and 28 wounded with 218 missing. General Tyler was among the dead, the last Confederate general to die in combat. LaGrange lost 7 killed and 29 wounded. The railroad at West Point, now in Union hands, was virtually annihilated with the destruction of 19 locomotives and 340 cars, further decimating the Confederacy's ability to transport goods.

Fort Tyler

The Fort Tyler earthwork is preserved in a park established by the Fort Tyler Association, which is responsible for its upkeep. The group maintains an excellent website that explains West Point, the fort, and its place in the War Between the States. Interpretive markers along a switchback trail leading to the fort's hilltop site describe the action. A Confederate monument, which was dedicated in 1901, was originally located on the east side of the river and was later relocated to the fort.

6th Ave.
(half block north of 10th St.)
West Point, GA
www.forttyler.com

Left to right: *The reconstructed Fort Tyler sits on the original site of the fort. The graves of General Tyler and his second in command, Captain C. Gonzales, in Pinewood Cemetery (Photos: Bob Price)*

Pinewood Cemetery

The casualities of the fighting at Fort Tyler, including Brigadier General Robert C. Tyler, are buried in Pinewood Cemetery along with the Confederates who died in local hospitals. Only nineteen of the seventy-six soldiers interred here are identified.

Off U.S. Hwy. 29 South on
East 11th St.
West Point, GA

THOMASTON, Upson County

Thomaston-Upson County
Chamber of Commerce
P.O. Box 827
Thomaston, GA 30286
706-647-9686
chamberinfo@alltel.net

The Civil War erupted on Thomaston's soil nine days after Confederate General Robert E. Lee's surrender at Appomattox, Virginia. Thomaston was a cotton-mill town ideally located on the Flint River along a spur off the Macon and Western Railroad. During the war, it housed two permanent and several temporary hospitals. On April 18, 1865, Union cavalry raiders moving from Columbus to Macon embarked on three days of devastation throughout Upson County. The raiders, led by Brigadier General James H. Wilson, looted homes, destroyed three textile mills, and set fire to a steam locomotive and train filled with Confederate stores.

In Thomaston, the Glenwood Cemetery's Confederate section holds fifty-four soldiers, six unknown, who died in local hospitals. The grave of Dr. Edward A. Flewellen, a noted Confederate surgeon and medical director for the Army of Tennessee, is located near this section. There is also a Confederate cemetery in the nearby town of Rock.

Thomaston's African American residents organized an emancipation celebration in 1866 that is still held annually in May and is believed to be the country's longest-running commemoration of the freedom from slavery.

Courthouse Square/First Cannonball Fired

Church St. and Center St.
Thomaston, GA

The Thomaston Courthouse Square contains several Civil War monuments, including the Woodmen of the World monument honoring Confederate dead from all states. In the 1930s the United Daughters of the Confederacy erected a monument to Georgia native Major General John B. Gordon, who was from Upson County. In addition, a single cannonball attached to a marble base reads, "First Cannon Ball fired

at Outbreak of the War Between the States at Fort Sumter, April 12, 1861." The story of the cannonball is further described with the inscription, "Presented to the UDC by Mrs. Sallie White to whom it was given in 1861 by P.W. Alexander, leading Confederate war correspondent who was present when the ball was fired and knew it to be the first. The first marker stating these facts was erected on this square in 1919."

Left: *Thomaston claims to have the first cannonball to bombard Fort Sumter. It is on display in the Courthouse Square. (Photo: Bob Price)*

Sidney Barron House (NRHP)

505 Stewart Ave.
Thomaston, GA 30286
706-647-9405

Wed.–Sat.: 11:00 a.m.–4:00 p.m.

Built in the early 1800s, the former home of Sidney Barron served as a hospital during the Civil War.

Thomaston-Upson Archives

Housed in the former R.E. Lee Institute library, the Thomaston–Upson Archives contains Confederate research materials and artifacts, such as the original battle flag of the 46th Georgia volunteer infantry regiment with its twenty–seven bullet holes. Many of the reference materials are primary sources, such as diaries, including a unique publication that contains the names of all Confederate troops hospitalized in Upson County during the Civil War.

301 South Centre St.
Thomaston, GA 30286
706-646-2437

Mon.–Fri.: 9:00 a.m.–5:00 p.m.
Second Sat. of each month: 9:00
a.m.–1:00 p.m.

COLUMBUS, Muscogee County

The Confederate interior, consisting of central and south Georgia and Alabama, served as the new nation's industrial belt. One of the centers of Southern manufacturing was the city of Columbus, Georgia, on the banks of the Chattahoochee River. Only Richmond, Virginia, produced more goods for the Confederacy.

Columbus was a transportation hub where water and rail transportation converged. Besides being the northernmost port along the Chattahoochee, Columbus was served by two railroads, one that ran westward toward Montgomery, Alabama, and the other a spur that reached northward to West Point, Georgia, where it connected with a rail line linked to several other Southern cities. Before the Civil War, cotton from inland farms was shipped by rail to Columbus, where it was loaded onto river-going vessels and transported to the Gulf of Mexico.

The city's foremost manufacturer during the war was a steel-rolling mill located on the Chattahoochee River. It produced a variety of war goods, including the materials needed to build gunboats for the Confederate navy that patrolled the river.

The CSS *Chattahoochee* was one of the gunboats built near Columbus. However, since the river was never the scene of heavy naval engagements, the gunboats saw limited duty. Late in the war, the city's shipyard also produced a Confederate ironclad, the CSS *Jackson*, which shortly after its completion was sunk to avoid capture.

Columbus was located well off the path of the major fighting the state witnessed in 1864. The ravages of war only touched the city late in the conflict when several hundred Confederate troops marched through in early 1865 en route to intercept Major General William T. Sherman's forces as they swept through South Carolina.

Late in the war in April 1865, days after General Robert E. Lee's surrender to General Ulysses S. Grant at Appomattox, Virginia, Union Brigadier General James H. Wilson's thirteen-thousand-man cavalry force rode toward Columbus to destroy the city's factories and mills. Confederate militia contested Wilson's presence but were eventually overwhelmed. The city fell within hours and was subsequently occupied by Wilson's troopers.

Historical markers scattered throughout Columbus mark the locations of hospitals; cannon, munitions, and sword factories; and textile mills that produced uniforms for the Confederate army.

Columbus CVB
900 Front Ave.
Columbus, GA 31902
706-322-1613/800-999-1613
www.columbusga.org

Below: *The Columbus Iron Works (now the Columbus, Georgia, Convention and Trade Center), burned during the war, was rebuilt, and burned down again in the early 1900s. (Courtesy of the Library of Congress)*

Battle of Columbus

Along the banks of the
Chattahoochee RIver
Columbus, GA

One of the final dramas of the Civil War occurred on the banks of the Chattahoochee River on Easter, April 16, 1865. The war in Virginia was over; General Robert E. Lee had surrendered to General Ulysses S. Grant at Appomattox. The long process of healing the nation's wounds and rebuilding was just beginning. But in Georgia, the fires of war were not yet extinguished. Union Brigadier General James H. Wilson's cavalry raiders attacked Columbus from the west banks of the Chattahoochee River and overwhelmed the makeshift force composed of a few thousand soldiers who were recovering in area military hospitals and local militias and further aided by elderly men and young boys. Wilson's troopers soon accomplished what they had set out to do, occupying the city in the early hours of April 17, and burned government and industrial properties as well as 125,000 bales of cotton.

Left: *Brigadier General James H. Wilson (Courtesy of the Library of Congress)*

Columbus Iron Works Convention and Trade Center (NRHP)

801 Front Ave.
Columbus, GA 31906
706-327-4522
www.columbusga.org/TradeCenter

Open when events are scheduled

Built in 1853 and known as the Confederate Naval Iron Works during the Civil War, the building was the second-largest iron works in the Confederacy. The factory supplied engines and parts to all Confederate shipyards in the Deep South. A sensitive renovation preserved the building's massive timbers, exposed beams, old brick walls, and manufacturing mechanisms. It now serves as a convention and meeting facility. The South Hall houses an exhibit of products manufactured in the 1800s, including "The Ladies' Defender," a cannon manufactured from brass cooking utensils donated by the women of Columbus, and displays of casting and armor from the CSS *Chattahoochee* and CSS *Jackson*.

Left: *The Columbus Naval Iron Works building, built on the original site of the iron works, is now a convention center. (Photo: Cara Pastore, Georgia Dept. of Economic Development)*

Columbus Museum

The Columbus Museum, one of the largest museums in the Southeast, focuses on American art and the cultural history of the Chattahoochee River valley region. It also offers exhibits relating to the significance of the Civil War in the Columbus area, including a collection of Confederate and Union weapons, as well as artifacts from local military units, such as the Columbus Guards.

1251 Wynnton Rd.
Columbus, GA 31906
706-748-2562
www.columbusmuseum.com

Tues., Wed., Fri., Sat.:
10:00 a.m.–5:00 p.m.
Sun.: 1:00 p.m.–5:00 p.m.

Linwood Cemetery (NRHP)

More than two hundred Confederate soldiers and sailors are buried in Linwood Cemetery, including Brigadier General Henry Lewis Benning, known by his troops as "The Rock" for his coolness and bravery, and Brigadier General Paul Jones Semmes, who died from wounds received at Gettysburg while leading his men across the Wheat Field. Many soldiers interred at Linwood died in Columbus' Confederate hospitals.

In the naval section of the cemetery, a 6.4-inch rifled gun from the ironclad CSS *Jackson* guards the graves. Among the sailors buried here are the crew of the CSS *Chattahoochee* who died in a spectacular engineering accident when the ship's boilers exploded. Others buried at Linwood include Louis Haiman, a Jewish tinsmith who produced excellent swords for the Confederacy; Dr. Francis O. Ticknor, a local physician who wrote the Civil War poem "The Little Giffen of Tennessee"; and Dr. John S. Pemberton, a wholesale druggist who developed the formula for Coca-Cola and formed a local Confederate militia company over which he served as captain, later becoming a lieutenant colonel in the 3rd Georgia Cavalry Battalion.

721 Linwood Blvd.
Columbus, GA 31902
706-321-8285
www.historiclinwood.org

Office: Mon.–Fri.: 9:00 a.m.–
3:00 p.m.
Cemetery: daily dawn to dusk

Right: *Linwood Cemetery (Photo: Bob Price).* Below: CSS Jackson *(Courtesy of the Library of Congress)*

National Civil War Naval Museum at Port Columbus (NRHP)

The National Civil War Naval Museum at Port Columbus is dedicated to the history of the navies of the North and South. Featured are the remains of two original Confederate navy vessels, the ironclad ram CSS *Jackson* and the wood gunboat CSS *Chattahoochee*. Also visibile are extensive naval artifacts and rare naval weapons, a torpedo, and a large collection of Civil War naval flags. The uniform collection includes the coat of Catesby Jones, who was in command of the CSS *Virginia (Merrimac)* during its battle with the USS *Monitor*.

Several large full-scale ship components have been reproduced, including the Confederate ironclad CSS *Albermarle* and U.S. Navy ships USS *Hartford* and USS *Monitor*. The Albermarle also houses a battle theater allowing visitors to experience Civil War naval combat from the point of view of a Confederate sailor on an ironclad.

Port Columbus' newest exhibit is a full-scale reproduction of a U.S. Navy sidewheel

1002 Victory Dr.
Columbus, GA 31902
800-742-2811
www.portcolumbus.org

Mon.–Sun.: 9:00 a.m.–5:00 p.m.

steamer, the USS *Water Witch*, which while on blockading duty in Savannah was captured by a Confederate navy commando-style raid. This replica is located in front of the museum next to the highway that makes finding the museum easy. Port Columbus also hosts several large-scale events each year, including living history programs.

National Infantry Museum and Soldier Center

1775 Legacy Way
Columbus, GA 31903
706-685-5800
www.nationalinfantrymuseum.com

Mon.–Sat.: 9:00 a.m.–5:00 p.m.
Sun.: 11:00 p.m.–5:00 p.m.

The new National Infantry Museum and Soldier Center opened in June 2009, just outside the gates of Fort Benning, the Home of the Infantry. The original museum was located on Fort Benning and was established in 1959. The new 190,000-square-foot museum is a tribute to infantrymen past, present, and future. Visitors take an interactive journey through every war fought by the United States over the past two centuries. The museum has a collection of fifty-seven thousand artifacts, an IMAX theater, a restaurant, and a gift store.

Patriot Park, where the museum is located, includes a parade field for Fort Benning Infantry School graduations, a memorial walk of honor, and a re-created World War II Company Street. The museum has a large Civil War collection, but the Civil War gallery will not be opened to visitors until 2011.

Fort Benning, the largest infantry training center in the world, was named in honor of Confederate Brigadier General Henry Lewis Benning, who was a brigade commander (Benning's brigade) in Hood's division, Longstreet's corps, Army of Tennessee, and fought at the Battle of Chickamauga.

ANDERSONVILLE, Sumter County

www.andersonvillega.com

Americus-Sumter Tourism Council
123 W. Lamar St.
Americus, GA 31709
229-928-6059/888-278-6837
www.therealgeorgia.com

The tiny middle-Georgia village of Andersonville was the site of the railroad depot that received the 49,485 Federal prisoners destined to become inmates at nearby Camp Sumter, the infamous prison camp that would come to represent the archetype of the horror of the prisoner-of-war system during the Civil War. In prisons across the North and South, captives suffered and died in horrendous conditions due to either a lack of available resources, wanton neglect and cruelty, or a combination. More Confederate prisoners died in Federal prison camps than Union prisoners in Confederate camps, a little-known fact about prisoner-of-war mortality rates during the War Between the States. One reason for this, besides a higher per capita Confederate prisoner population, was the U.S. government policy that stopped the prisoner exchange program in late 1863. The cessation of the program was due to the order of Union General Ulysses S. Grant, who reasoned that the Confederacy, with a chronic manpower shortage, would deplete its human reserves long before the North and shouldn't be given the advantage of freed prisoners of war to replenish the thinning ranks.

The Camp Sumter stockade at Andersonville was built to alleviate overcrowding at prison camps in Virginia. It had the capacity to accommodate about ten thousand prisoners in an area that encompassed 16.5 acres. Prisoners began arriving in late February 1864 and soon were coming at a rate of about four hundred a day. Although the stockade was enlarged to 26.5 acres in July 1864, it was not enough. By August the camp's population had increased to more than thirty-two thousand. Overcrowded con-

ditions, a lack of shelter, clothing shortages, malnutrition, and terrible inadequacies in sanitation quickly turned the enclosure into a quagmire of disease and death. Within fourteen months more than 13,000 of the 49,485 men who had been confined there died and were buried in the adjacent cemetery. After the war ended, camp commandant Captain Henry Wirz was arrested and charged with conspiring with Confederate officials to injure the health and destroy the lives of Union prisoners of war. Public opinion in the North demanded a scapegoat be identified and punished. Wirz was tried before a military tribunal, found guilty, and hanged on November 10, 1865. His execution as a war criminal is still the subject of controversy.

Above: *Union Private Thomas O'Dea's sketch of Andersonville Prison as he remembered it in August 1864 when it contained thirty-five thousand prisoners of war (Courtesy of the Library of Congress)*

Andersonville National Historic Site (NRHP)

The Andersonville National Historic Site Visitors Center houses displays and artifacts that relate the story of Camp Sumter and other Civil War prisons, both Union and Confederate, as well as an exhibit about American prisoners of war from all wars. The Andersonville National Cemetery, a beautiful yet somber site, is the resting place of the thirteen thousand soldiers who died at the prison, along with three thousand other Federal soldiers, veterans of other wars, and former prisoners of war. Eleven monuments in the cemetery pay tribute to the dead.

On GA 49, 1 mile east of Andersonville
Andersonville, GA 31711
229-924-0343
www.nps.gov/ande/

Left: *Andersonville National Historic Site (Photo: Barry Brown)*

Right: *Issuing rations at Andersonville Prison on August 17, 1864 (Courtesy of the National Archives)*

The National Prisoners of War Museum includes exhibits and a video presentation that tells the story of American prisoners of war in all of the nation's conflicts. The Camp Sumter stockade includes a reconstructed section of the timber wall and the infamous "deadline" (a line on the ground near the walls that if prisoners crossed they would be shot) built from information gained during archeological investigations. Also visible are sentry boxes and the makeshift shelters used by prisoners known as "shebangs." The Stockade Branch Stream served double duty as the prison's water source and sewer. The Providence Springhouse marks the site where lightning struck the ground during a thunderstorm and created a badly needed fresh water source that helped alleviate suffering.

Drummer Boy Civil War Museum

109 Church St.
Andersonville, GA 31711
229-924-2558
www.andersonvillegeorgia.com

Tues.–Sun.: 10:00 a.m.–5:00 p.m.
Closed in December

Housed in a c. 1900 store, the Drummer Boy Civil War Museum features memorabilia from both the North and South, including uniforms, guns, documents, flags, a naval history section, and a diorama of the Camp Sumter prison.

Right: *Drummer Boy Museum (Photo: Bob Price)*

Wirz Monument

Erected in 1909 by the Georgia Division of United Daughters of the Confederacy, the Wirz Monument memorializes Captain Henry Wirz, commandant of the Camp Sumter prison, for operating the facility under extremely difficult circumstances. Though Wirz's culpability for the terrible situation at Andersonville has long been debated, there is little debate that the U.S. government ran a prison system with systematic ill-treatment of Confederate captives in retaliation for conditions in the South. The Federal government needed a scapegoat for the infamous Andersonville prison and chose Wirz as a symbol of the inadequacies of the Civil War prison systems. He was tried, convicted, and hanged for war crimes by the U.S. government on November 10, 1865. Like the record of the man it pays tribute to, the monument remains controversial.

Andersonville Village
Andersonville, GA
www.andersonvillegeorgia.com

Left to right: *Depiction of Wirz's hanging, the Wirz Monument in Andersonville (Photo: Bob Price)*

AMERICUS, Sumter County

Americus was incorporated and made the seat of Sumter County on December 22, 1832. It was named for the Western continents. "Americus" is the masculine of "America."

Americus-Sumter Tourism Council
123 W. Lamar St.
Americus, GA 31709
229-928-6059/888-278-6837
www.therealgeorgia.com

Rees Park

The land for Rees Park was donated to the citizens of Americus by prominent local physician Dr. Albert Rees in 1846. Almost twenty years later, the park was dedicated to the memory of his son Lt. Lucius Gibson Rees of the 11th Georgia Regiment "Sumter Flying Artillery," who was killed in fighting around Petersburg, Virginia, in 1864. In an amazing feat, his body was returned to Americus by a family slave who had accompanied him to war. Rees is buried in Oak Grove Cemetery in Americus.

Taylor St. and Elm St.
Americus, GA

CORDELE, Crisp County

Cordele-Crisp County Chamber of
Commerce
302 E 16th Ave.
Cordele, GA 31015
229-273-1668
www. cordele-crisp-chamber.com

Cordele was incorporated on December 22, 1888.

Georgia Veterans Memorial State Park Museum

2459-A Hwy. 280 West
Cordele, GA 31015
229-276-2371
www.gastateparks.org

Mon.–Sun.: 8:00 a.m.–5:00 p.m.

Established as a memorial to U.S. veterans, the Georgia Veterans Memorial State Park Museum features uniforms, weapons, medals, and other artifacts from the Revolutionary War through the Persian Gulf conflict. Aircraft, armored vehicles, and guns from World War I through the Vietnam War are displayed on the grounds.

The museum's Civil War section includes rifles, carbines, pistols, swords, projectiles, photos, maps, and original artwork. The centerpiece is a three-inch naval cannon converted to field artillery with caisson. The museum also frequently hosts living-history interpretations and black-powder demonstrations.

HISTORIC HEARTLAND

Here, more than in any other section of Georgia, the storied plantation South survives. Antebellum homes abound in the towns of the Historic Heartland region, and almost every site included here is an architectural or cultural treasure. Residents of the area have been at the forefront of historic preservation and are eager to share their heritage with visitors.

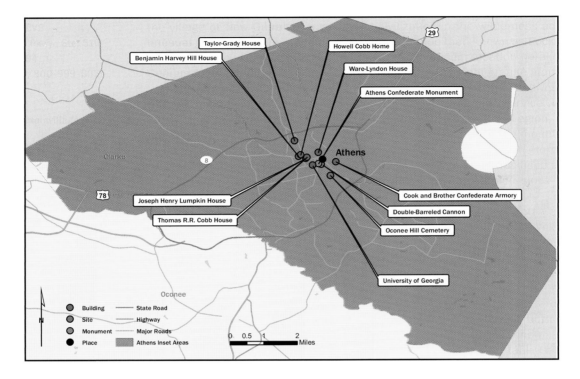

Taylor-Grady House

Benjamin Harvey Hill House

Howell Cobb Home

Ware-Lyndon House

Athens Confederate Monument

29

Clarke

8

Athens

78

Joseph Henry Lumpkin House

Cook and Brother Confederate Armory

Thomas R.R. Cobb House

Double-Barreled Cannon

Oconee Hill Cemetery

University of Georgia

Oconee

N

Building	State Road
Site	Highway
Monument	Major Roads
Place	Athens Inset Areas

0 0.5 1 2
Miles

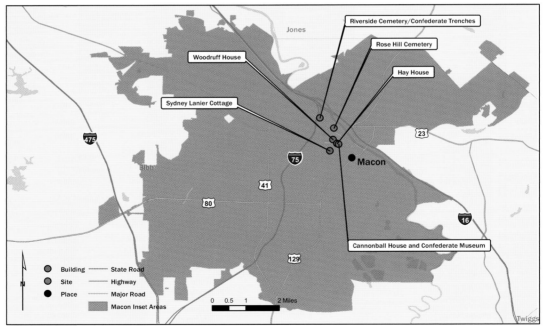

Jones

Riverside Cemetery/Confederate Trenches

Rose Hill Cemetery

Woodruff House

Hay House

Sydney Lanier Cottage

23

475

75

Macon

Bibb

41

80

16

Cannonball House and Confederate Museum

129

N

Building	State Road
Site	Highway
Place	Major Road
	Macon Inset Areas

0 0.5 1 2 Miles

Twiggs

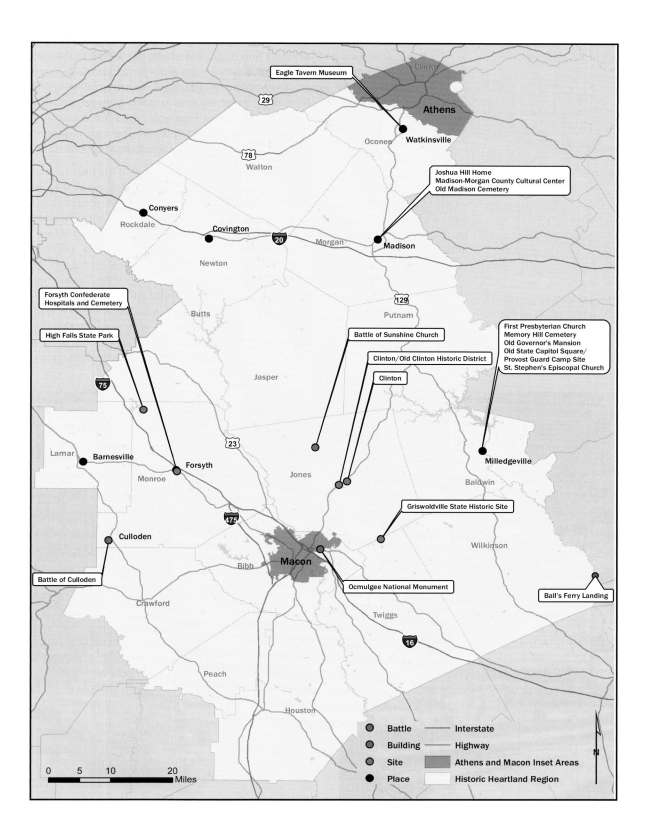

Eagle Tavern Museum

Joshua Hill Home
Madison-Morgan County Cultural Center
Old Madison Cemetery

Forsyth Confederate
Hospitals and Cemetery

High Falls State Park

Battle of Sunshine Church

Clinton/Old Clinton Historic District

Clinton

First Presbyterian Church
Memory Hill Cemetery
Old Governor's Mansion
Old State Capitol Square/
Provost Guard Camp Site
St. Stephen's Episcopal Church

Battle of Culloden

Griswoldville State Historic Site

Ocmulgee National Monument

Ball's Ferry Landing

Athens
Clarke
Watkinsville
Oconee
Walton
Conyers
Rockdale
Covington
Newton
Morgan
Madison
Putnam
Butts
Jasper
Lamar
Barnesville
Monroe
Forsyth
Jones
Milledgeville
Baldwin
Culloden
Macon
Bibb
Wilkinson
Crawford
Twiggs
Peach
Houston

Battle   Interstate
Building   Highway
Site   Athens and Macon Inset Areas
Place   Historic Heartland Region

0   5   10   20
Miles

N

ATHENS, Clarke County

Athens CVB
300 N. Thomas St.
Athens, GA 30601
706-357-4430/800-653-0603
www.visitathensga.com

Athens Welcome Center
Church-Waddel-Brumby House
280 E. Dougherty St.
Athens, GA 30601
706-353-1820

Antebellum Trail
www.antebellumtrail.org

Home to the University of Georgia, Athens had a home guard during the Civil War that successfully resisted Union cavalry at the Battle of Barber's Creek. Confederate earthworks from the battle on August 2, 1864, can still be clearly seen. Of special interest is the double-barreled cannon, the only one of its kind, that was used in the defense of Athens. It is believed to have been fired only once and with limited success. In addition to this most unusual relic, other sites of interest in Athens include historical monuments, a cemetery, and the homes and house museums of many Confederate leaders.

Athens is also the northern gateway to the one-hundred-mile Antebellum Trail, which winds south on the U.S. 441 Heritage Highway through Watkinsville, Madison, Eatonton, Milledgeville, Old Clinton, and Macon. Each of these communities is renowned for antebellum architecture, beautiful gardens, and Southern tradition.

Athens Confederate Monument

At Broad and Lumpkin streets
(across from the UGA Arch)
Athens, GA

Erected in 1871, the Athens Confederate Monument honors the Athens and Clarke County soldiers who gave their lives in defense of the South.

Left to right: *Athens Confederate Monument (Photo: Bob Price); Benjamin H. Hill House (Photo: Cara Pastore, Georgia Dept. of Economic Development)*

Benjamin H. Hill House

570 Prince Ave.
Athens, GA 30601

The Benjamin H. Hill House, which was built in 1858, has been faithfully restored by the University of Georgia and now serves as the private residence of the university president. Benjamin Harvey Hill graduated with honors from the university in 1844 and became an outstanding lawyer. He was elected to the state legislature in 1851 and the state senate in 1860. A voice of moderation, he opposed secession, but when Georgia left the Union he loyally supported the Confederate cause. He served in the Confederate Congress and was a close friend and adviser to President Jefferson Davis. After the war, Hill served terms in the U.S. House of Representatives and Senate and was one of the first powerful voices of the New South.

Cook and Brother Confederate Armory

Built in 1862, the Cook and Brother Confederate Armory manufactured Enfield-style rifles and carbines for the Confederate army. A state historical marker in front of the building details its history. After the Civil War, Chicopee Mills occupied the building until the 1970s. It is now owned by the University of Georgia and used for offices and physical plant space. The building is not open to the public.

East Broad St. at MLK Jr. Pkwy.
Athens, GA 30601

Above, left to right: *Cook and Brother Confederate Armory and the double-barreled cannon*
(Photos: Cara Pastore, Georgia Dept. of Economic Development)

Double-Barreled Cannon (NRHP)

In 1862 Athens resident John Gilleland designed the world's only double-barreled cannon, which was cast at the Athens Foundry and Machine Works in 1863. The concept involved loading the cannon with two balls connected by a chain several feet long. When fired, the whirling balls and chain would cut down any unfortunate enemy soldiers caught in their path. Though it never worked properly, a myth persists that the cannon was used to defend Athens without the cannonballs chained together. Some reports describe the cannon being fired only once or twice; then it malfunctioned and was never used again. It is now displayed on the city hall lawn and has become one of Athens' most famous landmarks.

At Hancock St. and College Ave.
(outside City Hall)
Athens, GA

Howell Cobb Homes

A University of Georgia graduate, Howell Cobb served in the U.S. Congress from 1843 to 1850 and was Speaker of the House in 1849. He was also governor of Georgia in 1851–1853 and secretary of the U.S. Treasury in 1856–1860. In 1861 Cobb was president of the Montgomery Convention, the body that created the Confederate States of America. During the Civil War he was a brigadier general in the Army

425 Hill St.
Athens, GA 30601

698 N. Pope St.
Athens, GA 30601

of Northern Virginia and later commanded the District of Georgia. Cobb is buried in Oconee Hill Cemetery in Athens. Howell Cobb once owned both of the houses, which are now private residences.

Left to right: *Howell Cobb (Courtesy of the UGA Hargrett Rare Book and Manuscript Library); one of his houses (Photo: Cara Pastore, Georgia Dept. of Economic Development)*

Joseph Henry Lumpkin House (NRHP)

248 Prince Ave.
Athens, GA 30601
706-569-5664

The 1830s Joseph Henry Lumpkin House has been restored and is currently used by the University of Georgia Law School. Joseph Henry Lumpkin attended the university and later became the first chief justice of the Georgia Supreme Court, serving from 1845 to 1867. He cofounded the UGA Law School with William Hope Hull and his son-in-law, Thomas R.R. Cobb. Lumpkin's four sons served in the Confederate army; one was killed at the Battle of Gettysburg, and another helped defend Athens at the Battle of Barber's Creek.

The house is currently used for meetings and seminars by the UGA Law School and may be rented to the public for special events.

Oconee Hill Cemetery

E. Campus Rd.
(behind Sanford Stadium)
Athens, GA 30601

The c. 1855 Oconee Hill Cemetery overlooks the banks of the Oconee River. Among the many Confederate soldiers buried here are four Confederate Civil War generals: Howell Cobb, Thomas R.R. Cobb, William M. Browne, and Martin L. Smith.

Right: *The Oconee Hill Cemetery (Photo: Cara Pastore, Georgia Dept. of Economic Development)*

Taylor-Grady House (NHL)

The Taylor-Grady House is a fine example of Greek Revival architecture. The home's thirteen columns represent each of the original colonies. Robert Taylor, the home's first owner, served as a general with the Georgia state troops. The second owner, Captain W.S. Grady, was killed at the Battle of Petersburg in Virginia. After the war, Grady's son, Henry W. Grady, as editor of the *Atlanta Constitution*, became a leading voice in reunifying the nation with his speeches about the New South. The house currently displays decorative arts and furniture of the period.

634 Prince Ave.
Athens, GA 30601
706-549-8688

Mon.–Thurs.: 9:00 a.m.–1:00 p.m.;
2:00 p.m.–5:00 p.m.

Thomas R.R. Cobb House (NRHP)

The Thomas R.R. Cobb House has had an active history. Its original Federal styling gave way to Greek Revival in 1852. Then in 1985 it was moved from its original site on Prince Avenue to Stone Mountain Park east of Atlanta. However, the park never restored the house, and in 2004 it was moved back to Athens, where it underwent restoration.

Thomas R.R. Cobb, Howell Cobb's younger brother, became a noted Georgia lawyer. He was one of the signers of the Georgia Ordinance of Secession and the principal author of the Confederate Constitution. He later served as a brigadier general in the Army of Northern Virginia and commanded Cobb's legion. He was killed in December 1862 at the Battle of Fredericksburg, ironically within sight of the Virginia birthplace of his mother. Cobb is buried in Athens' Oconee Hill Cemetery.

175 Hill St.
Athens, GA 30601
706-369-3513

Tues.–Sat.: 10:00 a.m.–4:00 p.m.

Above, left to right: *The recently restored Thomas R.R. Cobb House, which has been relocated near its original site in Athens (Photo: Cara Pastore, Georgia Dept. of Economic Development); the house before its restoration when it was located at Stone Mountain Park (Photo: Bob Price)*

University of Georgia

University of Georgia Visitors
Center at Four Towers Bldg.
400 River Rd.
Athens, GA 30602
706-542-0842

Visitors Center hours:
Mon.–Fri.: 8:00 a.m.–5:00 p.m.
Sat.: 9:00 a.m.–5:00 p.m.
Sun.: 1:00 p.m.–5:00 p.m.

Established in 1785, the University of Georgia is America's oldest state-chartered university. It was attended by many Georgia notables of the period, including Crawford W. Long, Alexander H. Stephens, Joseph Henry Lumpkin, Howell Cobb, Thomas R.R. Cobb, Benjamin Harvey Hill, Robert A. Toombs, and Henry W. Grady. After the war, the campus served as the headquarters for occupying Federal troops. Today, the main library houses the original Constitution of the Confederate States of America, which is displayed annually on Georgia's Confederate Memorial Day, April 26.

The historic north campus is listed in the National Register of Historic Places and contains many significant buildings, including Athens' oldest building, the c. 1802 Old College on the north campus where Stephens and Long were roommates. During the Civil War the Confederate army used Old College as a military hospital that specialized in the treatment of eye injuries. The 1824 Demosthenian Hall housed the Demosthenian Literary Society and Debate Club, of which Toombs and Hill were members. Stephens, Lumpkin, the Cobb brothers, and Grady belonged to the Phi Kappa Literary Society and Debate Club, which was housed in the 1836 Phi Kappa Hall. After the war the occupying Federal troops used this building as their headquarters. The 1832 University of Georgia Chapel was the site of antebellum church services and commencement exercises and is now home to George Cooke's painting of the interior of St. Peter's Cathedral in Rome, the largest framed oil painting in the world at the time of its completion. The Toombs Oak Marker, a Doric column pedestal outside the Commencement Chapel, notes the site of an oak tree where Toombs gave his legendary commencement speech in 1828 after having been expelled just prior to graduation. The 1858 University of Georgia Arch, which was modeled after the state seal, marks the entrance to the campus near the Old College. The arch was used on Georgia Confederate soldiers' uniform buttons and belt buckles. One of the nation's best collections of rare Confederate documents, including the Howell Cobb collection, is housed in the UGA Hargrett Rare Book and Manuscript Library on the historic old campus.

Left to right: *Demosthenian Hall, Phi Kappa Hall (Courtesy of the Library of Congress)*

Ware-Lyndon House (NRHP)

The c. 1850 Ware–Lyndon House, one of the few antebellum houses in the Athens area with Italianate elements, contains historic artifacts, documents, furniture, and medical items of the period. The house is named for two of its owners, Edward Ware and Edward Lyndon, who were Civil War–era physicians.

By 1863 most of Athens' male residents were away at war and the city was vulnerable to attack. The city's older men organized a militia unit for home defense called the Thunderbolts. Dr. Edward Ware served as an officer.

293 Hoyt St.
Athens, GA 30601
706-613-3623

Tues., Thurs.: Noon–9:00 p.m.
Wed., Fri., Sat.: 9:00 a.m.–5:00 p.m.

Left: *Ware-Lyndon House (Photo: Cara Pastore, Georgia Dept. of Economic Development)*

WATKINSVILLE, Oconee County

The town of Watkinsville grew up around the Eagle Tavern, which was built in 1801. Union Major General George Stoneman's raiders briefly rested here on August 2, 1864, before continuing northward, hoping to destroy "the armory and other Confederate works at Athens."

Local historians believe that the residents of Watkinsville tried to prepare for a possible Union attack by setting up a watch on the road from the town of High Shoals (today's Harden Hill/New High Shoals Road). However, when Stoneman's raiders arrived, they entered the town unmolested; having experienced so many false alarms, the townspeople had lowered their guard. The Federal cavalrymen took whatever they needed, including food, boots, and horses. A letter written by Mrs. Louisa Booth Ashford recounted the events, "They took all the watches they could find everywhere; made Mr. John Harris take his out of his pocket."

Oconee County
P.O. Box 145
Watkinsville, GA 30677
706-769-5120
www.visitoconee.com

Eagle Tavern Museum (NRHP)

Built in 1801, Eagle Tavern also served as a stagecoach stop. A persistent but unconfirmed story states that during the Civil War a Confederate soldier remained concealed for weeks in a hiding place in the loft behind the enormous chimney, which still stands today. Food and buckets of hot coals were handed up to him by slaves. The tavern has been restored to its 1840s appearance and includes a replica bedroom used by stagecoach travelers. A small museum displays artifacts from the early 1800s.

26 N. Main St. (U.S. Hwy. 441)
Watkinsville, GA 30677
706-769-5197
www.visitoconee.com

Mon.–Fri.: 10:00 a.m.–5:00 p.m.
Sun.: 1:00 p.m.–5:00 p.m.

Left: *Eagle Tavern Museum (Photo: Bob Price)*

CONYERS, Rockdale County

Conyers/Rockdale CVB
1184 Scott St.
Conyers, GA 30012
770-929-4270
www.conyersga.com

Conyers, an important stop on the Georgia railroad between Lithonia and Covington, was located on the Federal army's left wing on its second day of the March to the Sea. Conyers suffered from the destruction and theft that was typical of the march, while many of the town's inhabitants fled to nearby Social Circle. Though Conyers was not completely put to the torch, its rail line and depot were destroyed.

During Confederate President Jefferson Davis' flight to escape capture, part of his escort, including Major General Joseph Wheeler, was captured in Conyers on May 9, 1865, by pursuing Federal troops. Wheeler was released soon after in Athens, Georgia, but was rearrested and sent to Delaware with Davis to be imprisoned at Fort Delaware.

COVINGTON, Newton County

Covington-Newton County CVB
2101 Clark St.
Covington, GA 30014
770-787-3868/800-616-8626
www.newtonchamber.com

Elements of Federal General Kenner Garrard's cavalry entered Covington on July 22, 1864, on a mission to rip up rails and destroy bridges of the Georgia Railroad. While in the town they executed two residents who had put up a resistance, and they vandalized the community, burning the depot and a number of other buildings and stealing anything of use that could be carried away.

During the March to the Sea on November 18, 1864, the Federal XIV Corps headed by Major General William T. Sherman came through Covington, looting the town but sparing it from the torch. The troops were following Sherman's orders from a few days earlier to "forage liberally on the country" and seize "whatever is needed by the command."

Covington was an important hospital center from 1862 through 1864, treating thousands of patients. The First United Methodist Church and the "Old Church" were both used as Confederate hospitals. Confederate soldiers who did not survive are buried in Covington City Cemetery and at the Oxford Cemetery at Oxford College.

Right: *Sherman's troops foraging along the March to the Sea (Courtesy of the UGA Hargrett Rare Book and Manuscript Library)*

MANSFIELD, Newton County

Mansfield was incorporated on July 22, 1903. Previously it had been known as Carmel and Bob Lee.

Covington-Newton County CVB
2101 Clark St.
Covington, GA 30015
770-787-3868/800-616-8626
www.newtonchamber.com

Burge Plantation

The home of diarist Dolly Lunt Burge, Burge Plantation, which was established in 1809, suffered the privations of war when the left wing of the Federal army passed by on November 19, 1864. Her diary entry for that day included: "Like Demons they rush in! My yards are full. To my smoke-house, my Dairy, Pantry, Kitchen & Cellar, like famished wolves they come, breaking locks & whatever is in there way."

The house, outbuildings, and grounds, ransacked by soldiers all day, were spared from the torch, though all foodstuffs and livestock were removed. *The Diary of Dolly Lunt Burge, 1848–1879* provides a valuable window into the past, documenting life on a prosperous farm in rural Georgia during the late nineteenth century. The Burge home now sits across the street from its original location and can be visited by appointment.

2659 Hwy. 142
Mansfield, GA 30055
770-787-5152
www.burgeplantation.com

MADISON, Morgan County

Madison, one of Georgia's most beautiful antebellum towns, was incorporated and named the seat of Morgan County in 1809. During the Civil War, Madison was a Confederate hospital center, and during the March to the Sea it was on the route of Sherman's left wing under Major General Henry Slocum. Slocum destroyed sixteen miles of railroad track between Social Circle and Madison as well as railroad support facilities and industries he deemed useful to the Confederacy. Once in Madison, damage by Union troops included the Georgia Railroad depot and a building where cloth manufacturing and cotton ginning occurred as well as slave pens. After Slocum departed, Federal army stragglers committed acts of vandalism and looting; however, private homes were generally left unmolested. Previously, on August 1, 1864, a brigade of Union cavalry under Lt. Colonel Silas Adams, who was part of the Stoneman-McCook raid, stopped in Madison. Some supplies were burned but little permanent destruction was wrought.

This archetypical cotton-belt town was the home to many members of Georgia's cotton aristocracy. The homes are representative of the life-style of the rich southern planter. Historic groups in Madison sponsor tours during May and December.

Madison-Morgan County CVB
115 East Jefferson St.
Madison, GA 30650
706-342-4454/800-709-7406
www.madisonga.org

Joshua Hill Home

Joshua Hill was a U.S. senator with Unionist sympathies. He was outspoken in his opposition to secession but decided to resign his seat when the break with the Union became inevitable. In 1863 he attempted a bid for the governorship against

485 Old Post Rd.
Madison, GA 30650

Georgia's stalwart politician Joseph E. Brown but was unsuccessful. At the end of the war Hill became a Republican and participated in Reconstruction. Hill once again faced Brown, this time for a seat in the U.S. Senate. Hill succeeded, remaining in office until 1873. He is buried in Madison's Old City Cemetery. Hill's home, which was built in 1830, is privately owned and not open to the public.

Madison-Morgan County Cultural Center

434 S. Main St.
Madison, GA 30650
706-342-4743

Above: *Joshua Hill Home.*
Right: *Madison-Morgan County Cultural Center (Photos: Bob Price)*

The Madison-Morgan County Cultural Center is housed in a c. 1895 Romanesque Revival school building. A reconstructed section of an early nineteenth-century hand-hewn log cabin of heart of pine houses a Civil War exhibit. Included in the exhibit is a handmade coverlet that depicts fighting in Virginia as sketched by a Confederate soldier from Georgia's Oglethorpe County. After being wounded in Virginia, the soldier was sent to a Madison hospital, where he drew from memory the battle onto a hand-woven coverlet, which his wife then embroidered.

Old City Cemetery

On Central Ave. across the railroad tracks
Madison, GA

The Old City Cemetery contains the graves of one known and fifty-one unknown Confederates. Also buried here is a black hospital attendant with a headstone marked "Unknown Colored Hosp. Attend." Most of the soldiers interred here died in one of Madison's Confederate hospitals during 1862–1863.

HIGH FALLS STATE PARK, Monroe County

76 High Falls Park Dr.
Jackson, GA 30233
478-993-3053
http://gastateparks.org/info/highfall/

Right: *Unlike most sites that suffered damage and destruction during the war, High Falls was burned by Confederate forces to keep it out of the hands of the invading Federals. (Photo: Marla Bexley-Brown)*

Adjacent to the entrance of High Falls State Park off High Falls Park Drive are the stone foundations of a gristmill and other ruins of the antebellum manufacturing town of High Falls that once thrived here on the banks of the Towaliga River. Confederate Major General Joseph Wheeler's cavalry burned the town's buildings during Major General William T. Sherman's March to the Sea in an attempt to destroy supplies that would be useful to the Federal invaders. High Falls remained in existence until the 1880s, when, bypassed by the railroad, it was abandoned. The ruins and the falls can best be viewed from the remains of an iron bridge that partially spans the Towaliga River.

FORSYTH, Monroe County

The town of Forsyth was witness to more than its fair share of the suffering of war. As Major General William T. Sherman's army advanced closer to Atlanta, approximately eighteen thousand to twenty thousand sick and wounded Confederate soldiers were moved to Forsyth. Hotels, the courthouse, commercial establishments, private homes, and schools in the town and surrounding area were filled with the invalid and infirm, turning Forsyth into one of the state's major hospital centers.

Forsyth Confederate Hospitals and Cemetery

In the Confederate section of the Forsyth Cemetery are buried one known and 299 unknown Confederate soldiers. Most of these died in several Confederate hospitals located in Forsyth. Also buried here is Confederate female nurse Honora Sweeney, who died while serving the wounded in one of the city's hospitals. The Forsyth hospitals were known as Hardee and Clayton. Also in use as a hospital was the Forsyth Female College.

Newton Memorial Dr. and South Lee St.
Forsyth, GA

Left: *Forsyth Confederate Cemetery (Photo: Bob Price)*

CULLODEN, Monroe County

Culloden was first settled in 1739 when it was a junction of Indian trails that connected Columbus and Augusta. It was named in honor of William Culloden, a Scotch Highlander who opened a store here in 1780.

www.culloden.com

Battle of Culloden

Ten days after General Robert E. Lee's surrender in Virginia on April 19, 1865, Federal troops heading to Macon under Brigadier General James H. Wilson's command encountered the Worrill Grays, a reserve militia unit made up of two hundred boys, old men, and recuperating veterans. The Grays fought a valiant battle against overwhelming odds but were eventually forced to yield, leaving their dead and wounded on the field in Federal hands. Two members of the 17th Indiana Mounted Infantry, privates John Davis and Aaron Hudson, were awarded the Congressional Medal of Honor for capturing the Grays' flag during the fierce, if short, action.

At the cemetery on Church St. off Old U.S. 341
Culloden, GA

BARNESVILLE, Lamar County

A middle Georgia town on the Macon and Western Railroad, Barnesville, like many towns on the railroad, became a hospital center as wounded soldiers were transported south during the Atlanta Campaign. By July 1864, the following hospitals had relocated to Barnesville: Kingsville Hospital, Kingston Hospital, Medical College Hospital, Flewellen Hospital, and Erwin Hospital. Patients who died at the hospitals were buried in the Confederate section of Greenwood Cemetery.

One of the worst train accidents of the war occurred outside Barnesville at Lavender's Crossing on September 1, 1864. A supply train, or "up train," traveling north from Macon with an engine named the *Governor* collided with a southbound "down troop train" with an engine named the *Dispatch* that was evacuating wounded from soon-to-be-surrendered Atlanta. The collision caused approximately thirty casualties.

In one of the final episodes of the war on April 19, 1865, Brigadier General James H. Wilson's Federal cavalry, moving through Barnesville on the way to Macon, skirmished with a small Confederate force known as the Dixie Rangers. The Confederates, greatly outnumbered, were forced from the field and lost their flag to Federals from the 4th Indiana Cavalry.

Left: Confederate graves at the Greenwood Cemetery in Barnsville decorated for Christmas (Photo: Bob Price)

MACON, Bibb County

www.cityofmacon.net

Macon/Bibb CVB
450 Martin Luther King Jr. Blvd.
Macon, GA 31201
478-743-3401/800-768-3401
www.maconga.org

Built at the fall line of the Ocmulgee River, the geographic name for the point where a river is no longer navigable, Macon was the most important transportation center in central Georgia. It was also a manufacturing center supplying Confederate armies with the implements of war. Ammunition, cannons, and small arms were manufactured here at the enormous Confederate States Arsenal, which also maintained a large-scale small-arms repair operation. Camp Oglethorpe, a prisoner-of-war camp that housed as many as fifteen hundred Union officers, was located near the present Central City Park. The last session of Georgia's Confederate legislature also met in Macon in May 1865. For these reasons alone it seemed unlikely that the city would have survived the war given the Federal mission of destruction and penchant for retribution while it marched through Georgia. But Macon did survive, generally unscathed.

A hospital center, like many Deep South cities with a rail connection, Macon encountered its initial brush with combat when Major General George Stoneman made an attempt to subdue the city on July 30, 1864. Stoneman unlimbered his artillery near Dunlap Farm across the Ocmulgee River from Macon. A number of the shells struck the home of Judge Asa Holt—known today as the Cannonball House. With Confederate Major General Howell Cobb and the recently relieved Army of Tennessee commander General Joseph E. Johnston looking on, the Georgia militia, home guard, and a force of six hundred Tennessee Confederates successfully repelled Stoneman's cavalry.

Fighting again erupted on November 20–21, 1864, at Dunlap Farm during Major General William T. Sherman's March to the Sea. Federal Brigadier General Judson Kilpatrick attempted a feint movement on Macon while the Federal west wing bypassed the city to the east. Kilpatrick's troopers skirmished with elements of Major General Joseph Wheeler's cavalry, driving them back into Macon in an engagement known as the Battle of Walnut Creek. However, no pitched battle for the defense of Macon ever occurred.

Today, Macon has more churches per capita than any other U.S. city. A number of these beautiful buildings are relevant to Macon's Civil War history, such as the First Presbyterian Church and Christ Episcopal Church. Macon also boasts a number of historically significant homes that are open for tours year round.

Left: A depiction of the market in Macon (Courtesy of the UGA Hargrett Rare Book and Manuscript Library). Below: Macon's Cannonball House (Photo: Cara Pastore, Georgia Dept. of Economic Development)

Cannonball House and Confederate Museum (NRHP)

Constructed in 1853 for Judge Asa Holt, the Cannonball House gained fame during Federal Major General George Stoneman's artillery bombardment on July 30, 1864. A projectile fired from across the Ocmulgee River at Dunlap's Farm struck the building on the front elevation along Mulberry Street. The cannonball bounced off the sidewalk, grazed a support column, pierced the front façade, and landed in the hallway. Although little damage was done, the home gained local notoriety for having been damaged in the fighting.

Purchased by the Sidney Lanier Chapter of the United Daughters of the Confederacy, the home's two furnished parlors on the first floor honor Phi Mu, founded at nearby Wesleyan College and the first sorority established in the United States. At the rear of the house stands a two-over-two building that served as the kitchen with servants' quarters above. The building, which was constructed with bricks made by slaves, houses the Macon Confederate Museum, showcasing uniforms, weapons, and regimental flags.

856 Mulberry St.
Macon, GA 31201
478-745-5982
www.cannonballhouse.org

Mon.–Sat.: 10:00 a.m.–5:00 p.m.

Hay House (NRHP)

934 Georgia Ave.
Macon, GA 31201
478-742-8155
http://roadsidegeorgia.com/
site/hay_house.html

Tues.–Sat.: 10:00 a.m.–4:00 p.m.
Sun.: 1:00 p.m.–4:00 p.m.
(extended hours during summer)

A magnificent 18,000-square-foot four-level Italian Renaissance Revival home, the Hay House was completed in 1859. Unsubstantiated stories linked the Hay House with hidden gold from the Confederate treasury, a story made more palatable by the fact that the Confederate government had established an important treasury depository at Macon. A hidden room shown on the house tour that was supposedly used to conceal treasure has also helped to give the story a touch of credence over the years.

The home's large ornate cupola, visible to Major General George Stoneman's troops from their position at the Dunlap Farm across the Ocmulgee River, was used by Federal gunners to calculate range and trajectory during the bombardment of Macon. Regardless of the dubious story of hidden gold, the Hay House is a national treasure and a must-see site when visiting Macon.

Right: *Macon's Hay House (Photo: Jim Lockhart, Historic Preservation Division, Georgia Dept. of Natural Resources)*

Ocmulgee National Monument (NRHP)/ Battle of Dunlap's Farm

1207 Emery Hwy.
Macon, GA 31201
478-752-8257
www.nps.gov/ocmu

Daily: 9:00 a.m.–5:00 p.m.

The Ocmulgee National Monument is a Mississippian Indian site that was continually occupied for centuries and was purported to have been visited by Spanish explorer Hernando de Soto during his sixteenth-century trek across the Southeast. It was also the site of Union lines during fighting around Macon known as the Battle of Dunlap's Farm. On July 30, 1864, Major General George Stoneman used the farmhouse as his headquarters during the brief fighting, while his two pieces of light artillery shelled the city from the adjacent high ground. Federal artillery positions can still be seen on the property.

Though successful in destroying many miles of the Central of Georgia Railroad leading to Macon, along with several bridges and depots, Stoneman failed in his attempt to capture the city by storm and withdrew. After their departure, the Federal raiders were pursued into nearby Jones County, where they fought the Battle of Sunshine Church and were forced to surrender unconditionally. Ironically, Stoneman's objectives for the raid included freeing the prisoners at Macon's Camp Oglethorpe and Andersonville's Camp Sumter. Instead he and his men ended up as inmates at these facilities.

Right: The Union gun emplacement from the Battle of Dunlap's Farm (Photo: Bob Price)

Rose Hill Cemetery (NRHP)

Rose Hill Cemetery, an outstanding example of the nineteenth-century ideal of the cemetery as a public park, is located on the rolling hills above Riverside Drive overlooking the Ocmulgee River. Laid out by Macon resident Simri Rose in 1840, the fifty-acre site had five distinct sections: the Central Avenue District, Eglantine Square, Forest Hill, Magnolia Ridge, and Holly Ridge. Each section was originally separated by thick woodlands, but as the city grew, so did the cemetery. In the 1850s several more sections were added.

At the war's end, some twenty-seven thousand square feet were set aside for the re-interment of more than six hundred Confederate soldiers. They were buried in Soldiers Square on a hillside overlooking the Ocmulgee River next to a natural amphitheater that extends to the railroad tracks. Some of the Confederate notables include brigadier generals Edward Dorr Tracy and Philip Cook; Colonel John Basil Lamar, the aide-de-camp to General Howell Cobb; and governor and U.S. senator General Alfred H. Colquitt.

Remnants of a portion of the earthworks and an artillery battery used by Confederates in the defense of Macon can be seen in the postbellum Riverside Cemetery, directly adjacent to Rose Hill Cemetery and several blocks to the north off Riverside Drive. The earthwork is located in the back section above the Ocmulgee River.

1071 Riverside Dr.
Macon, GA 31201
478-751-9119
www.rosehillcemetery.org

Daily: 8:30 a.m.–sundown

Left: Casualties from area hospitals as well as the Battle of Griswoldville are buried in Rose Hill Cemetery. (Photo: Barry Brown)

Sydney Lanier Cottage (NRHP)

935 High St.
Macon, GA 31201
478-743-3851
www.historicmacon.org/slc

Mon.–Sat.: 10:00 a.m.–4:00 p.m.

Below, left to right: *Sydney La-nier Cottage, Woodruff House, the McCarthy-Pope House in Clinton (Photos: Bob Price)*

A man of many talents, Sydney Lanier was a great poet of the Southern tradition, as well as a linguist, musician, mathematician, and lawyer. He began his Civil War service as a private in the Macon Volunteers and was later transferred to the Confederate Signal Corps. Detailed to a blockade runner, he was captured on November 6, 1864, and imprisoned at the notorious prisoner-of-war camp in Point Lookout, Maryland, where he contracted tuberculosis. He was released in a prisoner exchange in February 1865. He later moved to the dry climate of San Antonio, Texas, to help improve his condition. He died of consumption in Lynn, North Carolina, on September 7, 1881, at the age of thirty-nine.

The poet laureate of Georgia and author of poems such as "Song of the Chattahoochee," Lanier was born in this cottage in 1842. Georgia's Lake Lanier near Gainesville and Lanier County are named after him. Today, the Sydney Lanier Cottage is the headquarters of the Historic Macon Foundation.

Woodruff House

988 Bond St.
Macon GA, 31201
478-301-2715

Built in 1836 by millionaire cotton planter Joseph Bond, this classical Greek Revival home gracing one of Macon's highest elevations was the headquarters for Union Brigadier General James H. Wilson during his occupation of the town in the spring of 1865. The Woodruff House also hosted President Jefferson Davis and his family during their visit to Macon in 1887 when a ball for Davis' daughter Winnie was held. The house is now owned by Mercer University and can be visited by appointment.

Clinton/Old Clinton Historic District (NRHP)

Clinton is located 12 miles northeast of Macon, 1.5 miles southeast of Gray, one block west off U.S. Hwy. 129

Clinton became a battleground during the Civil War when more than two thousand Union troops rode into town en route from Atlanta to Macon and Andersonville. They stole or destroyed over five hundred thousand dollars worth of property in Jones County, finally occupying Clinton by November 19, 1864. The Old Clinton Historical Society presents Clinton's War Days every May, a reenactment of the battles fought in and around Clinton. During War Days, the historical society displays Civil War memorabilia at the c. 1809 McCarthy-Pope House, the oldest remaining structure in town. Several historical markers are located along Georgia Highway 22, providing information about the town of Griswoldville, which ceased to exist after the war, and the Battle of Griswoldville.

CLINTON/GRISWOLDVILLE, Jones County

Clinton was incorporated on December 4, 1816, as the county seat. In 1860, Clinton was the third-largest city in the state after Savannah and Augusta.

Samuel Griswold came to Clinton in 1818 and established Georgia's first iron foundry, becoming the world's leader in cotton gin production. Griswold moved his foundry to the site of the railroad in 1849, and the town of Griswoldville was born. The town of Clinton almost disappeared due to destruction wrought by Federal soldiers as well as the residents rejection of having the railroad pass through the community.

Jones County–Gray Chamber of
Commerce & Visitors Center
161 W. Clinton St.
Gray, GA 31032
478-986-1123
www.jonescounty.org

Griswoldville State Historic Site

The Battle of Griswoldville was the only significant land battle fought along the route of Major General William T. Sherman's March to the Sea. On November 22, 1864, inexperienced troops from the Georgia militia made a courageous but tragic attack on Sherman's right wing. The Georgia troops suffered heavy losses before retiring to Macon. The slaughter of mostly old men and young boys was described by a Union commander as "a needless effusion of blood."

The wartime industrial center at Griswoldville was named for the Connecticut entrepreneur Samuel Griswold, who in 1820 established the first iron foundry in Georgia and a factory for making cotton gins, bricks, soap, and furniture. In 1862 Griswold converted his factory to manufacture a Colt-type pistol for the Confederacy. On November 21, 1864, Union cavalry Brigadier General Judson Kilpatrick's forces destroyed the town and factory. The town was never rebuilt.

Seventeen acres of the original Griswoldville battlefield were purchased through efforts of the Georgia Civil War Commission and were turned over to the state of Georgia in 1998. A tableau marker near the parking area orients visitors to the battle that occurred there. Currently, the nearby Jarrell Plantation Historic Site supervises the Griswoldville site.

Approximately 10 miles east of
Macon
Baker Rd. off Hwy. 57
Twiggs County
478-986-5172

Below: *The tableau marker at the Battle of Griswoldville site (Photo: Bob Price)*

Battle of Sunshine Church

A historical marker indicates the location of the Battle of Sunshine Church where on July 30, 1864, a Union cavalry force under Major General George Stoneman was stopped by Georgia militia at Macon. Stoneman retreated and was pursued by Confederate cavalry under Brigadier General Alfred Iverson Jr. With a much smaller force—but possessing knowledge of the territory, having been born in nearby Old Clinton—Iverson caught up to Stoneman at Sunshine Church. Deceiving Stoneman into believing he was surrounded, Iverson received the surrender of Stoneman and his seven hundred troopers and artillery.

North of Clinton on
U.S. Hwy. 29/GA Hwy. 11
Round Oak, GA

MILLEDGEVILLE, Baldwin County

Milledgeville/Baldwin CVB
200 West Hancock St.
Milledgeville, GA 31061
478-452-4687/800-653-1804
www.milledgevillecvb.com

Above: *Thomas Nast's An Incident of General Sherman's March through Georgia (Photo courtesy of Sotheby's, Inc. ©1997)*

Named after John Milledge, a Revolutionary War hero, Georgia governor, and U.S. senator, Milledgeville served as the capital of Georgia from 1807 to 1868. In 1864 Milledgeville was in the path of the left wing of Major General William T. Sherman's army on its March to the Sea. As the large Federal force approached the capital in the third week of November, the state government under Governor Joseph E. Brown evacuated the town and moved the seat of government to Macon. The Georgia militia troops who had remained in Milledgeville accompanied the fleeing legislature. The lead elements of the Federal XX Corps entered Milledgeville without opposition on November 22. Union soldiers looted the statehouse and state library, burned the state arsenal and railroad depot, and blew up the powder magazine. Sherman, headquartered in the Governor's Mansion, planned the next leg of his march from Milledgeville to Millen. The plan included continuing destruction of the Georgia Central Railroad and the release of Federal prisoners at Magnolia Springs six miles north of Millen. Both the left and right wings of Sherman's army departed Milledgeville on November 24.

First Presbyterian Church (NRHP)

Located on the Old State Capitol Square, the First Presbyterian Church was one of three churches erected in Milledgeville about the same time as the Old State Capitol. The church was occupied by Union forces during the war.

210 S. Wayne St.
Milledgeville, GA 31061
478-452-9394

Left: *First Presbyterian Church*
(Photo: Bob Price)

Old Governor's Mansion (NRHP)

This restored Greek Revival mansion served as the residence for eight Georgia governors from 1839 to 1868. When Major General William T. Sherman and his army occupied Milledgeville in November 1864, he used the mansion for his headquarters. Sherman slept in his bedroll on the floor since all furnishings had been evacuated to Macon along with Georgia governor Joseph E. Brown. Late in November, after Sherman had left Atlanta to begin the March to the Sea, Governor Brown returned to the mansion with his family and furnishings. In May 1865, Governor Brown was arrested at the mansion. The building was completely restored to its antebellum condition in 2005.

120 S. Clark St.
Milledgeville, GA 31061
478-445-4545
www.gcsu.edu/mansion

Tues.-Sat.: 10:00 a.m.-4:00 p.m.

Left to right: *Old Governor's Mansion, State Capitol Building (Photos: Bob Price)*

Old State Capitol Building and Museum (NRHP)

Serving as the seat of the state government from 1807 to 1868, this Gothic-style structure is one of the oldest public buildings in the United States. The Georgia Secession Convention took place in the Old State Capitol Building in January 1861. In 1864 Major General William T. Sherman's occupying troops held a mock session of the Georgia legislature in the building and repealed the Secession Act. In 1998 the Old State Capitol Building underwent significant renovation and restoration and now houses the administration and classrooms of Georgia Military College.

A museum was opened in 2006 on the ground floor with ten galleries depicting Georgia from the prehistoric period through the twentieth century. Three galleries are devoted to Secession, the Civil War, and the Reconstruction period following the war.

201 E. Greene St.
Milledgeville, GA 31061
478-453-1803
www.oldcapitalmuseum.org

Capitol Building:
Mon.-Fri.: 9:00 a.m.-5:00 p.m.

Museum:
Mon.-Fri.: 10:00 a.m.-4:00 p.m.
Sat.: Noon-4:00 p.m.

Old State Capitol Square (NRHP)/ Provost Guard Camp Site

201 E. Greene St.
Milledgeville, GA 31061

At the time of the Civil War, three churches and an arsenal, which was destroyed by General William T. Sherman's troops, stood around the Old State Capitol Square. The square witnessed the repeal of the Georgia Ordinance of Secession in a mock legislative session featuring drunken and rowdy Federal soldiers and the subsequent damaging of the interior of the capitol. A marker on the square denotes the area where the Federal provost guards pitched their tents on the grounds.

Memory Hill Cemetery (NRHP)

300 W. Franklin Street
(at Liberty Street)
Milledgeville, GA 31061
www.friendsofcems.org/
MemoryHill/

Originally called Cemetery Square, Memory Hill was designated as one of the four public cemetery squares of twenty acres each in the Milledgeville town plan of 1803. Many people associated with Milledgeville and Georgia are buried here, such as Congressman Carl Vinson; writer Flannery O'Connor; and Georgia governors, legislators, and soldiers. Also of historical significance is the large number of slave graves.

A Confederate Memorial at Memory Hill honors twenty-seven unknown Confederate soldiers. The monument was erected in the cemetery early in 1868 and is believed to be the first monument in Georgia to honor the state's fallen soldiers. Research done in 2003 resulted in the identification of the formerly unknown soldiers. One of the identified Confederates buried at Memory Hill is Edwin Francis Jemison, the young soldier whose photograph is among the best-known images associated with the War Between the States. Jemison was killed at Malvern Hill, Virginia, on July 1, 1862, at the age of seventeen.

Memory Hill Cemetery is maintained and controlled by the city of Milledgeville. However, grave lots are owned by individuals. A self-guided tour map is available at the cemetery, and guided tours may be arranged for groups of fifteen or more.

Above: *Edwin Francis Jemison (Courtesy of the Library of Congress)*

St. Stephen's Episcopal Church

Located on the Old State Capitol Square, St. Stephen's Episcopal Church is one of three churches built in Milledgeville around the same time as the Old State Capitol. In 1864 the church was damaged when Federal troops dynamited the nearby arsenal and powder magazine. In 1909, a new organ was presented to the church by George W. Perkins of New York, who heard that Major General William T. Sherman's men had stabled horses in the church, further damaging it and its contents. Hoofprints can still be seen in the floors.

220 S. Wayne St.
Milledgeville, GA 31061
478-452-2710

Right: *St. Stephen's Episcopal Church*
(Photo: Bob Price)

BALL'S FERRY LANDING, Wilkinson County

Ball's Ferry is named for John Ball, a Revolutionary War veteran who in 1806 established a ferry to provide transportation across the Oconee River. On the March to the Sea, Major General William T. Sherman's right wing skirmished with Confederate troops for three days before crossing the river at Ball's Ferry. Two markers along Georgia Highway 57 at the Oconee River describe the action of November 25, 1864.

At the end of the Civil War, Confederate President Jefferson Davis and his cabinet followed a route to Ball's Ferry, where they intended to camp but were diverted when they learned of an impending attack on Mrs. Davis, who was traveling separately. The ferry remained in operation until 1939, when the state of Georgia replaced it with a bridge.

More than five hundred acres surrounding the ferry landing has been purchased by the Ball's Ferry Historical Park Association and deeded to Georgia State Parks and Historical Sites for the site of a future state park.

8.0 miles east of Toomsboro on
GA Hwy. 57
Toomsboro, GA

Right: *Marker memorializing the events that took place at Ball's Ferry (Photo: Bob Price)*

CLASSIC SOUTH

The Classic South region is similar to Georgia's Historic Heartland in its abundance of homes in the *Gone with the Wind* tradition, especially in the Washington-Wilkes area. During the Civil War, Augusta was a major Confederate city, a rail junction, and home of the second-largest armament factory in the world.

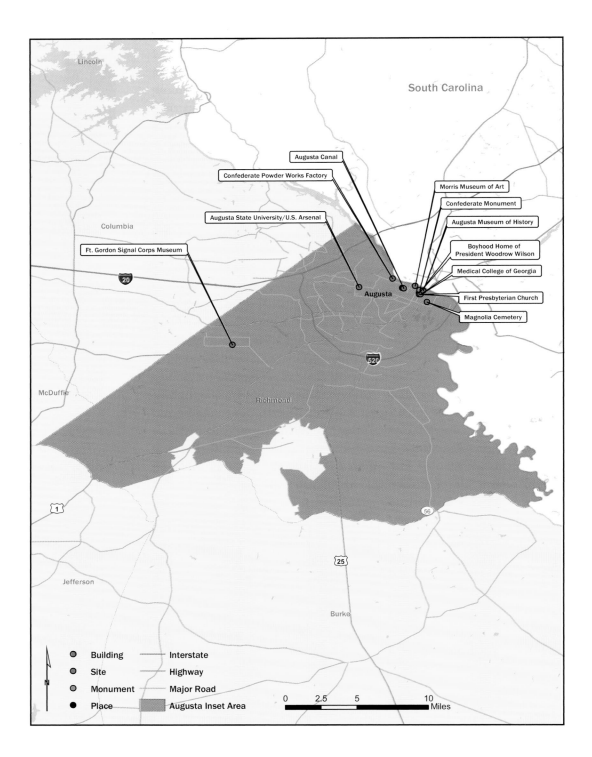

Lincoln

South Carolina

Columbia

Augusta Canal

Confederate Powder Works Factory

Morris Museum of Art

Confederate Monument

Augusta Museum of History

Augusta State University/U.S. Arsenal

Boyhood Home of
President Woodrow Wilson

Medical College of Georgia

Ft. Gordon Signal Corps Museum

20

Augusta

First Presbyterian Church

Magnolia Cemetery

520

McDuffie

Richmond

1

56

25

Jefferson

Burke

N

● Building   —— Interstate
● Site   —— Highway
● Monument   —— Major Road
● Place   Augusta Inset Area

0   2.5   5   10
                      Miles

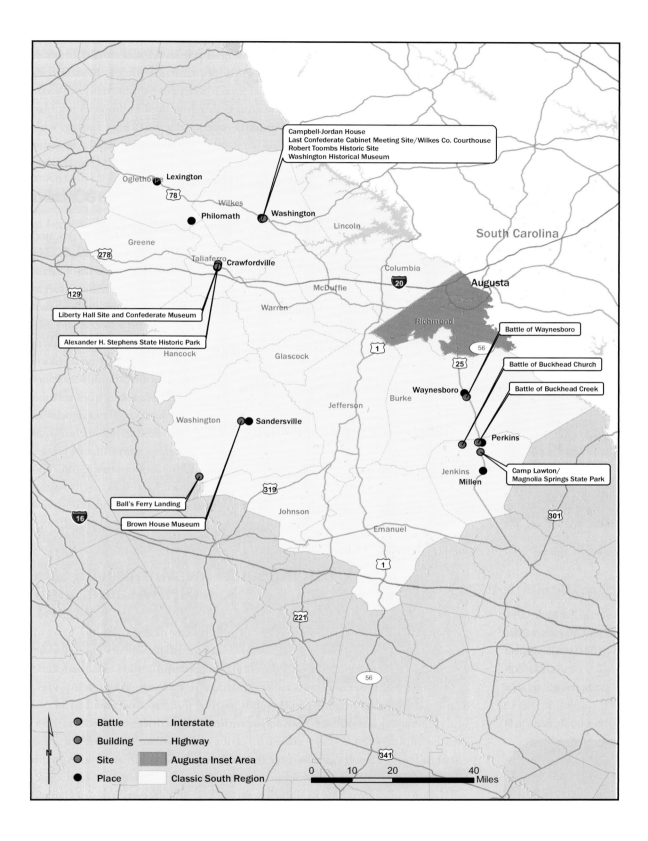

Campbell-Jordan House
Last Confederate Cabinet Meeting Site/Wilkes Co. Courthouse
Robert Toombs Historic Site
Washington Historical Museum

Oglethorpe Lexington
78
Wilkes
Philomath Washington
Greene Lincoln
South Carolina
278
Taliaferro Crawfordville
Columbia
129
McDuffie
Augusta
Liberty Hall Site and Confederate Museum
Warren
Richmond
Alexander H. Stephens State Historic Park
1
Battle of Waynesboro
Hancock
Glascock
56
25
Battle of Buckhead Church
Waynesboro
Battle of Buckhead Creek
Jefferson
Burke
Washington Sandersville
Perkins
319
Jenkins
Camp Lawton/
Magnolia Springs State Park
Ball's Ferry Landing
Millen
16
Johnson
Brown House Museum
Emanuel
301
1
221
56
341

Battle Interstate
Building Highway
Site Augusta Inset Area
N
Place Classic South Region

0   10   20   40
                          Miles

LEXINGTON, Oglethorpe County

Oglethorpe County Chamber of
Commerce
1158 Athens Rd.
Crawford, GA 30630
706-743-3113

Lexington, a lovely small town founded in the late 1700s, has at least twenty existing antebellum homes. Confederate Colonel Francis S. Bartow, killed early in the war at the Battle of First Manassas in Virginia, was considered the South's first Civil War hero. Bartow led the Oglethorpe Light Infantry, a regiment he raised in Savannah. It included the Oglethorpe Rifles, a company raised in the Lexington area.

In the nearby town of Crawford is the 1848 Crawford Railroad Station, which was a major storage and shipping center for supplies to the Confederate Army.

PHILOMATH (NHD), Oglethorpe County

Oglethorpe County Chamber of
Commerce
1158 Athens Rd.
Crawford, GA 30630
706-743-3113

On May 7, 1865, this quiet little village, then know as Woodstock, witnessed one of the Civil War's final dramas, the capitulation of approximately 350 Confederate cavalrymen who had ridden south with President Jefferson Davis during his efforts to escape capture. After the war, former Confederate Vice President Alexander H. Stephens renamed the town Philomath after the Greek term meaning "love of knowledge." Today, Philomath is recognized as a National Historic District.

WASHINGTON, Wilkes County

Washington-Wilkes County
Tourism and Main Street
22 West Square
Washington, GA 30673
706-678-2013
www.washingtonwilkes.org

Washington, which survived the March to the Sea, is filled with many outstanding examples of antebellum architecture. Chartered as the county seat in 1780, the town was named in honor of the Revolutionary War hero and first U.S. President George Washington. Even though it has firm eighteenth-century roots, Washington's most significant historical moments came at the close of the Civil War. On May 5, 1865, the last cabinet meeting of the Confederate States of America was held at the Heard House in Washington. In addition, Washington was the home of Robert A. Toombs, the nineteenth-century Georgia statesman and Confederate general often referred to as the "Unreconstructed Rebel." Brigadier General Edward Porter Alexander, the artillery commander for Robert E. Lee's Army of Northern Virginia at Gettysburg, was also a native of Washington.

Wilkes County, one of Georgia's original counties, carries the distinction of being the place where Eli Whitney perfected the cotton gin. First used in 1795 at the Mount Pleasant Plantation outside Washington, this labor-saving invention revolutionized cotton production and was an important component in changing the destiny of the nation. The cotton gin was able to take the place of ten men in the labor-intensive task of separating the cotton fiber from the seed, which allowed short staple cotton to become commercially viable. Because of the speed and volume with which it could process cotton, the device increased the demand for field workers, so more acreage could be converted to cotton production and more cotton harvested. As a result, the number of slaves increased throughout the cotton belt. As noted by a Scottish traveler through Georgia in 1844,

"Nothing was attended to but the rearing of cotton and slaves. The more cotton the more slaves and the more slaves the more cotton." Therefore during the early nineteenth century in a time when slavery was becoming less and less economically viable, Whitney, a New England native, became associated with making the South's peculiar institution more profitable, thus helping to set the stage for sectional conflict.

Campbell-Jordan House (NRHP)

John Archibald Campbell was born in this home in June 1811. His father, Colonel Duncan G. Campbell, was a distinguished lawyer involved in the 1824 Creek Indian land cessation. A graduate of the University of Georgia, John Campbell studied law and was admitted to the bar in 1829. He then moved to Montgomery, Alabama, where he served several terms in the state legislature. He was appointed associate justice of the U.S. Supreme Court in 1853, serving until his resignation in 1861. He exerted his considerable influence to prevent civil war, and although he opposed secession, he believed in a state's right to do so. Afterward, he became assistant secretary of war of the Confederate States and was appointed to meet with President Lincoln at Fort Monroe, Maryland, in February 1865 to help negotiate a peace to end the war. After the war he was arrested and lodged in Fort Pulaski on the Georgia coast near Savannah but was soon paroled and resumed his law practice in New Orleans. The house is privately owned and is not currently open to the public.

208 East Liberty St.
Washington, GA 30673

Left to right: *Campbell-Jordon House, Robert Toombs Historic Site (Photos: Bob Price)*

Robert Toombs Historic Site (NRHP)

During the antebellum period, Robert A. Toombs served in the Georgia Legislature and the U.S. House and Senate. When Georgia seceded from the Union, this prominent Washington, Georgia, statesman posed a significant challenge to Jefferson Davis for the presidency of the Confederate States. When Toombs failed to attain the office, he became a severe critic of the president and his policies. Toombs did serve the Confederacy as secretary of state and in the military as a brigadier general. The highlight of Toombs' Confederate military service, which helped to save the Army

216 East Robert Toombs Ave.
Washington, GA 30673
706-678-2226

Tues.–Sat.: 9:00 a.m.–5:00 p.m.

Above: *Robert A. Toombs*
(Courtesy of the Library of Congress)

of Northern Virginia, was in his magnificent defense of the right end of the Confederate line overlooking the Burnside's Bridge crossing at the Battle of Antietam in Maryland in 1862. He resigned his commission in 1863 and returned to Georgia to serve in defense of the state under General Gustavas W. Smith.

At the end of the war, Federal officials marked Toombs as one of the most wanted leaders from the vanquished Confederate government, and he fled the country for refuge in Cuba, Europe, and finally Canada before returning in 1867. Toombs refused to take an oath of loyalty to the Federal government and thus never served in public office again. Today he is remembered more for his firebrand oratory than his political acumen or military service.

Toombs' home, built between 1794 and 1801 and purchased by him in 1837, is an outstanding example of the type of dwelling owned by prosperous cavaliers during the antebellum period. Along the front elevation of this Greek Revival–style home, four Doric columns support the portico underneath and French windows open onto high-ceilinged rooms. An avid practitioner of Southern hospitality, Toombs believed it was better to have overnight guests stay in a home rather than a hotel. During the postbellum period, when a hotel was proposed for Washington, Toombs opposed it. Giving insight into Toombs' character, he stated, "If a respectable man comes to town, he can stay at my house. If he isn't respectable, we don't want him here."

Listed on the National Register of Historic Places, this nationally known landmark is open for tours and includes a film about Toombs' life.

Washington Historical Museum

308 East Robert Toombs Ave.
Washington, GA 30673
706-678-2105

Tues.–Sat.: 10:00 a.m.–5: 00 p.m.
Sun.: 2:00 p.m.–5:00 p.m.

A block from the Robert Toombs Historic Site, the Washington Historical Museum offers an excellent introduction to local history. The first two floors of this 1830s era house contain fine examples of eighteenth- and nineteenth-century furnishings, while the third floor will be of great interest to Civil War aficionados. It houses a Confederate-manufactured gun collection, examples of the Joe Brown Pike, uniforms, and period documents, papers, and diaries. Also on exhibit are the camp chest Jefferson Davis had with him when he was captured and other items of Confederate notables. Postwar items include a collection of Reconstruction-era carpetbags.

Left: *Washington Historical Museum (Photo: Bob Price)*

Wilkes County Courthouse/Last Confederate Cabinet Meeting Site

The Heard House, where the last Confederate cabinet meeting was held, was demolished in early 1904, and soon thereafter the present Wilkes County Courthouse was constructed on the site. Those attending the meeting on May 5, 1865, included President Jefferson Davis, Military Advisor General Braxton Bragg, Private Secretary Burton Harrison, Quartermaster General Alexander Robert Lawton, Postmaster John Reagan, Commissary General I.M. St. John, and Naval Purchasing Agent C.E. Thornburg. After the meeting ended, the group dispersed in different directions to escape the pursuing Union forces.

U.S. 78 in downtown Washington
Washington, GA 30673

Above: *Unfinished painting by Wilbur Kurtz depicting the last Confederate States of America cabinet meeting, which was held in Washington, Georgia (Courtesy of the Atlanta History Center)*

CRAWFORDVILLE, Taliaferro County

Crawfordville, the seat of Taliaferro County, was named in honor of William H. Crawford and is the site of Liberty Hall, home of Confederate Vice President Alexander H. Stephens.

http://crawfordville.georgia.gov

Alexander H. Stephens State Historic Park

456 Alexander St.
Crawfordville, GA 30631
706-456-2602
www.gastateparks.org

Tues.–Sat.: 9:00 a.m.–5:00 p.m.
Sun: 2:00 p.m.–5:00 p.m.

This 1,190-acre park is named for Alexander Hamilton Stephens, also known as "Little Alec." He was a Georgia political luminary and foremost statesman in state and national politics. Stephens also became vice president of the Confederate States of America. His home, Liberty Hall, built in 1875, and his burial site are both located in the Alexander H. Stephens State Historic Park. Next to Liberty Hall is an outstanding museum containing Confederate-era artifacts, both military and civilian, including dioramas and information on Civil War camp life. Other park attractions include fishing, boating, nature trails, picnicking, and camping.

Stephens was born in a log cabin near Crawfordville, Georgia, in 1812. A celebrated Whig turned Democrat, he cut his political teeth in the Georgia statehouse in 1836–1842 and served in the U.S. Congress from 1843 to 1859. A paradoxical believer in both states' rights and the maintenance of a strong union, he was a delegate to the Secession Convention in Milledgeville, Georgia, in 1861, where he voted against the Articles of Secession.

Stephens served as vice president of the Confederacy from 1861 to 1865 but was constantly at odds with Confederate President Jefferson Davis over numerous fundamental governmental issues. The result of these philosophical differences caused Stephens to spend most of the Civil War at his Crawfordville home instead of the Confederate capital in Richmond, Virginia. Physically frail and suffering from neuralgia and rheumatism, Stephens claimed to be too weak to make the journey from Georgia to Richmond. Reportedly, shortly after taking office he had lost faith in the Confederacy and Jefferson Davis. After the war, Stephens wrote *A Constitutional View of the War Between the States* in part to explain his wartime views. Voted governor of Georgia in 1882, Stephens died in office in Atlanta on March 4, 1883, and was buried in Oakland Cemetery in Atlanta. He was later reinterred at Liberty Hall.

Liberty Hall Historic Site and Confederate Museum

456 Alexander St.
Crawfordville, GA 30631
706-456-2221/706-456-2602

Tues.–Sat.: 9:00 a.m.–5:00 p.m.
Sun.: 2:00 p.m.–5:00 p.m.

Above: Alexander Hamilton Stephens (Courtesy of the National Archives). Right: Liberty Hall (Photo: Bob Price)

Liberty Hall, the home of Alexander H. Stephens, the vice president of the Confederacy and later governor of Georgia, displays his furniture, decorative arts, and personal papers and documents. A film offers insights into Stephens' personal life, as well as the causes and effects of the Civil War.

The Confederate Museum is in a separate building and houses a fine collection of Confederate artifacts, including uniforms, documents, swords, and arms.

AUGUSTA, Richmond County

Augusta, along with Macon, Columbus, and Atlanta, was part of a small web of Southern industrial cities that made Gerogia the most vital Confederate state in the Deep South. It was also a major transportation hub. Numerous Confederate industries crucial to Southern war efforts were established here, including the Confederate Powder Works, the Augusta Arsenal, and the Leech & Rigdon Revolver Factory. The city also served as a major hospital center with its five hospital complexes.

One of Augusta's most valuable manufacturing operations was its gunpowder factory. Built from scratch in 1862, the state-of-the-art gunpowder works produced 95 percent of the Confederacy's gunpowder and was by far the most important military facility in the Confederacy. Augusta, located deep in the South and linked to the battlefront by good rail connections, was an ideal site for producing gunpowder. The enterprise was so successful that Confederate forces never ran short of gunpowder in any engagement during four years of fighting.

As important as Augusta was to the Confederacy, the Federal army in its March to the Sea under Major General William T. Sherman, did not pass through the city. Union cavalry under Brigadier General Judson Kilpatrick twice feinted toward Augusta during the march but never entered the city.

Augusta CVB
1450 Greene St., Ste. 110
Augusta, GA 30903
706-823-6600/800-726-0243
www.augustaga.org

Augusta Visitor Information Center (lobby of the Augusta Museum of History)
560-B Reynolds St.
706-724-4067
www.augustaga.org

Mon.–Sat.: 10:00 a.m.–5:00 p.m.
Sun.: 1:00–5:00 p.m.

Augusta Canal (NRHP)

The nine-mile Augusta Canal first opened in November 1845, bringing power and water to Augusta. Canal transportation, waterpower, railroad facilities, and a central location safe from attack made Augusta the ideal location for the Confederacy's powder works. Today the canal and towpath are a recreation area and a source of water for Augusta.

A tour of the Canal Interpretive Center takes about an hour. The Petersburg Boat tour, departing from the Enterprise Mill docks, travels approximately half the length of the canal and lasts slightly less than an hour. The Augusta Canal is designated as a National Heritage Area and is on the National Register of Historic Places.

1450 Greene St.
(at Enterprise Mill)
Augusta, GA 30901
706-823-7089/706-823-0440
www.augustacanal.com

Mon.–Sat.: 10:00 a.m.–6:00 p.m.
Sun.: 1:00 p.m.–6:00 p.m.

Right: *Augusta Canal and Locks*
(Courtesy of the Library of Congress)

Augusta Museum of History

560 Reynolds St. (at 6th St.)
Augusta, GA 30901
706-722-8454
www.augustamuseum.org

Tues.-Sat.: 10:00 a.m.-5:00 p.m.
Sun.: 1:00 p.m.-5:00 p.m.

A significant part of the museum's permanent exhibit, Augusta's Story, is dedicated to the Civil War. The centerpiece is a twelve-pound Napoleon cannon made at the Augusta Foundry in 1864. Behind the cannon hangs the museum's largest Civil War flag, a ten-by-fifteen-foot Second National flag that was flown over the Augusta Arsenal. Also on exhibit are the Secession Flag of Georgia, the regimental flag of the 5th Georgia, and the flag of the cavalry battalion of Cobb's legion. Among the outstanding uniforms are a Confederate surgeon's frock coat and sash as well as an officer's uniform from the Clinch Rifles, a volunteer company from Augusta. Some of the most notable artifacts in the museum's collection are the architectural drawings of the famed Confederate Powder Works Factory.

Augusta State University/U.S. Arsenal (NRHP)

2500 Walton Way
Augusta, GA 30904
706-737-1444
www.aug.edu

Now part of the Augusta State University campus, this seventy-two-acre site served as a U.S. arsenal from 1829 to 1955. The university has retained several arsenal structures, including the original walled arsenal quadrangle with four original buildings (the arsenal storehouse, two officers quarters, and a barracks). Early in 1861 the Georgia militia seized the arsenal on behalf of the Confederacy, and thereafter until 1865 it served as an important war materiel production facility. Other surviving nineteenth-century buildings include the c. 1866 post guardhouse (now a small history museum, open daily at 9:00 a.m.) and the c. 1870 powder magazine. The university offers a walking tour that includes all historic buildings, as well as a military cemetery.

Left: *The storehouse building at the U.S. Arsenal*
(Courtesy of the Library of Congress)

Boyhood Home of President Woodrow Wilson (NHL, NRHP)

419 Seventh St. at Telfair Street
Augusta, GA 30901
706-722-9828
www.wilsonboyhoodhome.org

Tues.-Sat.: 10:00 a.m.-5:00 p.m.

The Boyhood Home of President Woodrow Wilson is Georgia's oldest presidential home. Thomas Woodrow Wilson lived here from 1860 to 1870. As a young boy, "Tommy" Wilson experienced the hardships and ravages of the Civil War and Reconstruction. These would later influence his decisions as the twenty-eighth president of the United States (1913–1921) as he once elucidated, "A boy never gets over his boyhood, and never can change those subtle influences which have become a part of him."

During the Civil War, Union prisoners were held on the grounds of the First Presbyterian Church, where his father was pastor and which was across the street from the Wilson home. Wounded Confederate soldiers were also treated in a hospital housed in the church sanctuary. In 1865, young Wilson observed from a window in the home the captured Confederate States of America President Jefferson Davis being escorted through Augusta.

The c. 1859 Victorian home with fourteen furnished rooms has been designated an official Save America's Treasures site. It is also a National Historic Landmark and is listed on the National Register of Historic Places.

Right: Woodrow Wilson's boyhood home
(Photo: John Harpring/Historic Augusta)

Confederate Monument (NRHP)

In 1878 the Ladies' Memorial Association erected this monument to the Confederates inscribed, "Honoring Richmond County Confederate Dead." A statue of an anonymous Confederate soldier tops the column in the place of honor above statues of four generals: Robert E. Lee, Stonewall Jackson, Thomas R.R. Cobb, and W.H.T. Walker.

700 block of Broad St.
Augusta, GA 30901

Right: The Confederate Monument in downtown Augusta.
Below: The Confederate-era chimney from the Confederate Powder Works (Photos: Bob Price)

Confederate Powder Works Factory (NRHP)

This towering chimney along the Augusta Canal is all that is left of the Confederate Powder Works Factory, the only permanent structure authorized and built by the Confederacy. Many existing buildings were pressed into Confederate service, but the two-mile-long gunpowder factory complex was unique as a new facility. The second-largest munitions factory in the world at the time, it produced thirty thousand pounds of gunpowder a day for the Southern war effort. The factory was dismantled after the war, but the 150-foot obelisk chimney was spared to serve as a monument to the Confederacy.

1717 Goodrich St.
Augusta, GA 30901

Textile factories that were built about a decade after the Civil War and are still in operation today sit on the site of the Confederate Powder Works. In 2006 the Georgia Civil War Commission gave a grant for restoration of the chimney.

First Presbyterian Church

642 Telfair St.
Augusta, GA 30901
706-823-2450
www.firstpresaugusta.org

The First Presbyterian Church was completed in 1809, five years after the congregation was organized. Its architecture was inspired by a design by Robert Mills, the architect of the Washington Monument. During the Civil War, the church and grounds were used as a military hospital and temporary detention camp for prisoners. Joseph R. Wilson, the church's pastor at the time of the war, was an ardent secessionist and the father of Woodrow Wilson, who as a boy witnessed Confederate President Jefferson Davis and his retinue taken through Augusta en route to prison.

Magnolia Cemetery (NRHP)

702 Third St.
Augusta, GA 30901
706-821-1746
www.augustaga.gov

Office hours:
Mon.-Fri.: 7:30 a.m.-4:00 p.m.

The sixty-acre Magnolia Cemetery, which covers seven city blocks, serves as the resting place for more than nine hundred Confederate soldiers and veterans, as well as seven generals: Edward Porter Alexander, Goode Bryan, Victor Jean Baptiste Girardey, John King Jackson, William Duncan Smith, Marcellus A. Stovall, and Ambrose Ransom Wright. Some Union troops who died while prisoners of war are also buried in a small Federal section. The cemetery's eastern wall was a defensive line for the city in 1864 and bears patches from wartime cannon emplacements.

Above, left to right: *Grave markers for seven Confederate generals located in Magnolia Cemetery (Photo: Bob Price); the Medical College of Georgia (Courtesy of the Library of Congress)*

Medical College of Georgia (NRHP)

598 Telfair St.
Augusta, GA 30912
706-721-7238
www.mcg.edu

Mon.-Fri.: 9:00 a.m.-4:00 p.m.

Georgia architect Charles B. Cluskey designed the Medical College of Georgia, which was the first medical school in the state and one of the first in America. During the Civil War, the Greek Revival structure served as a military hospital, and Confederate surgeons used the Medical College building as their headquarters. The college resumed normal functions at the war's end.

Morris Museum of Art

This gem of a museum offers a stroll through the history of painting in the South. The first museum in the country devoted to the art and artists of the South, the Morris Museum of Art's collection includes a Civil War gallery with eyewitness paintings by soldier-artists and artist-correspondents of the war, such as Edwin Forbes. The museum also houses the Center for the Study of Southern Art with an extensive research library.

1 Tenth St.
Augusta, GA 30901
706-724-7501
www.themorris.org

Tues.–Sat.: 10:00 a.m.–5:00 p.m.
Sun.: Noon–5:00 p.m.

Library:
Tues.–Fri.: 10:00 a.m.–5:00 p.m.

FORT GORDON U.S. ARMY SIGNAL CORPS MUSEUM,
Richmond County

The Signal Corps Museum collection contains signal-related artifacts pertaining to the military dating back to 1860, including a Beardslee Magneto telegraph, a wigwag flag, a signal torch and lantern, a keying device and repeater, and original items belonging to Albert J. Myer, a Federal officer and founder of the Signal Corps. Augusta native and General Robert E. Lee's Chief of Artillery Brigadier General Edward Porter Alexander was a student under Myer.

504 Chamberlain Ave.
Conrad Hall (Bldg. 29808)
Fort Gordon, GA 30905
706-791-2818
www.gordon.army.mil/ocos/
museum

Tues.–Fri.: 8:00 a.m.–4:00 p.m.
Sat.: 10:00 a.m.–4:00 p.m.

SANDERSVILLE, Washington County

Located in a rural section of central Georgia with a strong cotton-based economy, Sandersville was connected with the Central Railroad at Tennille, Georgia, via a spur track. With the start of the war in 1861, Washington County was known throughout Georgia for producing fifteen companies of Confederate soldiers in spite of its rural location.

On the March to the Sea, the left wing of the Federal Army marched through Sandersville on November 26, 1864. On the previous night thirteen Federal prisoners had been executed by a vigilante mob of Sandersville residents. Upon hearing of the egregious

Washington County Chamber of Commerce
131 W. Haynes St.
Sandersville, GA 31082
478-552-3288
www.washingtoncountyga.com

Left: *Depiction of Sandersville on November 26, 1964, as Sherman's troops passed through town (Courtesy of the Library of Congress)*

act, Major General William T. Sherman decided to set fire to the entire town but was dissuaded from committing total destruction by the pleadings of the Reverend J.D. Anthony. The courthouse and downtown districts were burned before the Federals departed, but the rest of the town was spared. On May 6, 1865, President Jefferson Davis made a stop in Sandersville while fleeing through Georgia from pursuing Federal cavalry.

An unmarked brick mausoleum in the Old City Cemetery is purported to contain the remains of the thirteen executed Federal prisoners.

Left: The unmarked mausoleum in the Old City Cemetery (Photo: Barry Brown)

Brown House Museum

268 N. Harris St.
Sandersville, GA 31082
478-552-1965

The restored 1852 Brown House now functions as a house museum and research center for the Washington County Historical Society.

Right: The Brown House (Photo: Barry Brown)

PERKINS, Jenkins County

Millen/Jenkins County Chamber
of Commerce
548 Cotton Ave.
Millen, GA 30442
478-982-5595
www.jenkinscountyga.com

Perkins is an unincorporated community in Jenkins County.

Battle of Buckhead Creek

Take U.S. 25 north from Millen
for 7.5 miles; go left at CR81 at
the Perkins Community. Go west
for 3.5 miles to Big Buckhead
Church. Buckhead Creek is just
beyond the church.

After the two wings of his army had crossed the Ogeechee River on the March to the Sea, Major General William T. Sherman's plan was to feign a movement toward Macon with the right wing while feigning a movement toward Augusta with the left wing. This caused the Confederates to move troops and resources needlessly to areas where they were not actually needed while trying to second guess Sherman's true intentions. Sherman never wavered from his objective: the city of Savannah.

Confederate cavalry under Major General Joseph Wheeler maintained a constant harassment of the Federals, causing a number of running cavalry skirmishes with Brigadier General Judson Kilpatrick throughout late November 1864. On November 24, 1864, Kilpatrick was ordered to feign northeastward toward Augusta, burn the railroad trestle over Briar Creek and, if possible, free the Union prisoners being held at Camp Lawton near Millen.

Wheeler, believing that the true Federal objective was Augusta, moved his forces there. When he realized his mistake, he ordered his men to ride furiously to the southeast. They eventually caught up with the rear guard of Kilpatrick's force on November 26, 1864, and prevented the Briar Creek trestle from being destroyed. Having discovered that Camp Lawton had been evacuated of all prisoners, Kilpatrick made camp near Buckhead Creek on the evening of November 27, 1864.

On the morning of November 28, 1864, Wheeler attacked Kilpatrick's force while the Federals were crossing Buckhead Creek. The Federals were forced to fight a rear guard action and used a dismounted regiment supported by artillery that succeeded in stopping the Confederate advance, allowing Kilpatrick's men to burn the Buckhead Creek bridge.

Wheeler's men were forced to cross further upstream and continued to follow the Federals, who had found a defensive position near Reynolds' plantation. With the Confederates on the offensive, fighting continued until darkness set in, and Kilpatrick's forces retreated toward Louisville, Georgia, where Sherman's left wing was encamped.

Estimated casualties from the fighting at Buckhead Creek are as high as six hundred for the attacking Confederates, while only forty-six for the Union.

Above: *The site of the Battle of Buckhead Creek (Photo: Bob Price)*

MILLEN, Jenkins County

During the time of the Civil War, Millen was located in Burke and Screven counties. Named for Captain John Millen, a civil engineer for the railroad, the town was first called Old 79 because of its distance from Savannah. In 1881 Millen was incorporated as the seat of the newly formed Jenkins County.

Jenkins County Chamber
Development Authority
548 Cotton Ave.
Millen, GA 30442
478-982-5595
pauladepot@bellsouth.net

Magnolia Springs State Park/Camp Lawton

1053 Magnolia Springs Dr.
Millen, GA 30442
478-982-1660

Daily: 7:00 a.m.–10:00 p.m.

Camp Lawton, the largest prisoner-of-war camp built by either side during the Civil War, could hold forty thousand prisoners. It was designed with the intention of avoiding the pitfalls of poor planning that plagued the overcrowded Camp Sumter stockade at Andersonville. The small stream running through the stockade at Andersonville was inadequate in both purity and flow and was a major cause of the high mortality rate. In contrast, the Camp Lawton site had an abundance of clean, clear water from Magnolia Springs. The site also had the prerequisite access to rail transportation through the Augusta and Savannah Railroad for easily transporting prisoners and supplies.

By November 1864, the prison held only 10,299 Federals, transferees mostly from Andersonville, which had began shutting down in the fall, evacuating prisoners to other locations. The same fate befell Camp Lawton when it was abandoned in the wake of the March to the Sea only two months after the arrival of its first prisoners.

Today, little remains of the prison; however, earthen berms that formed its boundary are visible. Fort Lawton was located on the ridge to your right as you enter Magnolia Springs State Park. The stockade measured approximately 1,500 feet by 2,000 feet, with the longer axis aligned north to south. The creek used for drinking water originated at Magnolia Springs and bisected the stockade. The park offers visitors a twenty-eight-acre lake, rental cottages, and campsites.

Right: This fanciful historic print shows guards behind the deadline, a feature at Camp Sumter in Andersonville but not at Camp Lawton. (Courtesy the UGA Hargrett Rare Book and Manuscript Library)

WAYNESBORO, Burke County

Waynesboro is located in Burke County, one of the eight original Georgia counties. It was named after the Revolutionary War hero "Mad" Anthony Wayne. The town was laid out in 1783 but not incorporated until 1883.

Burke County Chamber of Commerce
216 East 6th St.
Waynesboro, GA 30830
706-554-5451
www.burkecounty-ga.gov

Battle of Waynesboro

On the morning of December 4, 1864, Brigadier General Judson Kilpatrick's division of cavalry, supported by two full brigades of infantry, advanced from Thomas' Station and formed a line of battle. Kilpatrick's intention was to attack Waynesboro, burn the bridges over Brier Creek, and destroy the Confederate cavalry under Major General Joseph Wheeler, who had been harassing the Federals constantly during the March to the Sea.

Outside of Waynesboro, Kilpatrick's advance encountered Wheeler's skirmishers, and the attack began. The skirmishers were driven back by the superior force at their front and retreated to a strong defensive line of barricades that were soon overrun by the quickly advancing Federals. As the Union advance continued, they encountered even more barricades manned by Wheeler's dismounted troops that had to be overrun. Wheeler's small force retired into Waynesboro, where another line of defensive barricades had been set up in the streets. Seeing his situation as hopeless, Wheeler ordered a charge by Texas and Tennessee troops to gain time to quickly extricate his force out of town, cross Brier Creek, and then travel some eight miles in order to block the road to Augusta. Confederate loses at Waynesboro included twenty-three dead and forty-one wounded, while Kilpatrick reported a loss of two hundred.

Once in possession of Waynesboro, the Federals burned the bridges over Brier Creek and set fire to the town, though the flames were extinguished before great damage occurred. No longer needing to feign a movement on Augusta, the Federals continued their march in a southeasterly direction toward Savannah.

Downtown Waynesboro

Below: *A depiction of the Battle of Waynesboro on December, 4, 1864 (Courtesy of the Library of Congress)*

PLANTATION TRACE

Large plantations and hunting preserves popular with tourists still survive in the Plantation Trace region. This land was the breadbasket of the Confederacy, and the region's still largely agricultural focus stands as evidence of its importance.

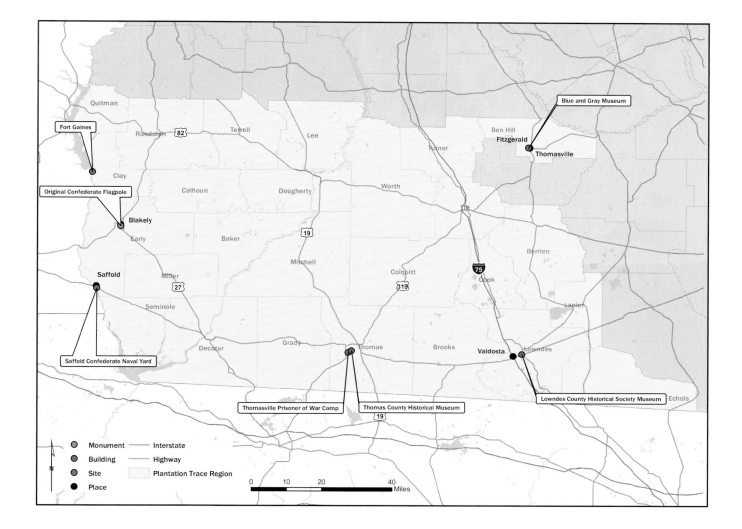

Quitman

Fort Gaines

Randolph
US 82

Terrell

Lee

Turner

Ben Hill

Blue and Gray Museum

Fitzgerald

Thomasville

Clay

Original Confederate Flagpole

Calhoun

Dougherty

Worth

Blakely

Early

Baker

19

Mitchell

Tift

Saffold

Miller
27

Colquitt
319

Berrien

Cook
75

Lanier

Seminole

Saffold Confederate Naval Yard

Decatur

Grady

Thomas

Brooks

Valdosta

Lowndes

Thomasville Prisoner of War Camp

Thomas County Historical Museum
19

Lowndes County Historical Society Museum

Echols

Monument   Interstate
Building   Highway
Site   Plantation Trace Region
Place

N

0   10   20   40
                          Miles

FORT GAINES, Clay County

www.fortgaines.com

For walking tours of the fort:
Clay County Library
229-768-2248
George T. Bagby State Park
800-864-7275

Fort Gaines was constructed in 1816 on a high bluff overlooking the Chattahoochee River to guard against incursion by Creek Indians during the Creek War of 1814–1815. Steamboat traffic on the Chattahoochee began in 1827, and Fort Gaines became a boomtown, dubbed the Queen City of the Chattahoochee. During the War Between the States, Fort Gaines again became useful as a defense against Federal gunboats traveling upstream to capture the important Confederate manufacturing center of Columbus. Three large guns were strategically placed at Fort Gaines to control river traffic but were never tested in battle since no fighting occurred there. Today, one of the three original guns can still be seen in its original position at Fort Gaines.

Left: *Fort Gaines and one of the three original guns (Photo: Bob Price)*

BLAKELY, Early County

Early County Chamber of
Commerce
52 Court Square
Blakely, GA 31723

Blakely, named after Captain Johnson Blakely, who was lost at sea during the War of 1812, has been the seat of Early County since 1825. The town was officially incorporated in 1870.

Original Confederate Flagpole

Early County Courthouse
52 Court Square
Blakely, GA 31723

Thirty-two days after the firing on Fort Sumter on May 16, 1861, the Confederate government erected a flagpole on the courthouse lawn in Blakely. Today, the flagpole is still standing and is considered the only remaining Confederate-era flagpole in the state.

Right: *Original Confederate flagstaff (Photo: Bob Price)*

SAFFOLD, Early County

Saffold is a rural community on the banks of the Chattahoochee River nineteen miles south of Blakely. The town is named after a prominent plantation family from the area.

Early County Chamber of Commerce
52 Court Square
Blakely, GA 31723
www.blakelyyearlychamber.com

Saffold Confederate Naval Yard

A Confederate Naval Yard was located in Early County at Saffold on the lower Chattahoochee River. The gunboat *Chattahoochee* was constructed and launched here in 1862. Today, the ship's remains are housed in the National Civil War Naval Museum in Columbus, Georgia.

www.civilwaralbum.com/misc2/saffold_georgia1.htm

Left: *Site where the gunboat Chattahoochee was most likely constructed and launched (Photo: Bob Price)*

FITZGERALD, Ben Hill County

Fitzgerald saw no action during the Civil War because it did not exist. Its story is unique in America—the only town founded in harmony by Union and Confederate veterans. This planned community emerged in 1895 out of one thousand acres of woodlands. Seven of the fourteen north-south streets are named for Union generals: Grant, Sherman, Sheridan, Thomas, Logan, Meade, and Hooker. The others bear the names of Confederate generals: Hill, Bragg, Gordon, Longstreet, Jackson, Johnston, and Lee. Veterans from both sides are buried in Fitzgerald's Evergreen Cemetery, including Private William J. Bush, Company B, 14th Regiment, Georgia Infantry, who was the longest-living Confederate veteran from Georgia. Evidence of this town's remarkable story of reunification can be found in the Blue and Gray Museum, on an architectural tour of the town, in Evergreen Cemetery, and in the manner in which Fitzgerald still functions today.

Fitzgerald Main Street Office
119 S. Main St.
Fitzgerald, GA 31750
912-426-5033
www.fitzgeraldga.org

Right: *1908 bird's-eye view of Fitzgerald (Courtesy of the Library of Congress)*

Blue and Gray Museum

116 N. Johnston St.
Fitzgerald, GA 31750
229-426-5069
www.fitzgeraldga.org/
Blue&GrayMuseum.htm

Tues.–Sat.: 10:00 a.m.–4:00 p.m.
Sun.: 1:00 p.m.–5:00 p.m.

Located in a historic railroad depot, the museum contains more than twelve hundred objects, photos, and rare artifacts that tell the unique story of Fitzgerald and its Civil War connection, including the names of the veterans who founded the city, a display of rare swords and canes, a Congressional Medal of Honor, and a Southern Cross of Honor. Also on view is the Confederate flag used to drape the coffin of Fitzgerald resident William J. Bush. Bush was the last survivor of the 125,000 Georgians who fought for the South; he died in 1952 at the age of 107. A documentary film portrays the founding story of Fitzgerald through archival photographs.

Right: *A display at the Blue and Gray Museum (Photo: Bob Price)*

THOMASVILLE, Thomas County

Thomasville-Thomas County
Historic Plantations Convention
and Visitors Bureau
401 S. Broad St.
Thomasville, GA 31799
229-228-7977/866-577-3600
www.escapetothesoutheast.com/
GA-DMO-Thomasville.asp

Harper's Weekly proclaimed Thomasville the "best winter resort in three continents." For decades, the town had been a haven where wealthy planters spent their summers, avoiding the epidemics associated with the coastal lowlands. The area was an ideal site for growing crops. Large tracts of land were purchased for agricultural use, often by Northerners, and as the landowners became wealthy, they constructed plantations in the classic antebellum Greek Revival style. Fifty-nine of these beautiful plantations are currently open for tours.

During the war, Thomasville was the site of an outburst of anti-Semitic activity, an uncommon occurrence in the Confederacy as several high-ranking officials were Jewish, including Secretary of State Judah Benjamin. Unlike in the North, where anti-Semitism was endemic, Jews living in the South were widely accepted and were strong supporters of Southern independence.

Thomasville had an instance of anti-Semitism in August 1862. Colonel J.L. Seward, a former congressman, warned of the military threat and danger associated with rapidly rising prices and scarcity of food and supplies. Ignoring the law of economics that ties inflation to supply and demand, as well as the Anaconda Plan blockade of Southern ports, Seward railed against the local German Jewish population. The Jews were given ten days to leave town, and a committee of vigilance was created to enforce the order.

The resolutions, however, did not stand, quashed by the combined influence of the residents of Macon and Savannah, both Gentile and Jew alike, because, as was stated at the time, no one could question the Southern Jews' "devotion to the Confederacy."

Thomas County Historical Museum

The Thomas County Historical Museum contains Civil War artifacts including local regimental flags and other memorabilia from the area regiments raised for Confederate service.

725 North Dawson St.
Thomasville, GA 31792
229-226-7664
http://www.thomascountyhistory
.org

Highlights of the Thomas County Historical Museum (right) *include Confederate regimental flags from Thomas County troops. (Photo: Bob Price)*

Thomasville Prisoner of War Camp

Like Camp Lawton in Millen, Georgia, the prisoner-of-war camp at Thomasville was quickly constructed in late 1864 to house Union prisoners of war evacuated from Camp Sumter at Andersonville, Georgia, during the March to the Sea. In December 1864, five thousand prisoners were brought and held here. Covering an area of only seven acres, the camp was defined by a ditch eight feet wide and twelve feet deep. However, the camp was not surrounded by a log fence, requiring it to be guarded by numerous soldiers and artillery pieces. Once the Federal army had taken Savannah, the Thomasville prison camp was closed, and the prisoners were sent back to Andersonville, arriving on December 24, 1864. Hundreds of prisoners died of disease while at the prison and were buried in the First Methodist Church Cemetery in Thomasville, although they were later reinterred at the Andersonville National Cemetery. Remnants of the border ditch as well as barrier berms are still visible. The site is marked by a state historical marker.

Wolfe St.
Thomasville, GA

Left: *The city park contains a portion of the boundary ditch of the temporary prisoner-of-war camp located in Thomasville. (Photo: Bob Price)*

VALDOSTA, Lowndes County

Valdosta/Lowndes County CVB
One Meeting Place
Valdosta, GA 31601
229-245-0513/800-569-8687
www.valdostatourism.com

Valdosta raised a number of volunteer militia companies for the Southern cause, although most ended up participating in the Virginia campaigns. In the winter of 1864, Confederate troops moving from Savannah disembarked at Valdosta and were fed by local residents before continuing on to nearby Florida, where they engaged Union forces successfully at the Battle of Olustee on February 20, 1864. In 1865, Federal troops from Company G, 103rd U.S. Colored Troops, were stationed in Valdosta.

Right: *Confederate Monument in front of the county courthouse (Photo: Bob Price)*

Lowndes County Historical Society Museum (NRHP)

305 West Central Ave.
Valdosta, GA 31601
229-247-4780
www.valdostamuseum.org

Mon.–Fri.: 10:00 a.m.–5:00 p.m.
Sat.: 10:00 a.m.–2:00 p.m.

Exhibits in the Lowndes County Historical Society Museum highlight local Civil War participation and include uniforms and original documents. Most unique is the Thomas A. Faries collection. Faries was a Confederate colonel who fought in the Louisiana Red River Campaign and was a close associate of General Pierre G.T. Beauregard. After the war, he became adjutant general of Louisiana. Faries' uniform is on display at the museum along with his bugles and the sheet music he wrote for bugle and fife tunes.

Left to right: *Lowndes County Historical Society Museum, Civil War holdings on display at the museum (Photos: Bob Price)*

MAGNOLIA MIDLANDS

Several fascinating Civil War–related sites are located in the Magnolia Midlands region: Jefferson Davis Memorial Park at Irwinville, the site of the Confederate president's capture while evading Federal forces after the war's end, and Doctortown, an important transportation center that was successfully defended by a Confederate garrison during the March to the Sea.

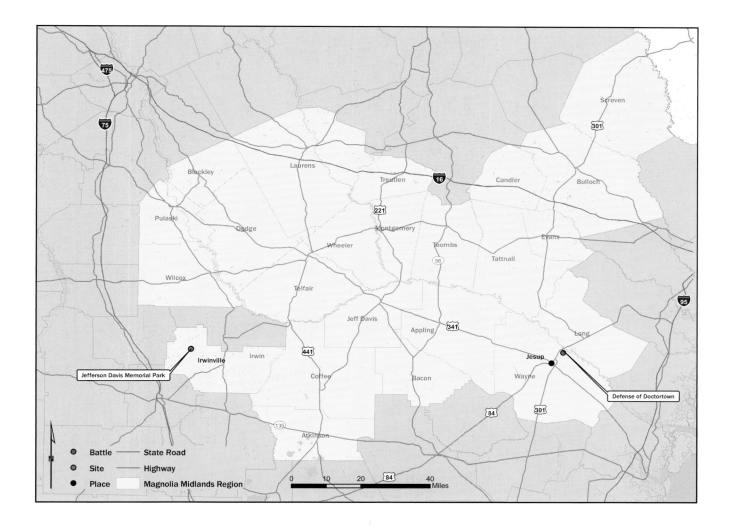

Battle — State Road

Site — Highway

Place ▢ Magnolia Midlands Region

Jefferson Davis Memorial Park

Defense of Doctortown

IRWINVILLE, Irwin County

Ocilla-Irwin County Chamber of
Commerce
P.O. Box 104
Ocilla, GA 31774
229-468-9114
www.ocillachamber.net

Irwinville, located ten miles from the current county seat of Ocilla, was the county seat of Irwin County from 1831 to 1906. The county's most famous incident was the capture of Confederate president Jefferson Davis, a mile north of Irwinville, by Union forces in 1865.

Right: *Entry gates and Civil War Museum at the Jefferson Davis Memorial Park (Photo: Bob Price)*

Jefferson Davis Memorial Park

338 Jeff Davis Park Rd.
(1 mile north of Irwinville)
Fitzgerald, GA 31750
229-831-2335
www.gastateparks.org/info/
jeffd/

Wed.–Sat.: 9:00 a.m.–5:00 p.m.
Sun.: 2:00 p.m.–5:30 p.m.

Below: *Civil War Museum at the Jefferson Davis Memorial Park (Photo: Bob Price)*

During his flight from Richmond, Virginia, which began April 2, 1865, Confederate President Jefferson Davis and his cabinet first set up a temporary center of government in Danville, Virginia, and from there wound their way through the Carolinas to Georgia. With Davis were advisers John Reagan, Judah Benjamin, John Breckinridge, and Burton Harrison and a small elite military escort. Following the last Confederate cabinet meeting in Washington, Georgia, on May 5, 1865, much of the group dispersed.

By the night of May 8, 1865, the remaining party, which now included Davis' wife, Varina, and their children (who had joined the president in Dublin, Georgia, the day before), stopped for the night in Abbeville, Georgia. The party was doggedly pursued by a detachment of Brigadier General James H. Wilson's cavalry, who were under the false assumption that Davis had been involved in the assassination of Abraham Lincoln. A one-hundred-thousand-dollar bounty had been put on Davis' head, making his capture all that much more enticing. In the predawn hours of May 9, 1865, the pursuing cavalrymen, who planned to pounce at the first light of dawn, surrounded Davis' party. What they didn't know was that a separate detachment of Federal cavalry had also caught up with the Confederate president, and fighting broke out between the Union forces. Before the chaos ended, two Federals were killed and several wounded by friendly fire.

In the confusion, Davis had accidentally grabbed his wife's shawl as he ran for his horse in an attempt to escape. He was stopped by the drawn gun of a Federal officer and ordered to halt. Varina Davis ran over to put her arms around her husband

Above: *Relief detail on the statue commemorating the site where Davis was taken into Federal custody (Photo: Bob Price).* Right: *Jefferson Davis (Courtesy of the National Archives)*

fearing he would be shot. At that moment, the president of the now defunct Confederacy became a prisoner. One of the pursuers, Lt. Colonel B.D. Pritchard is said to have stated, "Well Old Jeff, we got you at last."

The main building of the thirteen-acre Jefferson Davis Memorial Park houses a museum with artifacts relating to the Confederacy and the saga of Jefferson Davis' escape and capture. A few hundred yards from the building is the twelve-foot monument topped with a bronze bust that marks the spot where Davis was arrested. Beside the monument is a walking trail with markers explaining the encirclement and capture of Davis' party.

JESUP, Wayne County

Jesup is named in honor of General Thomas Sidney Jesup, who rendered valuable service during the Creek War of 1836. Jesup was incorporated as a town on October 24, 1870.

Jesup-Wayne County Chamber and Tourism Board
124 NW Broad St.
Jesup, GA 31545
912-427-2028
www.waynechamber.com

Left: *Aerial view of Doctortown near Jesup and the bridge over the Altamaha River, which was successfully defended by Confederate forces in December 1864 (Source: Bob Price)*

Defense of Doctortown

The place where the Altamaha River passes through Doctortown has been a vital river crossing since the Alachua Indian trading paths crossed there. In 1857, the Savannah, Albany and Gulf Railroad built a one-hundred-foot trestle across the

From Jesup, travel north on U.S. 301, turn right on Doctortown Rd.
www.co.wayne.ga.us

Altamaha River at Doctortown, turning the town into a shipping hub where freight carried by riverboat was transferred to rail cars. Due to its important role in transporting goods and materials, Doctortown became an objective for Major General William T. Sherman's Savannah Campaign.

The defending Confederates, approximately one thousand Georgia militia under Brigadier General Henry McCay, built earthworks on the south bank at the trestle. They employed two 32-pound field guns mounted on the Altamaha River bluff and a third Campbell Siege Gun mounted on a flatcar pushed by a locomotive to guard the trestle. Their position was surrounded on three sides by marshland, thus preventing a Federal flanking movement.

On December 16, 1864, Sherman sent Brigadier General Judson Kilpatrick's cavalry and Brigadier General William B. Hazen's infantry, then in the vicinity of Savannah, to destroy the railroad between the Ogeechee River and the Altamaha River at Doctortown. After destroying a smaller trestle to the north at Lake Morgan, a brigade of Federals mounted three frontal assaults against the Doctortown bridge and its defenders, damaging parts of the trestle but not gaining their objective. Unable to complete their mission, Kilpatrick and Hazen withdrew to Savannah on December 19, 1864.

One of the guns from this engagement was later placed in front of the Ware County Confederate Monument at Phoenix Park in Waycross, Georgia. Today, Doctortown is the site of the world's largest pulp mill, owned by the Rayonier Company. The company controls access to the Doctortown Park west of the railroad trestle; permission is required to visit the site.

Above: *Doctortown historical marker.* Right: *The bridge over the Altamaha River (Photos: Barry Brown)*

GEORGIA'S COAST

Along with Richmond, Virginia; Charleston, South Carolina; Mobile, Alabama; and New Orleans, Louisiana, one of the Confederacy's premier cities was the colonial capital of Savannah. Today Savannah remains the jewel of historic cities in Georgia. Its historic riverfront and squares contain many of the same buildings and homes that greeted Major General William T. Sherman when his army occupied the city.

Georgia's Coast also contains many of the fortifications designed to defend the state from Federal naval assault. Fort Pulaski on Cockspur Island, represents the pre–Civil War technology of using brick and mortar as building materials that proved unable to withstand bombardment from rifled cannon and fell after a short siege in April 1862. Located at Richmond Hill is Ft. McAllister, an earthen fort designed to absorb the impact of artillery ordnance. Impervious to iron shot and shell, it remained in Confederate control until its capture by a land assault in December 1864.

To the north of Savannah in Effingham County is the colonial town of New Ebenezer, the site of the oldest public building in Georgia and the center of much activity during General Sherman's Savannah Campaign. To the south of Savannah is the town of Darien, once one of the most active ports in Georgia and burned during the Civil War by the 54th Massachusetts Colored Infantry, a scene depicted in the movie *Glory*.

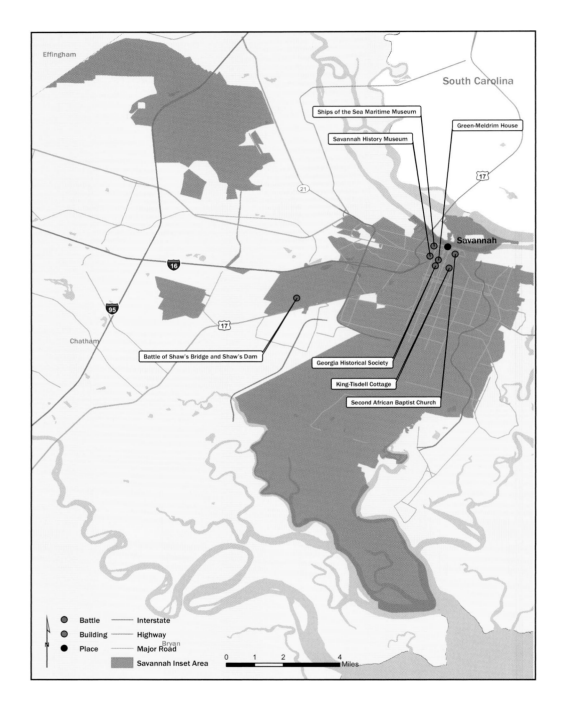

Effingham

South Carolina

Ships of the Sea Maritime Museum

Green-Meldrim House

Savannah History Museum

Savannah

Chatham

Battle of Shaw's Bridge and Shaw's Dam

Georgia Historical Society

King-Tisdell Cottage

Second African Baptist Church

Bryan

Battle
Building
Place

Interstate
Highway
Major Road
Savannah Inset Area

0   1   2   4
                         Miles

CROSSROADS OF CONFLICT

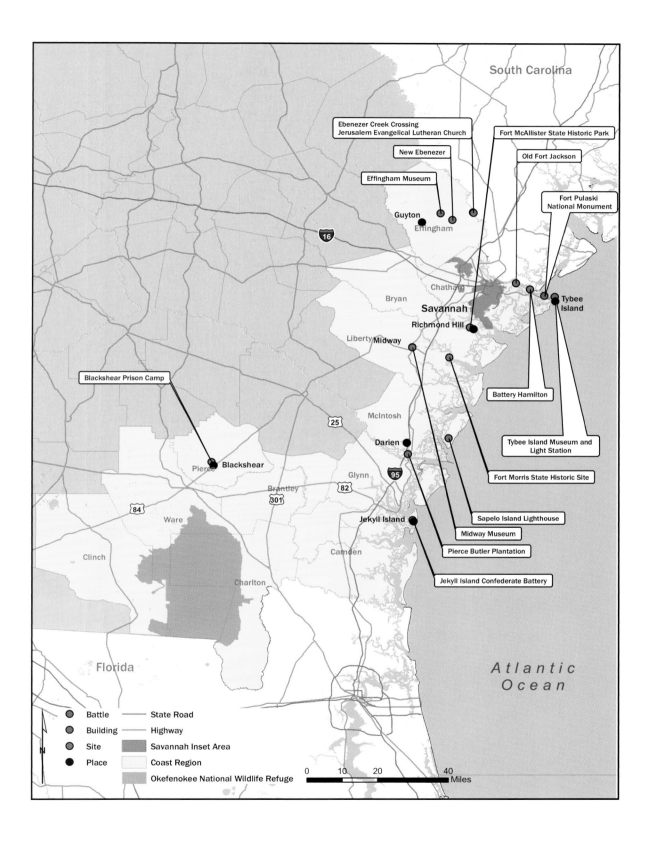

Ebenezer Creek Crossing
Jerusalem Evangelical Lutheran Church

New Ebenezer

Effingham Museum

Fort McAllister State Historic Park

Old Fort Jackson

Fort Pulaski
National Monument

Guyton

Effingham

South Carolina

Chatham

Bryan

Savannah

Richmond Hill

Tybee
Island

Liberty Midway

Battery Hamilton

Blackshear Prison Camp

McIntosh

Tybee Island Museum and
Light Station

Darien

Pierce   Blackshear

Glynn

Brantley

Fort Morris State Historic Site

Sapelo Island Lighthouse

Midway Museum

Pierce Butler Plantation

Jekyll Island

Ware

Camden

Jekyll Island Confederate Battery

Clinch

Charlton

Florida

Atlantic
Ocean

Battle   State Road

Building   Highway

Site   Savannah Inset Area

N

Place   Coast Region

Okefenokee National Wildlife Refuge

0   10   20   40
                    Miles

NEW EBENEZER, Effingham County

Effingham County Chamber of
Commerce
P.O. Box 1078
Springfield, GA 31329
912-754-3301
www.effinghamcounty.com

Originally settled by Salzburgers, Protestant Germans who had fled Salzburg, Austria, in 1734 in search of religious freedom, New Ebenezer is the site of their second and permanent settlement from 1736. The Salzburgers formed a prosperous community and built the Jerusalem Evangelical Lutheran Church in 1767. The British captured and occupied the town in 1779 during the Revolutionary War, and almost a century later, New Ebenezer was again captured, this time by the Federal XIV Corps during Major General William T. Sherman's March to the Sea.

Effingham County held importance during the Civil War due to the Central of Georgia Railroad, which traversed the county, as well as its location near the city of Savannah, the Savannah River, and South Carolina. The town of Guyton was a transportation hub that became a hospital center as well as a training camp for Confederate troops from southeast Georgia and north Florida.

Effingham County was in the line of march for the columns of Federal soldiers approaching Savannah and became heavily contested ground due to its proximity to Chatham County and the city of Savannah. Fighting erupted between Major General Joseph Wheeler's Confederate cavalry and units of Federal cavalry at Cypress Swamp near Sister's Ferry on December 7, 1864, and on the Augusta Road near the Chatham County line at Cuyler's Plantation on December 9, 1864.

Near the town of New Ebenezer is the site of the Ebenezer Creek crossing of the Savannah-Augusta Road. On December 7, 1864, the Federal XIV Corps under Brigadier General Jefferson C. Davis crossed Ebenezer Creek heading south and stranded hundreds of slaves who had been following the army. An undetermined number of the escaped bondsmen drowned in the swollen creek in an attempt to follow the Federals. The incident was picked up by northern newspapers and had ramifications all the way to the White House, becoming one of the more infamous events of Sherman's Savannah Campaign.

Right: *A prewar view of New Ebenezer (Courtesy of the UGA Hargrett Rare Book and Manuscript Library)*

Effingham Museum

The Effingham Museum, housed in the Old Springfield Jail, was established in 1994. Exhibits include prehistoric as well as Native American artifacts. Several rooms are reserved for Civil War artifacts, many excavated from battlefields, campgrounds, and hospitals located in Effingham County. The museum sells books specializing in local Civil War history and contains a genealogical research library on the first floor.

The Historic Effingham Society's current project is a living history exhibit using original and reconstructed buildings located adjacent to the museum. The buildings range in age from the late eighteenth century to the early twentieth century and were moved here only when threatened with demolition.

1002 Pine St.
Springfield, GA 31329
912-754-2170
www.historiceffinghamsociety.org

Below: *Jerusalem Evangelical Lutheran Church (Photo: Barry Brown)*

Jerusalem Evangelical Lutheran Church

While marching through Effingham County on the Savannah-Augusta Road, the Federal XVI Corps came upon the historic town of New Ebenezer, which at the time was recorded by Major James A. Connolly of the 123rd Illinois Infantry as being made up of "one old church and two houses." The church, the Jerusalem Evangelical Lutheran Church, was built in 1767 by the early Georgia settlers, the Salzburgers. It is the oldest church in the state and the oldest Lutheran congregation in the country.

The XVI Corps spent several nights in New Ebenezer, plundering the church and destroying the wooden fence surrounding the cemetery. The parsonage, a few miles from the church, was also burned to the ground.

In April 1906 the wartime pastor of the church traveled to Columbia, South Carolina, to give a deposition to the U.S. District Court in a legal action filed regarding reimbursement in the amount of $1,565 for the losses inflicted by occupying Federal forces. The final judgment was made by the court in 1915, fifty years after the army passed through, granting $225 in compensation from the U.S. Congress.

2966 Ebenezer Rd.
Rincon, GA 31326
912-754-3915

Augusta Road Crossing of Ebenezer Creek

An incident occurred at the Ebenezer Creek crossing on the old Savannah-Augusta Road during the March to the Sea that would raise questions about the Federal army's attitude toward and treatment of African Americans. This would be juxtaposed against the very real problems faced by an army traveling deep within enemy territory with no supply line. Due to Major General William T. Sherman's stubborn demeanor, no black soldiers fought in his army during the Atlanta Campaign or the March to the Sea. However, the Federal army did employ large numbers of blacks known as "pioneers," who worked ahead of the advance column, clearing roads of obstructions and often building labor-intensive wooden "corduroy" roads that were passable by heavy wagons. The pioneers were made up of escaped slaves; their work was hard and dangerous but necessary to the forward momentum of the army. They were paid with rations for their work; no money exchanged hands.

The Ebenezer Creek crossing site is located on private property and is accessible by appointment only. Arrangements must be made in advance by calling the Effingham Museum at 912-754-2170.

Right: *Site of the Ebenezer Creek crossing incident. The bridge supports are postwar.* (Photo: Barry Brown)

Blacks who could not work or cook were known as "contraband" and were perceived by the Federal army as a problem. Often consisting of women, children, and the elderly, they were extra mouths to feed that exacerbated food shortages, slowed movement, and required protection. Federal commander Brigadier General Jefferson C. Davis was keenly aware that a quicker-moving army would make it easier to evade and defend against pursuing Confederate horseman.

General Davis, leading Sherman's XIV Corps, was known for much more than the name he shared with the Confederate president; this unfortunate similarity resulted in the derisive nickname "General Reb." A committed veteran of the regular army, Davis loved to fight. His temper was legendary, notably after having shot and killed his superior Major General William Nelson during a dispute in a Cincinnati hotel room in 1862. Never tried for this crime due to protection from powerful political allies, Davis had the reputation of being intolerant of blacks and maintaining proslavery views.

On December 7, 1864, as the XIV Corps approached Ebenezer Creek near Springfield, Georgia, some twenty-five miles northeast of Savannah, Davis discovered that the bridge had been destroyed by retreating Confederate militia. Ebenezer Creek, a swampy black stream was approximately 150 feet wide and ten feet deep and was swollen by recent rains. Davis realized that he would need to order the 58th Indiana Pontonniers to lay a bridge for the crossing.

The pontoon bridge was put in place, and by daylight on December 9 the rear guard of the XIV Corps finished crossing. When the last troops had reached the south bank, the pontoon bridge was taken up, stranding the black refugees on the north bank, where they were likely to be captured by Confederate cavalry. Many panicked and jumped in the water. Some drowned before reaching the other side, while others made it safely across. The number of deaths is unknown; there is no report of the incident from General Davis in the *Official Records.* However, Confederate Major General Joseph Wheeler did mention the incident in a report: "A great number of negroes were left in our hands, whom we sent back to their owners. The whole number of negroes captured from the enemy during the movement being nearly 2,000."

The incident was brought to the attention of the Senate Military Commission in Washington, D.C., by a letter sent by a Major James A. Connolly of the 123rd Illinois Infantry. Newspapers picked up the story, and reports of it were picked up by Secretary of War Edwin W. Stanton. Stanton traveled to Savannah on January 11, 1865, with an investigation into the matter as an item on his agenda.

The Ebenezer Creek incident caused both Sherman and Davis to experience scrutiny from officials in Washington, including their superior, Army Chief of Staff Major General Henry Halleck. Because of what happened at Ebenezer Creek and Sherman's refusal to use blacks as combat soldiers, the accusation was made that he "manifested an almost criminal dislike to the negro." Sherman denied the charges, and after a meeting with Halleck and a group of prominent black ministers in Savannah in January 1865, the matter was officially dropped.

Guyton

In early 1862, Guyton, located west of Springfield on the Central of Georgia Railroad, was chosen for the site of Camp Davis, the third regional training camp in the state. Located two miles north of Guyton, it served as the training ground for the 47th, 48th, 49th, 50th, and 51st Georgia Volunteer Infantry regiments. The camp was closed in mid–1862, and the camp hospital was moved to Guyton, where it was expanded and became known as the Guyton Confederate General Hospital. Located in the center of town on the railroad, the hospital had 270 beds and a staff of sixty-seven during its peak in mid–1863. Today, much of the site of the camp is an overgrown field and woods containing no visible physical remnants of the camp.

At the intersection of GA Hwy. 119 and GA Hwy. 17

http://guyton.georgia.gov

SAVANNAH, Chatham County

This beautiful Southern port city escaped the ravages of the Civil War from its beginning in 1861 to December 1864 when Major General William T. Sherman's army approached Savannah's defenses. The capture of nearby Fort Pulaski on April 11, 1862, had rendered Savannah ineffective as a Confederate port, but the city's strong defense lines discouraged any inland attacks during the subsequent three and a half years.

As Federal forces approached Savannah early in December 1864, culminating the March to the Sea, Sherman planned for a siege rather than a direct attack on the city's strong defenses. Sherman's force of sixty-two thousand dug in west of the city and began long-range shelling with siege guns. The Confederate commander in Savannah, Lt. General William Hardee, had earlier been given permission to evacuate the city in order to preserve the integrity of his force of ten thousand troops. Not waiting for Sherman's assault plans to unfold, Hardee's troops spiked their cannons, dumped ammunition into the river, and scuttled and burned naval vessels, including the ironclad CSS *Georgia*. During the night of December 20, all Confederate forces evacuated Savannah.

Savannah CVB
101 E. Bay St.
Savannah, GA 31401
912-644-6401/877-728-2662
www.savannahvisit.com

Right: *Sherman's army entering Savannah in December 1864 (Courtesy of the UGA Hargrett Rare Book and Manuscript Library)*

The next day Federals under Brigadier General John W. Geary cautiously advanced on the defense lines and, finding them abandoned, walked into the open city. Geary was met by the mayor and city officials who presented him with a letter addressed to General Sherman surrendering the city. When Sherman himself arrived in the now-occupied city on December 22, he penned a message to President Lincoln, "I beg to present to you as a Christmas-gift, the city of Savannah."

Besides its importance during the Civil War, Savannah is rich in architectural splendor and Southern charm. Georgia's first city, founded in 1733, boasts hundreds of magnificent homes that were standing in 1861–1865. Thankfully, Sherman spared the city from the torch after he received its surrender.

In addition to Civil War attractions, sites of interest include the Historic Railroad Shops and Roundhouse Railroad Museum; Wormsloe Historic Site; the home of the founder of the Girl Scouts, the Juliette Gordon Lowe House; Ralph Mark Gilbert Civil Rights Museum; and the Mighty Eighth Air Force Heritage Museum outside Savannah.

Battle of Shaw's Bridge and Shaw's Dam

Savannah Christian Preparatory
School
Parkway Campus
1599 Chatham Pkwy.
Savannah, GA 31410

Savannah was not prepared to weather a siege as the majority of the city's defenses were directed to cover the islands and coastal approaches to the east, with little attention given to the land approaches to the north and west. As Major General William T. Sherman approached, the city's western defenses were ordered to be erected on December 3, 1864.

Battery Acee, one of the most active batteries in the western defense of Savannah, stood at the head of the dam across Shaw's rice field on the Savannah-Ogeechee Canal. On December 10, 1864, the first of several Federal assaults was made to capture Battery Acee and the Confederate earthworks covering the causeway across the Savannah-Ogeechee Canal. All attempts to overwhelm the position by force were repulsed until it was abandoned on December 20, 1864, following the fall of Fort McAllister.

Today, the earthworks at Shaw's Dam, located in the marsh behind the Savannah Christian Preparatory School, are one of the few surviving examples of Savannah's western defensive line. The area is surrounded by wetlands and is protected under the stewardship of the school and is not open to the public at this time.

Left: *The XVII Corps crossing the Ogeechee River (Courtesy of the Library of Congress)*

Fort Jackson (NHL)

Designated a National Historic Landmark, Fort Jackson, the oldest standing brick fortification in Georgia, was named in honor of James Jackson, a Revolutionary War officer and governor of Georgia. During the Civil War, the fort served as headquarters for the Confederate defenses of the Savannah River, part of a system of nine fortifications that protected the river with a total firepower of nearly one hundred heavy guns. Fort Jackson was never taken by Union naval vessels.

1 Fort Jackson Rd.
Savannah, GA 31404
912-232-3945
www.chsgeorgia.org

Daily: 9:00 a.m.–5:00 p.m.

Today, a museum at Old Fort Jackson depicts the fort's history from the 1740s, featuring artifacts from the ironclad CSS *Georgia* and Civil War–era cannons, with frequent cannon firing demonstrations and interpretations by uniformed soldiers. The site is operated by the Coastal Heritage Society.

Left: *Fort Jackson (Photo: Bob Price)*

Georgia Historical Society (NRHP)

Founded in 1839 and headquartered in the historic 1876 Hodgson Hall, the Georgia Historical Society tells the story of Georgia through educational programs, publications, research services, and exhibits. The society is home to the oldest collection of materials related to Georgia history and the oldest Civil War collection in the state, including documents, photographs, weapons, uniforms, flags, and portraits. The collection is open for research and is occasionally on exhibit.

501 Whitaker St.
Savannah, GA 31401
912-651-2125/912-651-2128
www.georgiahistory.com

Tues.–Sat.: 10:00 a.m.–5:00 p.m.

Green-Meldrim House (NRHP, NHL)

1 West Macon St.
Savannah, GA 31401
912-232-1251

Tues., Thurs.-Sat.:
10:00 a.m.-4:00 p.m.

Closed mid-Dec. through mid-
Jan. and two weeks prior to Easter

Right: *The Green-Meldrim
House, Sherman's headquar-
ters in occupied Savannah
(Courtesy of the UGA Hargrett
Rare Book and Manuscript
Library)*

The Green-Meldrim House is one of the finest examples of Gothic Revival architecture to be found in the South. It was constructed in the early 1850s as the residence of Charles Green, an Englishman who came to Savannah in 1833.

During the Civil War, when the city surrendered to Major General William T.
Sherman in December 1864, Green invited the Union general to use the house for
his headquarters. It was here that Sherman learned that his seventh child, whom he
had never seen, had died of pneumonia. A later owner of the house was Judge Peter
Meldrim, a mayor of Sa-
vannah, whose beautiful
daughters gave tours of
the magnificent inte-
rior for many years. The
house is now owned and
operated by St. John's
Episcopal Church.

King-Tisdell Cottage (NRHP)

514 East Huntingdon St.
Savannah, GA 31401
912-234-8000
www.kingtisdell.org

The cottage is currently under
renovation. Call before visiting.

The King-Tisdell Cottage was named for its African American owners, Eugene and
Sarah King, and Sarah King and Robert Tisdell. When renovation is complete a
museum in the cottage will interpret slavery in Savannah, including documents that
reveal the role blacks played during the Civil War.

The nearby Beach Institute African-American Cultural Center (502 E. Harris
Street) once served as the home of Savannah's first school for freed slaves. The institute was built in 1867 by the Freedman's Bureau funded by the American Missionary Association. The institute building houses the Ulysses Davis Folk Art Collection
with 238 wood sculptures in its permanent collection.

Savannah History Museum (NRHP, NHL)

303 Martin Luther King Jr. Blvd.
Savannah, GA 31401
912-238-1779
www.chsgeorgia.org

Mon.-Fri.: 8:30 a.m.-5:00 p.m.
Sat.-Sun.: 9:00 a.m.-5:00 p.m.

The Savannah History Museum is housed in the restored nineteenth-century Central of Georgia Railroad passenger station, a National Historic Landmark. The museum contains exhibits about the 1779 Battle of Savannah during the Revolutionary
War and Civil War memorabilia, including artifacts from the CSS *Georgia*. There is
a gift shop and a theater showing an eighteen-minute video about the history of
Savannah. Portions of the movie, *Glory*, about the 54th Massachusetts Colored Infantry, were filmed at the nearby railroad roundhouse.

Second African Baptist Church

In December 1864, Pastor John Cox and members of the Second Baptist Church, as it was then known, hosted Major General William T. Sherman when he occupied Savannah after its surrender. Sherman had requested Dr. William Pollard, a veterinarian and deacon of the First Bryan Baptist Church, "to assemble all persons of color in Chatham County and the surrounding areas to meet in the square opposite the Second Baptist Church to hear the reading and explanation of the Proclamation of Emancipation."

The crowd was too large to fit into the Second Baptist Church; all assembled outside in what is now known as Greene Square. It is reported that Sherman stood on the steps of Second Baptist Church and explained the Emancipation Proclamation to the gathered crowd. He is said to have promised forty acres and a mule to each of the newly freed slaves. A few weeks later, in January 1865, U.S. Secretary of War Edwin M. Stanton arrived in Savannah. Stanton and Sherman crafted Field Order 15, which "set aside Georgia's Sea Islands and abandoned rice fields 30 miles inland for newly freed slaves."

In Greene Square opposite the Second African Baptist Church is a marker commemorating the historic event of Sherman's attendance at Second Baptist Church.

123 Houston St.
Savannah, GA 31401
912-233-6163
www.secondafrican.org

Ships of the Sea Maritime Museum (NRHP)

The Ships of the Sea Maritime Museum, which was founded in 1966, exhibits ship models, paintings, and maritime antiques principally from the great era of Atlantic trade and travel between England and America during the eighteenth and nineteenth centuries. Its collection includes large-scale models of the greatest ships in Savannah's history, a display of navigational instruments and other seafaring artifacts, and video presentations.

In 2003 the permanent exhibit Savannah and the Civil War at Sea opened. Paintings, prints, drawings, and ship models tell the story of four tumultuous years of blockading adventures and battles at sea. Large ship models on display include the Confederate gunboat *Savannah*, the racing-yacht-turned-blockade-runner *America*, the privateer *Rattlesnake*, the U.S. monitor *Montauk* and four of her sister ships who came to Georgia waters, and the ironclad CSS *Atlanta*. The exhibit also includes a panoramic painting and sketches by famous maritime artists.

The museum is housed in the William Scarbrough House. Built in 1819, the house is one of the earliest examples of Greek Revival architecture in the South. Its garden is also the largest in Savannah's historic district.

William Scarbrough House
41 Martin Luther King Jr. Blvd.
Savannah, GA 31401
912-232-1511
www.shipsofthesea.org

Tues.–Sun.: 10:00 a.m.–5:00 p.m.

Right: *The USS* Water Witch, *which was captured by Confederates in June 1864. The ship's wreckage was discovered in October 2007 in a riverbed near Savannah. (Courtesy of the Library of Congress)*

FORT PULASKI, Chatham County

Savannah CVB
101 E. Bay St.
Savannah, GA 31401
912-644-6401/877-728-2662
www.savannahvisit.com

Located on Cockspur Island approximately eighteen miles east of Savannah, Fort Pulaski is named after the American Revolutionary War hero Polish Count Casimir Pulaski. Completed in 1847, the fort enclosed five acres and could mount 146 guns. The brick walls were seven and a half feet thick and thirty-five feet high and were surrounded by a twenty-five-foot-wide moat. In 1829–1830, while the fort was under construction, twenty-two-year-old U.S. Army Lt. Robert E. Lee was assigned to build the dikes and drainage system for the island.

On January 3, 1861, Georgia militia troops raised the Georgia flag over Fort Pulaski. In late 1861, Federal forces had captured nearby Fort Walker and occupied Tybee Island only one mile from Fort Pulaski. Under the command of Union Brigadier General Thomas W. Sherman, Captain Quincy Adams Gillmore's troops moved heavy artillery and rifled cannons into siege position.

On April 10, 1862, Union artillery on Tybee Island began shelling Fort Pulaski, reducing the walls to half their thickness and disabling all of the fort's forty-eight heavy guns.

Above: Fort Pulaski (Photo: Cara Pastore, Georgia Dept. of Economic Development)

At dawn on April 11, Captain Gillmore's gunners continued to enlarge the breech. By noon shells were passing through an opening and exploding on the powder magazine, which housed forty thousand pounds of gunpowder. To avoid total destruction, Confederate Colonel Charles H. Olmstead surrendered the fort, along with its garrison of 385 Georgia infantry militia. Each side had lost one man, and the Union army had expended 5,275 artillery rounds during the thirty-hour bombardment.

Rifled artillery guns, unlike smoothbore cannons, cause their projectiles to spin, resulting in greater accuracy, range, and penetration power and causing massive damage. This event marked the obsolescence of brick masonry forts. Furthermore, the Georgia–South Carolina coastal defense system, which had taken nearly fifty years to establish, was rendered impotent in just two days. Fort Pulaski stands today as a memorial to personal commitment and valor as well as visionary inventiveness.

Fort Pulaski played a significant role as a haven for former slaves who were freed on April 13, 1862, shortly after the fall of the fort. With the aid of the vast Underground Railroad network, the newly freed slaves made their way to the new Union command at Fort Pulaski. They took up residence in the fort's old construction village, carving out a simple existence along the occupied Georgia coast. Many of the men who arrived at Fort Pulaski later joined together to form one of the first colored troops units during the Civil War, the 1st and 3rd South Carolina Colored Volunteers, who saw action late in the war.

Fort Pulaski National Monument (NRHP)

Within weeks of the bombardment and surrender of Fort Pulaski on April 11, 1862, occupying Federal troops began repairing the fort. Total restoration began in the 1930s, and today Fort Pulaski is an excellent example of the type of pentagonal fort that comprised the Confederate coastal defense system. Around the grounds visitors can view a variety of mounted artillery pieces as well as the shell-battered walls. The moat has been filled. Uniformed rangers and living-history interpreters give talks, and audio stations describe various points of interest in the casemates, including a prison and refurbished officer's quarters, the powder magazine, barbette tier, and parade ground. For larger touring groups, reenactors load a powder charge and fire one of the large artillery pieces. An annual Siege and Reduction Weekend is staged by living-history reenactors on the weekend closest to the battle anniversary (April 10–11). A picnic area and visitors center are also on the grounds.

1 Cockspur Island Rd.
Savannah, GA 31410
912-786-5787
www.nps.gov/fopu

Daily: 9:00 a.m.–5:00 p.m.
(extended summer hours)

Right: *The effects of rifled cannon on the brick and mortar walls of Fort Pulaski began the era of earthen fortifications.* (Photo: Bob Price)

TYBEE ISLAND, Chatham County

Savannah CVB
101 E. Bay St.
Savannah, GA 31401
912-644-6401/877-728-2662
www.savannahvisit.com

Below: *Battery Hamilton as seen from Fort Vulcan (Courtesy of the Library of Congress)*

A barrier island sixteen miles east of Savannah, Tybee Island has been variously occupied by Native Americans, the Spanish, the French, and the English. Because of its location at the mouth of the Savannah River, in 1736 General James Oglethorpe ordered a lighthouse and a small fort to be constructed on the island to ensure control over access to the river.

In December 1861, Confederate forces withdrew from Tybee Island to Fort Pulaski on Cockspur Island under orders of General Robert E. Lee to defend Savannah and the Savannah River. Federal forces under Captain Quincy Adams Gillmore took control of Tybee and began constructing cannon batteries on the island's west side facing Fort Pulaski approximately one mile away. On April 11, 1862, the batteries, using rifled cannon, reduced portions of Fort Pulaski to rubble, making the brick-and-mortar fort obsolete and changing forever the way coastal fortifications would be constructed.

Battery Hamilton

On Bird Island in the Savannah River off Tybee Island

www.nps.gov/seac/pulaski/batteryhamiltonbrochure.pdf

Battery Hamilton is located on what was once the north end of Bird Island, a marsh habitat in the Savannah River. Its sister fort, Battery Vulcan, was built on the South Carolina side of the river but has long since disappeared underwater. The Union army constructed the sandbag, timber, and earthen forts in February 1862 as a means of controlling traffic on the Savannah River during the siege of Fort Pulaski. The forts successfully blocked Confederate vessels from bringing men and supplies to Fort Pulaski. After the capitulation of Fort Pulaski on April 12, 1862, the batteries had served their purpose and were abandoned.

Although it is in a fair state of preservation, Battery Hamilton is not visible above the high marsh grass that covers the surface of Bird Island. The once five-foot-high earthworks have been considerably eroded by tidal action and the marsh-mud environment. The Georgia Department of Transportation (GDOT), the island's owner, is currently removing the silt deposits that have collected over the years as a result of continual dredging of the shipping channel in the Savannah River. The GDOT along with the Federal Highway Administration has sponsored a study to determine the best stabilization plan for this fragile environmental setting.

Battery Hamilton is one of Georgia's lesser-known Civil War resources as well as one of only a handful of earthen fortifications that remain from the War Between the States. Battery Hamilton is not open to the public.

Tybee Island Museum and Light Station

Tybee Island has played a significant military role throughout Georgia and U.S. history, including during the Revolutionary War and the War of 1812. In 1861, Confederate troops occupied the island but early in 1862 withdrew to nearby Fort Pulaski by order of General Robert E. Lee to defend Savannah and the Savannah River. Before leaving, the Confederates burned the lighthouse stairs to prevent the Federals from using it for observation. Union forces soon moved onto Tybee Island and constructed cannon batteries, which included rifled cannon, under the command of Captain Quincy Adams Gillmore. On April 10–11, 1862, Union batteries opened fire on Fort Pulaski from Tybee. The newly employed and highly accurate rifled artillery destroyed a wall of the brick fort, causing its surrender and making such defensive forts forever obsolete.

The Tybee Island Museum is housed in Fort Screven's Battery Garland, constructed in 1898–1899. The battery served as part of America's coastal defense system through the Spanish-American War of 1898, World War I, and World War II. It was decommissioned in 1945. Exhibits in the museum include dioramas, paintings, and weapons, as well as a continuously running slideshow, all depicting over four hundred years of Tybee's history. Civil War exhibits contain photos and lithographs that illustrate Tybee's role in the war, plus uniforms, weapons, and soldiers' personal items.

30 Maddin Dr.
Tybee Island, GA 31328
912-786-5801
www.tybeelighthouse.org

Wed.–Mon.: 9:00 a.m.–5:30 p.m.

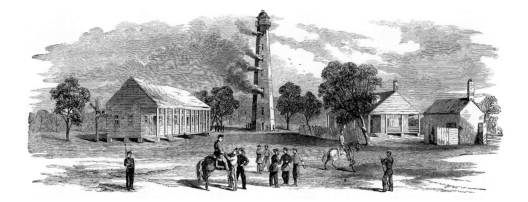

Left: *A depiction of the Confederate burning of the lighthouse on Tybee Island (Courtesy of the Library of Congress)*

RICHMOND HILL, Bryan County

Richmond Hill was incorporated on May 3, 1962. The Richmond Hill State Park comprises 191 acres and is located on the Ogeechee River ten miles east of Richmond Hill adjacent to Fort McAllister.

Richmond Hill CVB
11460 Hwy. 441
Richmond Hill, GA 31324
www.richmondhillcvb.org

Fort McAllister State Historic Park (NRHP)

3894 Fort McAllister Rd.
Richmond Hill, GA 31324
912-727-2339
www.fortmcallister.org

Daily: 8:00 a.m.–5:00 p.m.

Fort McAllister is a vast earthwork that anchored the southern end of the defenses of Savannah. During the Civil War it withstood seven major naval attacks from the coastal side, some involving the largest guns used by the Union navy. When the fort fell to Major General William T. Sherman's invading land forces who attacked from the landward side on December 13, 1864, the Confederate hold on Savannah was no longer tenable, making its fall inevitable.

A museum at the site offers a documentary film, gift shop, and relics from the war. A major expansion in 2004 added an outside shed that protects large pieces of the CSS *Nashville*, including the turbine and massive tools used to repair the ship.

Right: *Fort McAllister*
(Photo: Barry Brown)

MIDWAY, Liberty County

Liberty County CVB
425 West Oglethorpe Hwy.
Hinesville, GA 31313
912-368-3580

In 1754 Congregationalists established the Midway community and in 1758 created St. John's Parish, one of the original colonial parishes. The parish took an early stand for independence from Britain and produced many influential patriots, including two signers of the Declaration of Independence, Dr. Lyman Hall, a Midway Church member, and Button Gwinnett. In 1777, because of their devotion to independence, St. John's Parish and the nearby St. Andrew's and St. James' parishes formed Liberty County. The Revolutionary War came to the Southern provinces in 1778, and the Midway Church community saw action by American Continentals and militiamen attempting to thwart British forces under General Augustine Prevost. Many Midway structures, including the church, were burned by the retreating British.

Midway again became a target for an invading army in December 1864. Union Major General William T. Sherman's cavalry under Brigadier General Judson Kilpatrick ravaged the entire area, plundering plantations and corralling animals in the walled, two-acre cemetery. Kilpatrick used Midway Church as his temporary headquarters.

Many attractions in the Midway area are part of the Historic Liberty Trail, a self-guided driving tour that includes the Sunbury Cemetery, with markers dating from 1788 to 1911, and the rebuilt 1792 Midway Church, which can be entered by obtaining a key from the Midway Museum next door. Other sites on the Liberty Trail with a Civil War connection are the Fort Morris State Historic Site, the Fort Stewart Museum on the Army installation at nearby Hinesville, and Seabrook, a Civil War–period school for freed slaves and now an African American living history village.

Right: *The Midway Church served as the Union quartermaster's headquarters in 1864. (Photo: Bob Price)*

Fort Morris State Historic Site (NRHP)

Fort Morris was built in 1776 to protect the nearby seaport of Sunbury from British invasion. By 1778 it was garrisoned by two hundred patriots under command of Colonel John McIntosh. In November 1778, British forces surrounded the fort and demanded its surrender. The fiery McIntosh replied, "We, Sir, are fighting the battle of America.... As to surrendering the fort ... Come and Take It!" The fort was bombarded into submission and fell on January 9, 1779. Renamed Fort Defiance, it was once again used to defend against the British during the War of 1812.

Early in the Civil War, Confederate militia were mustered into service and some were stationed near the fort to keep watch over the Union fleet operating in St. Catherine's Sound. In 1864 Union cavalry under Brigadier General Judson Kilpatrick burned nearby Sunbury Baptist Church as a signal to Federal troops that the town had been secured. There were no Confederate troops at Fort Morris at the time, and Union forces did not take over the fort.

Visitors to Fort Morris can stand within the remaining earthworks and view scenic St. Catherine's Sound. A museum and documentary video describe the site's history, including archeological artifacts. Paintings in the museum depict an encampment of the Savannah Mounted Rifles in June 1861, the mustering into Confederate service of the Liberty Independent Troop in August 1861, and the burning of Sunbury Baptist Church by Kilpatrick's cavalry in 1864.

2559 Fort Morris Rd.
Midway, GA 31320
912-884-5999
www.gastateparks.org
www.fortmorris.org

Wed.–Sun.: 9:00 a.m.–5:00 p.m.

Right: *Fort Morris, originally constructed during the colonial era, was manned by Confederate troops during the Civil War. (Photo: Bob Price)*

Midway Museum

491 N. Coastal Hwy./GA Hwy. 17
Midway, GA 31320
912-884-5837
www.quantumtour.com

Tues.–Sat.: 10:00 a.m.–4:00 p.m.
Sun.: 2:00 p.m.–4:00 p.m.

The furnished Midway Museum, a reproduction of a late eighteenth-century raised cottage, interprets coastal Georgia history. Exhibits include Civil War documents, books, swords, and a uniform, plus a gift shop and a library for researchers that contains Civil War material. The Midway Museum is located within the Midway National Historic District and is a stop on the Historic Liberty Trail.

DARIEN, McIntosh County

McIntosh County Chamber of Commerce/Welcome Center
105 Ft. King George Dr.
Darien, GA 31305
912-437-6684
www.mcintoshcounty.com

www.coastalga.com/darien/

Established as a port on the Altamaha River in 1736 by Scottish Highlanders under the leadership of John McIntosh Mohr, Darien has a long martial tradition and hosted the first military parade in Georgia on February 22, 1736. Georgia's founder, James Oglethorpe, was in attendance, reviewing the Highland Company from Scotland, which had aided him in many campaigns along the East Coast, including the Battle of Bloody Marsh against the Spanish in 1742.

By 1863 Darien had become one of the great ports along the eastern seaboard. Besides shipping staples like cotton and lumber, the port was used by blockade runners. Due to its notoriety and economic importance, Darien became a target of Union forces invading the Southern coast.

On June 11, 1863, Darien saw some of the first Civil War action by black troops, the USCT (United States Colored Troops) of the 54th Massachusetts. The regiment was commanded by twenty-five-year-old Colonel Robert Gould Shaw, the son of wealthy and prominent Boston abolitionists. Stationed at St. Simon's Island, Shaw received orders from his superior, Kentucky Colonel James Montgomery, to march on Darien. Under protest from Colonel Shaw, who saw the order as immoral, the town was looted and burned by the USCT regiments, including the 54th Massachusetts.

Rebuilt in the 1870s, Darien again became an important seaport, shipping lumber throughout the world until depletion of the area's forests in the early twentieth century forced an end to its prominence. Today, the remains of tabby warehouses and buildings dating from the nineteenth-century sacking of the town can be seen along the river in the area beneath the U.S. 17 bridge and behind the visitors center. The Methodist Church on Vernon Square was partially destroyed during the 1863 fire but was rebuilt in 1884.

Above right: William H. Carney, a sergeant in the 54th Massachusetts and the first African American to receive the Congressional Medal of Honor. Left: Still visible along the Darien waterfront are ruins from the town's burning by the 54th Massachusetts as depicted in the movie Glory. (Photo: Barry Brown)

Pierce Butler Plantation (NRHP)

Directly south of Darien at the southern end of the U.S. 17 bridge over the Altamaha River is the site of Captain Pierce Butler's rice plantation. Though the current house dates to after the Civil War, the seventy-five-foot-high chimney from the plantation's antebellum rice mill still stands in a marshy section of the front yard. This mill, along with much of the island, were the setting of the 1840 book *Journal of a Residence on a Georgia Plantation* by Fanny Kemble, a British actress of note and Pierce Butler's wife. The book, a study of the treatment of the plantation's slaves, is a scathing indictment of the institution of slavery. It is said to have influenced Northern and British attitudes toward slavery and had a similar, though not as profound, influence as Harriet Beecher Stowe's *Uncle Tom's Cabin* in setting the stage for the War Between the States.

On U.S. 17, 0.25 miles south of Darien. The site can be viewed from a pull off along U.S. 17.

Left: The chimney from the Pierce Butler Plantation's rice mill still stands today. (Photo: Barry Brown)

Sapelo Island Lighthouse (NRHP)

The Sapelo Island Lighthouse was built and activated in 1820 to help lead ships safely into the port at Darien at the mouth of the Altamaha River. Upgraded with a more efficient lighting apparatus in 1854, the machinery and lens were dismantled by Confederate forces as they evacuated Sapelo Island in March 1862 just ahead of a Federal landing force. The machinery was replaced and the light again reactivated in 1868 when the lighthouse received its distinctive red- and white-striped paint.

Note: Sapelo Island can only be reached by ferry, and visits must be arranged by calling the visitors center at 912-437-3224.

www.lighthousefriends.com

Tours:
Sat: 9:00 a.m. – 1:00 p.m.
Fri., June – Labor Day:
8:30 a.m. – 12:30 p.m.

Visitors Center:
Tues. – Fri.: 7:30 a.m. – 5:30 p.m.
Sat.: 8:00 a.m. – 5:30 p.m.
Sun.: 1:30 p.m. – 5:00 p.m.

Left: Sapelo Island Lighthouse (Photo: Cara Pastore, Georgia Dept. of Economic Development)

JEKYLL ISLAND, Glynn County

Jekyll Island CVB
100 James Rd.
Jekyll Island, GA 31527
912-635-4155
www.jekyllisland.com

Jekyll Island was named in January 1734 by General James Oglethorpe in honor of Sir Joseph Jekyll, who helped finance Oglethorpe's colonial venture. The du Bignon family purchased the island as part of a consortium in 1791 and by 1800 owned the entire island. The family became cotton planters whose fortunes waxed and waned throughout most of the nineteenth century.

With the outbreak of the Civil War, Confederate forces built a battery on the island but abandoned it a year later when the island's residents moved to the mainland. Federal forces dismantled the battery in January 1863 to strengthen fortifications further up the coast.

Jekyll Island Confederate Battery

On Horton Rd. adjacent to the fence around the Jekyll Island Airport
Jekyll Island, GA

In order to defend Jekyll Island, in 1861 Confederate forces built a five-gun heavy artillery battery consisting of one 42-pound gun and four 32-pound navy guns, each having about sixty rounds of shot and shell. Casements, a hot furnace, and magazines were constructed here as well. On February 10, 1862, General Robert E. Lee, then in charge of coastal defenses, requested permission from Governor Joseph E. Brown to dismantle the position since the island's residents had moved to the mainland. The guns were relocated to Savannah for the city's protection.

On March 9, 1862, the USS *Mohican* landed a rifle company and marines on Jekyll Island and raised the U.S. flag. In January 1863 a Federal force removed the battery's protective railroad irons to strengthen fortifications further up the coast at Port Royal, South Carolina.

The battery site is marked by a state historical marker adjacent to the fence around the runway of the Jekyll Island Airport. The battery is just inside the fence.

BLACKSHEAR, Pierce County

Pierce County Chamber
of Commerce
318 East Taylor St.
Blackshear, GA 31516
912-449-7000

The town of Blackshear was named in honor of General David Blackshear, who in 1814 led the troops who constructed the Blackshear Trail between Hartford and the Flint River. Blackshear's Mill was the name of the post office in 1878. Later the town became known as Blackshear.

Blackshear Prison Camp

Blackshear Prison Camp was one of a number of Andersonville's satellite camps throughout Georgia and the Carolinas where Union prisoners of war were transferred in November 1864 during Major General William T. Sherman's March to the Sea. Weary and emaciated soldiers were loaded onto railroad cars and transported south to this small South Georgia town where only 333 households were listed in the 1860 census. Some of the soldiers who were sick from their imprisonment in the Andersonville stockade died during the journey as neither the train nor the tracks were in serviceable condition and breakdowns were frequent. Finally arriving in Blackshear in early December, they were marched to the outskirts of town (on today's Highway 203) in what some accounts describe as a "pine barren forest," and waited. Guarded by young boys, old men, and disabled veterans from the 2nd and 4th Georgia Reserves, the prisoners were kept out in the open for several weeks while a suitable enclosure was being constructed in Thomasville.

After the war, U.S. government officials traveled throughout the country in search of Union soldiers buried on the fields of battle and reinterred them in Federal cemeteries. They found twenty-seven soldiers buried at Blackshear and moved them to the Beaufort National Cemetery in Beaufort, South Carolina; only two are identified.

On GA Hwy. 203 north of Blackshear
Blackshear, GA

Right: *The Blackshear Prison Camp was one of several temporary sites where Union prisoners from Camp Sumter were moved during the March to the Sea. (Photo: Bob Price)*

GPS Coordinates

1867 Train Depot/Welcome Center   –84.35434300000, 33.52166700000
5th Indiana Battery Site   –84.64855500000, 33.99860800000

Adairsville   –84.93409200000, 34.36879700000
Adairsville Depot   –84.93479400000, 34.36780800000
Alexander H. Stephens State Historic Park   –82.89366200000, 33.56738100000
Alfred R. Waud Grave Site   –84.55006600000, 33.95528900000
Allenbrook   –84.35740534000, 34.00910249000
Alta Vista Cemetery and Longstreet's Grave Site   –83.83557900000, 34.28901500000
Americus   –84.23218000000, 32.07211400000
Andersonville   –84.14064100000, 32.19600000000
Andersonville National Historic Site   –84.12933500000, 32.19791800000
Archibald Smith Plantation   –84.35942500000, 34.02352100000
Athens   –83.37327400000, 33.96009700000
Athens Confederate Monument   –83.37544400000, 33.95763700000
Atlanta   –84.31806000000, 33.77023300000
Atlanta Campaign Pavilion #1   –85.10275900000, 34.90946700000
Atlanta Campaign Pavilion #2   –85.01182300000, 34.80124400000
Atlanta Campaign Pavilion #3   –84.94915500000, 34.60432900000
Atlanta Campaign Pavilion #4   –84.85526700000, 34.23363700000
Atlanta Campaign Pavilion #5   –84.7905500000, 33.958056600000
Atlanta History Center   –84.38633300000, 33.84184800000
Augusta   –81.98196700000, 33.47719400000
Augusta Canal   –81.98049700000, 33.47683600000
Augusta Museum of History   –81.96072400000, 33.47443800000
Augusta State University/U.S. Arsenal   –82.02571900000, 33.47831300000
Augustus Hurt House Site   –84.35597100000, 33.76734500000

Ball's Ferry Landing   –82.95850900000, 32.78182500000
Barnesville   –84.15577100000, 33.05466800000
Barnsley Gardens   –84.98048400000, 34.30137700000
Bartow History Center and Museum   –84.79513100000, 34.16664000000
Battery Hamilton   –80.96101379000, 32.06090927000
Battle at Moore's Mill   –84.44305600000, 33.82611100000
Battle of Allatoona Pass   –84.71561000000, 34.11424100000
Battle of Atlanta   –84.33045600000, 33.74779000000
Battle of Brown's Mill   –84.84494800000, 33.33347400000

Battle of Buckhead Church   -82.02330700000, 32.90245800000
Battle of Buckhead Creek   -81.96670400000, 32.91071800000
Battle of Columbus   -84.99689000000, 32.46354000000
Battle of Culloden   -84.09599000000, 32.86605000000
Battle of Ezra Church   -84.43906800000, 33.75084800000
Battle of Jonesboro   -84.36659600000, 33.53260600000
Battle of King's Tanyard   -83.77360900000, 34.03616500000
Battle of Kolb's Farm   -84.59708800000, 33.91056100000
Battle of Peachtree Creek   -84.40309200000, 33.81048400000
Battle of Pine Mountain   -84.64468700000, 33.98882200000
Battle of Ringgold Gap   -85.10023000000, 34.90719600000
Battle of Ruff's Mill/Concord Covered Bridge/Gann House   -84.55846383000, 33.84898601000
Battle of Shaw's Bridge and Shaw's Dam   -81.16721000000, 32.05365000000
Battle of Smyrna Camp Ground   -84.51381800000, 33.88296000000
Battle of Sunshine Church   -83.61335300000, 33.09077200000
Battle of Utoy Creek   -84.47330100000, 33.71990100000
Battle of Waynesboro   -82.00794300000, 33.07905200000
Bellevue Plantation, Home of Benjamin Harvey Hill   -85.03954585000, 33.04163986000
Benjamin Harvey Hill House   -83.38644700000, 33.96178500000
Blackshear   -82.24135800000, 31.30262000000
Blackshear Prison Camp   -82.25009300000, 31.31786700000
Blakely   -84.93398700000, 31.38303900000
Blue and Gray Museum   -83.25788200000, 31.71578900000
Blunt House   -84.97189369000, 34.76657983000
Booth Western Art Museum   -84.79632500000, 34.16825100000
Boyhood Home of President Woodrow Wilson   -81.96524100000, 33.47172600000
Brown House Museum   -82.81011700000, 32.98752300000
Buckhead   -84.38217400000, 33.84029400000
Bulloch Hall   -84.36656800000, 34.01514500000

Camp Lawton/Magnolia Springs State Park   -81.95819400000, 32.87542800000
Camp McDonald Site   -84.61665800000, 34.02222000000
Camp Stephens   -84.27407000000, 33.27551800000
Campbell-Jordan House   -82.73750391000, 33.73360215000
Cannonball House and Confederate Museum   -83.63206200000, 32.84012500000
Cartersville   -84.79676300000, 34.16390700000
Cartersville Depot   -84.79590400000, 34.16590800000
Cascade Springs Nature Preserve   -84.48118000000, 33.71971000000
Cassville   -84.85274100000, 34.24378300000
Cassville Confederate Cemetery   -84.84606200000, 34.25114500000
Cave Spring   -85.33167600000, 34.10566800000
Chattahoochee River Crossing   -84.35054500000, 34.00433500000
Cheatham Hill   -84.60636000000, 33.94414000000
Cheney-Newcomer Plantation House   -84.61839866000, 33.88725265000
Chickamauga and Chattanooga National Military Park   -85.26028600000, 34.91821300000
Chickamauga/Fort Oglethorpe   -85.26028600000, 34.91821300000
Clayton County Courthouse   -84.29454500000, 33.76931200000

Clayton House   -84.71780900000, 34.11375100000
Clinton/Griswoldville   -83.53882000000, 33.00798500000
Clinton/Old Clinton Historic District   -83.55763800000, 32.99918500000
Clisby Austin House   -85.03935142000, 34.83832665000
Columbus   -84.99429300000, 32.46330500000
Columbus Iron Works Convention and Trade Center   -84.99568800000, 32.46160300000
Columbus Museum   -84.97453100000, 32.46616500000
Confederate Cemetery and Monument   -84.97913200000, 34.76718700000
Confederate Monument   -81.96435700000, 33.47489700000
Confederate Powder Works Factory   -81.99185000000, 33.48721000000
Conyers   -84.01653200000, 33.65916200000
Cook and Brother Confederate Armory   -83.36598700000, 33.95864300000
Cook-Huff House   -84.96945400000, 34.77516200000
Cooper's Iron Works   -84.77061638000, 34.15830954000
Cordele   -83.77931700000, 31.96351000000
Courthouse Square/First Cannonball Fired   -84.32673300000, 32.88755500000
Covington   -83.86318300000, 33.59686700000
Crawford W. Long Museum   -83.57268200000, 34.11817500000
Crawfordville   -82.89672900000, 33.55464000000
Crestlawn Memorial Park   -84.43892600000, 33.80998400000
Crown Gardens and Archives   -84.97250100000, 34.78163100000
Culloden   -84.09389000000, 32.86306000000
Cyclorama and Grant Park   -84.37161300000, 33.73417800000

Dallas   -84.84134300000, 33.92449400000
Dalton   -84.97023900000, 34.76982500000
Dalton Depot   -84.96731900000, 34.77372600000
Darien   -81.45141700000, 31.39962500000
Decatur   -84.29489000000, 33.77561900000
Decatur Cemetery   -84.29177800000, 33.77800900000
Defense of Doctortown   -81.83261100000, 31.65031500000
DeKalb History Center's Jim Cherry Museum   -84.29652000000, 33.77511000000
Dexter Niles House Site   -84.41160900000, 33.77949800000
Disney Trail   -85.00916700000, 34.79933100000
Double-Barreled Cannon   -83.37633900000, 33.95995900000
Dr. Hamilton House   -84.17093300000, 33.80575900000
Drummer Boy Civil War Museum   -84.14248800000, 32.19603000000
Dug Gap Battlefield Park   -85.01505400000, 34.74283300000
Duncan Norton House   -84.94446100000, 34.58008000000

Eagle Tavern Museum   -83.40965200000, 33.86400300000
Ebenezer Creek Crossing   -81.18261000000, 32.37873000000
Effingham Museum   -81.31606200000, 32.37473000000

Fair Oaks   -84.56039000000, 33.96505400000
Fayette County Historical Society   -84.45437800000, 33.44089300000
Fayetteville   -84.45512700000, 33.44865400000

First Presbyterian Church -83.22601000000, 33.07962700000
First Presbyterian Church -81.96479200000, 33.47065500000
First Presbyterian Church of Rome -85.17196500000, 34.25298900000
Fitzgerald -83.25255600000, 31.71492700000
Forsyth -83.93825200000, 33.03433100000
Forsyth Confederate Hospitals and Cemetery -83.93690000000, 33.03155200000
Fort Gaines -85.05056026000, 31.60759515000
Fort Gordon U.S. Army Signal Corps Museum -82.15417700000, 33.41771100000
Fort McAllister State Historic Park -81.19486468000, 31.89180033000
Fort Morris State Historic Site -81.27877838000, 31.76377984000
Fort Norton -85.16319800000, 34.26681400000
Fort Pulaski National Monument -80.90406000000, 32.02700300000
Fort Tyler -85.18640400000, 32.88031300000
Fort Walker -84.36864900000, 33.73051100000
Fort Wayne -84.93845062000, 34.57996164000

Gainesville -83.82409900000, 34.29835700000
Georgia Historical Society -81.09646100000, 32.07051600000
Georgia Military Institute Site/Colonel Arnoldus Brumby House -84.55219300000, 33.94377500000
Georgia School for the Deaf/Fannin Hall -85.33245400000, 34.10704200000
Georgia State Capitol and Museum -84.38813400000, 33.74912800000
Georgia Veterans Memorial State Park -83.73661600000, 31.95690100000
Gilgal Church and Pine Knob Battle Sites -84.66442800000, 33.97223900000
Glover-McLeod-Garrison Mansion -84.54740340000, 33.93527670000
Gordon-Lee Mansion -85.29427200000, 34.87144900000
Green Bone Creek -84.42710300000, 33.82599300000
Green-Meldrim House -81.09493360000, 32.07369206000
Griffin -84.26379900000, 33.25227800000
Griswoldville State Historic Site -83.45988800000, 32.86966100000
Guyton -81.39167000000, 32.33611000000

Hamilton House -84.97196500000, 34.78133100000
Hay House -83.63285500000, 32.84050300000
High Falls State Park -84.01537700000, 33.18114100000
Historic Utoy Church and Cemetery -84.44977000000, 33.71541000000
Holliday-Dorsey-Fife House Museum -84.45583500000, 33.44826000000
Howell Cobb Home -83.38531100000, 33.96265900000

Irwinville -83.38593100000, 31.66459700000

Jefferson -83.57416900000, 34.11393900000
Jefferson Davis Memorial Park -83.38703100000, 31.66373400000
Jekyll Island -81.42397600000, 31.06371700000
Jekyll Island Confederate Battery -81.42800140000, 31.07095337000
Jerusalem Evangelical Lutheran Church -81.18096200000, 32.37654700000
Jesup -81.88181500000, 31.60411200000

John A. White Park –84.44974100000, 33.72543400000
John B. Gordon Hall –85.28157700000, 34.70824200000
Johnson–Blalock House –84.35449800000, 33.52397500000
Johnston's River Line –84.52023200000, 33.78903100000
Jonesboro –84.35376400000, 33.52158700000
Joseph Henry Lumpkin House –83.38239743000, 33.96050397000
Joshua Hill Home –83.47344100000, 33.59141400000
Judge William A. Wilson House and Cemetery –84.51053800000, 33.73740400000

Kennesaw –84.61550500000, 34.02336700000
Kennesaw House/Marietta Museum of History/GWTW Museum –84.55054300000, 33.95278400000
Kennesaw Mountain National Battlefield Park –84.59499800000, 33.95477300000
King-Tisdell Cottage –81.08941981000, 32.06932041000
Kingston –84.94412400000, 34.23714000000
Kingston Civil War Museum and Woman's History Museum –84.94619400000, 34.23508300000
Kingston Confederate Cemetery –84.94616200000, 34.23001300000
Kingston Depot –84.94555400000, 34.23647800000
Kingston Methodist Church –84.94499700000, 34.23517000000

LaFayette –85.28104600000, 34.70867400000
LaFayette Presbyterian Church –85.28203800000, 34.70535100000
LaGrange –85.03371500000, 33.03670500000
Lake Allatoona Vicinity –84.71129900000, 34.10813100000
Last Confederate Meeting Site/Wilkes County Courthouse –82.73915400000, 33.73768500000
Lee & Gordon's Mill –85.26688808000, 34.88361899000
Lemuel P. Grant Mansion –84.37691100000, 33.74054400000
Lexington –83.11210000000, 33.86965200000
Liberty Hall Historic Site and Confederate Museum –82.89580600000, 33.55834100000
Linwood Cemetery –84.98381000000, 32.47592900000
Lionel Hampton/Utoy Creek Park –84.47238200000, 33.73787700000
Lithonia –84.10517300000, 33.71236900000
Longstreet Home Site and Vineyards –83.82525800000, 34.31487700000
Lovejoy Station –84.32475000000, 33.44890500000
Lovejoy's Station –84.37161100000, 33.48105400000
Lowndes County Historical Society Museum –83.28280600000, 30.83049600000

Macon –83.62633700000, 32.83419700000
Madison –83.46792300000, 33.59564500000
Madison-Morgan County Cultural Center –83.47097900000, 33.59156700000
Magnolia Cemetery –81.95707100000, 33.46242600000
Marietta –84.55022400000, 33.95277000000
Marietta City Cemetery/Confederate Cemetery –84.54958300000, 33.94580400000
Marietta Depot –84.55022400000, 33.95277000000
Marietta National Cemetery –84.54123600000, 33.95130400000
Marsh House –85.28123300000, 34.70944600000
Mary Gay House –84.30470000000, 33.77259400000

McAfee's Bridge   -84.26230800000, 33.97342600000
McCravey-Johnston House   -84.94372000000, 34.23548100000
McLemore's Cove   -85.38705682000, 34.73947296000
Medical College of Georgia   -81.96335300000, 33.47070600000
Memory Hill Cemetery   -83.22910000000, 33.07581500000
Midway   -81.43076400000, 31.80736400000
Midway Museum   -81.43069800000, 31.80558500000
Milledgeville   -83.22204000000, 33.08246800000
Millen   -81.94928200000, 32.80506700000
Monument to Confederate General W.H.T. Walker   -84.32711800000, 33.73992900000
Monument to Federal General James B. McPherson   -84.34133400000, 33.74414900000
Moore's Bridge Park and Horace King Historic Site   -84.88798000000, 33.48401300000
Morris Museum of Art   -81.96897600000, 33.47938900000
Mozley Park   -84.43864700000, 33.75289500000
Myrtle Hill Cemetery   -85.17967000000, 34.25226100000

Nancy Harts   -85.03130500000, 33.03941600000
Nash Farm Battlefield   -84.29124000000, 33.45868000000
National Infantry Museum   -84.95706400000, 32.38094500000
New Ebenezer   -81.26769700000, 32.34640000000
New Hope Church Monument and Battle Site   -84.79055000000, 33.95789900000
Newnan   -84.79968100000, 33.38068900000
Newton Male Academy Museum   -84.80269600000, 33.37854700000
Noble Brothers Foundry   -85.16490700000, 34.26244100000

Oak Hill Cemetery   -84.80820000000, 34.17564200000
Oak Hill Cemetery   -84.25632100000, 33.24655300000
Oak Hill Cemetery   -84.79855500000, 33.38190700000
Oakland Cemetery   -84.37509200000, 33.74807400000
Ocmulgee National Monument/Battle of Dunlap's Farm   -83.60113300000, 32.84500500000
Oconee Hill Cemetery   -83.36888300000, 33.95088200000
Old Fort Jackson   -81.03602711000, 32.08184230000
Old Governor's Mansion   -83.23161300000, 33.07964100000
Old Madison Cemetery   -83.47238900000, 33.59510000000
Old State Capitol Square/Provost Guard Camp Site   -83.22492400000, 33.08003800000
Old Stone Presbyterian Church   -85.07694700000, 34.90645400000
Oostanaula River Bridge   -84.94103400000, 34.57762100000
Original Confederate Flagpole   -84.93367800000, 31.37748000000

Palmetto   -84.66958500000, 33.51837800000
Patrick R. Cleburne Memorial Confederate Cemetery   -84.35148400000, 33.52990600000
Perkins   -81.95286200000, 32.90973600000
Philomath   -82.98802600000, 33.72674200000
Pickett's Mill State Historic Site   -84.77306800000, 33.97997000000
Pigeon Hill   -84.59026000000, 33.96536000000
Piedmont Hotel   -83.82337247000, 34.29303853000
Pierce Butler Plantation   -81.44787938000, 31.35312944000

Pinewood Cemetery   -85.17271800000, 32.87797600000
Port Columbus National Civil War Naval Museum   -84.97622600000, 32.44579600000
Prater's Mill   -84.92064994000, 34.89504760000

Railroad Tunnel through Chetoogeta Mountain   -85.03326100000, 34.83866200000
Rees Park   -84.22458400000, 32.06729500000
Resaca   -84.94939300000, 34.60426900000
Resaca Confederate Cemetery   -84.94375900000, 34.60640500000
Richmond Hill   -81.17936600000, 31.88428500000
Ringgold   -85.10940100000, 34.91569200000
Ringgold Depot   -85.10767730000, 34.91541537000
Riverside Cemetery/Confederate Trenches   -83.64018000000, 32.85083000000
Robert Toombs Historic Site   -82.73397683000, 33.73639321000
Rome   -85.16555600000, 34.26083700000
Rose Hill Cemetery   -83.63420200000, 32.84737200000
Roselawn   -84.80278813000, 34.16527361000
Ross House   -85.28472495000, 34.97499168000
Roswell   -84.36270600000, 34.01530100000
Roswell Manufacturing Company Mill Ruins   -84.35527600000, 34.01336200000
Roswell Mill Workers Monument   -84.36000700000, 34.01516400000
Roswell Presbyterian Church   -84.36296900000, 34.01908000000
Roswell Town Square   -84.36330700000, 34.01489300000

Saffold   -85.03333600000, 31.12146200000
Saffold Confederate Naval Yard   -85.03143700000, 31.11253600000
Sandersville   -82.78197300000, 32.98732300000
Sapelo Island Lighthouse   -81.28116366000, 31.41941637000
Savannah   -81.09015900000, 32.08066700000
Savannah History Museum   -81.09921400000, 32.07565300000
Second African Baptist Church   -81.08636000000, 32.07670700000
Ships of the Sea Maritime Museum   -81.09718100000, 32.08107100000
Shrine of the Immaculate Conception   -84.38956000000, 33.75052700000
Sidney Barron House   -84.32181480000, 32.88222059000
Site of James J. Andrews Execution   -84.38305800000, 33.77376700000
Site of Solomon Luckie's Mortal Wounding   -84.39091300000, 33.75353500000
Site of the First Federal Shell to Fall in Atlanta   -84.38597600000, 33.75849700000
Site Where Battle of Decatur Began   -84.29552200000, 33.76993200000
Smyrna   -84.51417800000, 33.88397800000
Sope Creek Mill Ruins/Federal Crossing Point   -84.43749900000, 33.94029400000
Southern Museum of Civil War and Locomotive History   -84.61413700000, 34.02351900000
Springvale Park   -84.35741600000, 33.75617400000
St. Stephen's Episcopal Church   -83.22598500000, 33.07875100000
Stately Oaks Plantation   -84.34091500000, 33.47194900000
Statue of General Joseph E. Johnston   -84.96812900000, 34.77153100000
Stillwell House   -84.17251000000, 33.80763600000
Stone Mountain Confederate Cemetery   -84.17161400000, 33.81278400000
Stone Mountain Depot   -84.17056400000, 33.80663900000

Stone Mountain Park   -84.16192900000, 33.81246300000
Stone Mountain Village   -84.17116400000, 33.81207100000
Stonewall Confederate Cemetery and Memorial Park   -84.25152800000, 33.24609200000
Surrender of Atlanta Site   -84.40735900000, 33.77622400000
Swanton House   -84.30522982000, 33.77203283000
Sweetwater Creek State Conservation Area   -84.63940900000, 33.75411400000
Sydney Lanier Cottage   -83.63595600000, 32.83731200000

Tanyard Creek Park   -84.40205900000, 33.80875900000
Taylor-Grady House   -83.38868397000, 33.97057044000
Thomas County Historical Museum   -83.98372300000, 30.84572700000
Thomas R.R. Cobb House   -83.38176618000, 33.96114733000
Thomaston   -84.32509700000, 32.88630100000
Thomaston-Upson Archives   -84.32585300000, 32.88084200000
Thomasville   -83.25788200000, 31.71578900000
Thomasville Prisoner of War Camp   -83.99719700000, 30.83736000000
Tunnel Hill   -85.04315600000, 34.84009400000
Tunnel Hill Heritage Center   -85.04233700000, 34.84000100000
Tybee Island   -80.84635700000, 32.00302500000
Tybee Island Museum and Light Station   -80.84793714000, 32.02221085000

University of Georgia   -83.373583300000, 33.9580566000000
U.S. Army Corps of Engineers Visitors Center   -84.74023500000, 34.18589600000

Valdosta   -83.31821300000, 30.82286200000
Varnell   -84.97444300000, 34.90005800000
Vinings   -84.46433200000, 33.86479100000
Vining's Station   -84.47950200000, 33.86425600000

Wallis House   -84.61309373000, 33.96504191000
Ware-Lyndon House   -83.37561000000, 33.96388800000
Warren House   -84.353534700000, 33.532751000000
Washington   -82.73927300000, 33.73689700000
Washington Historical Museum   -82.73197100000, 33.73599400000
Watkinsville   -83.40965200000, 33.86400300000
Waynesboro   -82.01554300000, 33.09273500000
West Point   -85.18322800000, 32.87795300000
Westview Cemetery   -84.44199400000, 33.74725700000
Whitesburg   -84.91384700000, 33.49404900000
Whitman-Anderson House   -85.10915945000, 34.91760231000
Windemere Plantation   -84.61928745000, 33.49149414000
Winder   -83.72310700000, 33.99199000000
Winnie Davis Memorial Hall and Navy Supply Corps Museum   -83.40207900000, 33.96390300000
Wirz Monument   -84.14005000000, 32.19464100000
Woodruff House   -83.63461600000, 32.84216300000

Yellow River Post Office   -84.06907300000, 33.87700000000

The Civil War in Georgia

A Brief Summary of the Principal Events

January 1, 1861	Georgians go to the polls to vote on either a pro-Union or a pro-Secession slate of delegates for the state convention to be held in Milledgeville. The referendum is won by the pro-Secession vote.
January 3, 1861	Colonel Alexander Lawton and 134 men from the 1st Volunteer Regiment of Georgia seize Fort Pulaski. At the time, the fort is manned only by a caretaker and an ordnance sergeant. Captain Francis Bartow will be the first Confederate commander of Fort Pulaski.
January 19, 1861	Georgia votes to leave the Union at the Secession Convention in Milledgeville.
January 22, 1861	A "statement of protest" is issued by the six convention delegates who refuse to sign the Ordinances of Secession.
September 11, 1861	Joseph E. Brown is elected to a third term as governor.
February 10, 1862	General Robert E. Lee requests permission from Governor Joseph E. Brown to dismantle the Confederate batteries on Jekyll Island since its residents have abandoned the island. The guns are sent to strengthen the defenses around Savannah.
March 9, 1862	Federal troops occupy Jekyll Island.
April 10–11, 1862	The siege of Fort Pulaski takes place. Areas of the fort's wall are reduced to rubble by the use of rifled cannon by the Federals under Captain Quincy Adams Gillmore, thus forever ending the era of the masonry fort.
April 12, 1862	Union raiders in civilian clothing seize the Confederate engine *General* at Big Shanty on a mission of sabotage. The plot falls apart due to rain, poor decision making, and a tenacious band of Confederates in hot pursuit. The raiders are eventually captured but later receive the first Medals of

Honor (some posthumously) bestowed by the U.S. government.

July 1862 The Griswold Cotton Gin Company produces its first Colt-patterned revolvers under Confederate contract.

July 1, 1862 Federal navy assault on Fort McAllister.

July 29, 1862 Federal navy assault on Fort McAllister.

January 27, 1863 Federal navy assault on Fort McAllister.

February 28, 1863 Federal gunships, including the monitor U.S.S. *Montauk*, move up the Ogeechee River past Fort McAllister to destroy the Confederate privateer *Rattlesnake* (formerly *Nashville*).

March 3, 1863 Federal Naval assaults on Fort McAllister resume.

May 3, 1863 Confederate Major General Nathan Bedford Forrest captures Colonel Abel D. Streight's raiders in western Alabama before they reach their goal of Rome, Georgia.

June 11, 1863 The coastal town of Darien is burned by the USCT of the 54th Massachusetts.

September 19–20, 1863 The Battle of Chickamauga ends in Confederate victory and leads to the siege of Chattanooga.

October 10, 1863 Confederate President Jefferson Davis arrives in north Georgia to visit with Army of Tennessee commander General Braxton Bragg and to mediate a growing feud between Bragg and his generals.

November 27, 1863 Federal pursuit of the Confederate Army of Tennessee fleeing Chattanooga is stopped by the ambuscade under Major General Patrick R. Cleburne at the Battle of Ringgold Gap.

December 16, 1863 Confederate General Braxton Bragg resigns command of the Army of Tennessee and is replaced by General Joseph E. Johnston at Dalton. The Army of Tennessee spends the winter of 1863–1864 headquartered at Dalton.

January 2, 1864 Major General Patrick R. Cleburne presents a proposal to the Army of Tennessee high command to offer freedom to slaves who volunteer to fight for the Confederate army. A topic of great controversy, the proposal presented at the Dr. James Black house in Dalton never gets off the ground.

February 22–27, 1864   Major General George H. Thomas probes Confederate lines around Dalton after General Joseph E. Johnston dispatches two divisions to aid Lt. General Leonidas Polk in the west. Thomas withdraws on February 27 after realizing Johnston could counter any Federal threat.

February 25, 1864   The first five hundred Federal prisoners arrive at Andersonville Station and are marched one-third of a mile east to the barren and unfinished stockade known as Camp Sumter.

May 5–7, 1864   The Atlanta Campaign begins as the Federal XIV Corps drives the Confederate outpost from Tunnel Hill to Buzzard's Roost.

May 8–11, 1864   The battles of Rocky Face Ridge and Dug Gap occur while Federal troops probe Buzzard's Roost Gap in unsuccessful attempts to dislodge the Confederates.

May 8–13, 1864   Major General James B. McPherson attempts a flanking movement around Confederate forces at Dalton through the Snake Creek Gap, establishing the pattern for the entire campaign. The plan is to get between the Confederate army and Atlanta at Resaca. A small force of Confederates stationed at Resaca causes McPherson to hesitate and lose the advantage.

May 14–15, 1864   The Battle of Resaca ends in a draw, but the Confederate Army is forced to head south to protect its flanks.

May 16, 1864   The Battle of Rome Crossroads and fighting near Calhoun.

May 17, 1864   Fighting at Adairsville and in the vicinity of Rome.

May 18–19, 1864   General Johnston's attempted assault on a portion of Major General William T. Sherman's pursuing forces at Cassville falls short when Lt. General John B. Hood, fearing a threat on his flank, fails to act.

May 20, 1864   The Federal army crosses the Etowah River, moving ever closer to Atlanta. However, Major General William T. Sherman, wishing to avoid a frontal assault on well-entrenched Confederates in the Allatoona Mountain range, leaves the railroad and attempts to flank General Joseph E. Johnston to the west.

May 25, 1864	The Battle of New Hope Church occurs after Confederates rush west into Paulding County to counter Major General William T. Sherman's threat there. Heavy casualties result after two hours of fighting stops the Federal advance.
May 26–June 1, 1864	Fighting on the New Hope–Dallas line in Paulding County as the Atlanta Campaign becomes a war of entrenchment.
May 27, 1864	A Federal flanking movement is stopped with heavy casualties at the Battle of Pickett's Mill.
June 14, 1864	Lt. General Leonidas Polk is killed atop Pine Mountain.
June 9–23, 1864	Operations west of Marietta, including fighting at Pine Mountain, Lost Mountain, Brushy Mountain, Gilgal Church, Mud Creek, Noonday Creek, and Noyes Creek. The Confederates are forced back to the "Gibraltar of Georgia," the Kennesaw Mountain Line.
June 22, 1864	At the Battle of Kolb's Farm, General John B. Hood's assaults are all stopped with a bloody repulse, though the Federal flanking movement around Kennesaw Mountain is temporarily averted.
June 27, 1864	The Federals launch a morning assault on what are considered weak points in the Confederate line and are repulsed at all points with heavy losses at the Battle of Kennesaw Mountain.
July 3–4, 1864	The Confederate army abandons the Kennesaw line to avoid a Federal flanking movement and moves back to the Smyrna-Ruff's Mill Line. Federals assault the line at both Smyrna Station and Ruff's Mill.
July 5–9, 1864	The Johnston's River Line is occupied. The Federals build a line parallel and constant skirmishing ensues.
July 5–17, 1864	Operations along the Chattahoochee River with fighting at Howell's, Turner's, and Pace's ferries.
July 18, 1864	General Joseph E. Johnston, after having failed to stop the Federal advance towards Atlanta, is relieved of command by President Jefferson Davis and replaced by General John B. Hood.

July 18–20, 1864	Operations commence around Peachtree Creek, including fighting at Moore's Mill, Green Bone Creek, and Stone Mountain east of the Atlanta.
July 20, 1864	The Battle of Peachtree Creek is the first of Hood's three unsuccessful sorties during July designed to destroy, piecemeal, elements of Major General William T. Sherman's army.
July 21, 1864	Combat for control of Leggett's Hill.
July 22, 1864	The Battle of Atlanta and the Battle of Decatur. Federal Major General James B. McPherson and Confederate Major General W.H.T. Walker are killed.
July 22–24, 1864	Federal Brigadier General Kenner Garrard's cavalry raid on Covington.
July 23–August 26, 1864	Siege operations begin and last through most of August.
July 27–31, 1864	Brigadier General Edward M. McCook leads cavalry raid on the Atlanta and West Point and the Macon and Western railroads.
July 28, 1864	The Battle of Ezra Church.
July 30, 1864	Battle at Dunlap Farm and shelling of Macon by Major General George Stoneman's raiders.
July 31, 1864	Battle of Sunshine Church. Major General George Stoneman and six hundred men surrender to Confederate Brigadier General Albert Iverson Jr.
August 3, 1864	Battle of King's Tanyard.
August 5–7, 1864	Battle of Utoy Creek. Fighting around Atlanta's West End.
August 10–Sept. 9, 1864	Confederate Major General Joseph Wheeler's cavalry raid into north Georgia and east Tennessee.
August 18–22, 1864	Federal Brigadier General Judson Kilpatrick's raid on Lovejoy Station.
August 31–Sept. 1, 1864	Battle of Jonesboro. General John B. Hood's eighty railroad cars of supplies and munitions are burned.

September 2, 1864	Mayor James M. Calhoun surrenders Atlanta to Federal forces. Federal troops begin to occupy the city.
September 25, 1864	President Jefferson Davis visits General John B. Hood's headquarters at Palmetto to confer on the military situation after the fall of Atlanta.
September 28, 1864	President Jefferson Davis wires General John B. Hood from West Point, Georgia, to relieve Lt. General William Hardee from the Army of Tennessee and send him to command the Department of South Carolina, Florida, and Georgia. Hardee's new assignment will be headquartered in Savannah.
October 5, 1864	Following several days' march north from Palmetto, General John B. Hood dispatches Major General Samuel G. French's division to capture the Federal garrison at Allatoona Pass. After a severe combat, French withdraws without the garrison's capitulation.
November 8, 1864	Lincoln is reelected as president of the United States.
November 15, 1864	Major General William T. Sherman, after organizing his army into right and left wings, begins his double-pronged march across Georgia from Atlanta to Savannah. All items of use to the Confederates in the city of Atlanta are burned.
November 19, 1864	Governor Joseph E. Brown calls for all men between the ages of sixteen and fifty-five to oppose General William T. Sherman but is unable to raise a significant force.
November 22, 1864	The Battle of Griswoldville ends in Confederate defeat. The state capitol at Milledgeville falls to the Federal invaders.
November 28, 1864	Cavalry action at Buckhead Creek and Reynolds Plantation.
December 4, 1864	The Battle of Waynesboro. Major General Joseph Wheeler's cavalry resists the Federal advance.
December 7, 1864	The Ebenezer Creek incident occurs at the Augusta-Savannah Road.
December 13, 1864	Fort McAllister falls, leading to the evacuation of Savannah.
December 16, 1864	Doctortown, on the Altamaha River, is successfully defended against several Federal assaults.

December 20-21, 1864   The city of Savannah falls to the invading Federals while Lt. General William Hardee's army escapes into South Carolina.

April 16, 1865   Brigadier General James H. Wilson's Federal raiders enter Georgia and attack at West Point and Columbus. The Battle of West Point ends with the fall of Fort Tyler and the death of Brigadier General Robert C. Tyler. Columbus is captured, and its naval works are burned along with the ship CSS *Jackson*.

May 10, 1865   Confederate President Jefferson Davis and family are captured near Irwinville.

May 12, 1865   Confederate Brigadier General William T. Wofford surrenders the last significant body of Confederate troops in Georgia to the Federals, ending the war in Georgia.

Bibliography

GUIDES TO CIVIL WAR SITES

Gelbert, Doug. *Civil War Sites, Memorials, Museums and Library Collections: A State-by-State Guidebook to Places Open to the Public.* Jefferson, NC: McFarland & Company, 1997.

Georgia Department of Natural Resources. *Georgia Civil War Markers.* 2nd ed. Atlanta: State Parks, Recreation & Historical Sites Division, Georgia DNR, 1982.

Georgia Department of Natural Resources and Georgia Department of Industry, Trade, and Tourism. *Crossroads of Conflict: A Guide for Touring Civil War Sites in Georgia.* Atlanta: Historic Preservation Division, Georgia DNR; and Georgia Tourist Division, Georgia DITT, 1995.

Kelly, Dennis. *Kennesaw Mountain and the Atlanta Campaign: A Tour Guide.* Marietta, GA: Kennesaw Mountain Historical Association, 1990.

Kennedy, Frances H., ed. *The Civil War Battlefield Guide.* 2nd ed. The Conservation Fund. New York: Houghton Mifflin Company, 1998.

Lenz, Richard J. *The Civil War in Georgia: An Illustrated Traveler's Guide.* Watkinsville, GA: Infinity Press, 1995.

McCarley, J. Britt. *The Atlanta Campaign: A Civil War Driving Tour of Atlanta-Area Battlefields.* Atlanta: Cherokee Publishing Company, 1989.

McKay, John. *Insider's Guide to Civil War Sites in the Southern States.* 3rd ed. Guilford, CT: Globe Pequot Press, 2005.

Miles, Jim. *Civil War Sites in Georgia.* Nashville: Rutledge Hill Press, 1996.

———. *Fields of Glory: A History and Tour Guide of the Atlanta Campaign.* Nashville: Rutledge Hill Press, 1989.

————. *To the Sea: A History and Tour Guide of Sherman's March*. Nashville: Rutledge Hill Press, 1989.

Roth, Darlene R. *Architecture, Archaeology and Landscapes: Resources for Historic Preservation in Unincorporated Cobb County, Georgia*. Marietta, GA: Cobb County Historic Preservation Commission, 1988.

Wertz, Jay, and Edwin C. Bearss. *Smithsonian's Great Battles and Battlefields of the Civil War: A Definitive Field Guide*. New York: William Morrow & Company, Inc., 1997.

Wiggins, David N. *Georgia's Confederate Monuments and Cemeteries*. Charleston, SC: Arcadia Publishing, 2006.

SUGGESTIONS FOR FURTHER READING

Angle, Craig. *The Great Locomotive Chase: More on the Andrews Raid & the First Medal of Honor*. State College, PA: Jostens Printing, 1992.

Arnsdorff, Jimmy E. *Those Gallant Georgians Who Served in the War Between the States*. Greenville, SC: Southern Historical Press, 1994.

Bailey, Ronald H., and the editors of Time-Life Books. *The Civil War: Battle for Atlanta, Sherman Moves East*. Alexandria, VA: Time-Life Books, 1985.

Barnard, George N. *Photographic Views of Sherman's Campaign*. New York: Dover Publications, 1977.

Barrow, Charles Kelly. *Black Confederates*. Gretna, LA: Pelican Publishing, Inc., 1995.

————. *Black Southerners in Confederate Armies: A Collection of Historical Accounts*. Gretna, LA: Pelican Publishing Company, Inc., 1995.

————. *Sons of Confederate Veterans Georgia Division: The First One Hundred Years 1896–1996, A Short History*. Thomasville, GA: Craigmiles & Assoc., Inc., 1996.

Bragg, C.L., Charles D. Ross, Gordon A. Blaker, Stephanie A. T. Jacobe, and Theodore P. Savas. *Never for Want of Powder: The Confederate Powder Works in Augusta, Georgia*. Columbia: University of South Carolina Press, 2007.

Bragg, William Harris. *Griswoldville*. Macon, GA: Mercer University Press, 2000.

Bierce, Ambrose. *Ambrose Bierce's Civil War*. New York: Random House, 1956.

Boyd, Kenneth W. *Georgia Historical Markers—Coastal Counties*. Atlanta: Cherokee Publishing, 1991.

Bryan, T. Conn. *Confederate Georgia*. Athens: University of Georgia Press, 1953.

Castel, Albert. *Decision in the West: The Atlanta Campaign of 1864*. Lawrence: University Press of Kansas, 1992.

Cook, Ruth Beaumont. *North Across the River: A Civil War Trail of Tears*. Birmingham, AL: Crane Hill Publishers, 1999.

Cozzens, Peter. *This Terrible Sound: The Battle of Chickamauga*. Urbana: University of Illinois Press, 1992.

Davis, Robert S. Jr., ed. *Requiem for a Lost City: A Memoir of Civil War Atlanta and the Old South*. Macon, GA: Mercer University Press, 1999.

Davis, William C., and Bell I. Wiley. *A Photographic History of the Civil War: Fort Sumter to Gettysburg*. New York: Black Dog & Leventhal Publishers, 1994.

————. *A Photographic History of the Civil War: Vicksburg to Appomattox*. New York: Black Dog & Leventhal Publishers, 1994.

Evans, David. *Sherman's Horsemen: Union Cavalry Operations in the Atlanta Campaign*. Bloomington: Indiana University Press, 1996.

Garrett, Franklin M. *Atlanta and Environs: A Chronicle of its People and Events*. Athens: University of Georgia Press, 1954.

Hitt, Michael D. *Charged with Treason: Ordeal of Four Hundred Mill Workers during Military Operations in Roswell, Georgia*. Monroe, NY: Library Research Associates, 1992.

Howard, Annie Hornady. *Georgia Homes and Landmarks*. Atlanta: Southern Features Syndicate, 1929.

Jones, James Pickett. *Yankee Blitzkrieg: Wilson's Raid through Alabama and Georgia*. Athens: University of Georgia Press, 1976.

Joslyn, Mauriel Phillips. *Charlotte's Boys: Correspondence of the Branch Family of Savannah*. Charlottesville, VA: Howell Press, 1996.

————, ed. *Confederate Women*. Sarasota, FL: Pelican Press, 2004.

————. *Immortal Captives: The Story of 600 Confederate Officers and the United States Prisoner of War Policy*. Shippensburg, PA: White Mane Publishing, 1996.

Kerlin, Robert H. *Confederate Generals of Georgia and Their Burial Sites*. Fayetteville, GA: Americana Historical Books, 1994.

Livingston, Gary. *Fields of Gray: Battle of Griswoldville, November 22, 1864*. Jacksonville, NC: Caisson Press, 1996.

Long, E.B., with Barbara Long. *The Civil War Day by Day: An Almanac 1861–1865*. New York: Doubleday & Co., 1971.

Marvel, William. *Andersonville: The Last Depot*. Chapel Hill: University of North Carolina Press, 1994.

McElfresh, Earl B. *Maps and Mapmakers of the Civil War*. New York: Harry N. Abrams, Inc., 1999.

McMurry, Richard M. *Atlanta 1864: Last Chance for the Confederacy*. Lincoln: University of Nebraska Press, 2001.

McPherson, James M. *Battle Cry of Freedom: The Civil War Era*. New York: Ballantine Books, 1988.

McTyre, Joe, and Rebecca Nash Paden. *Historic Roswell Georgia*. Charleston, SC: Arcadia Publishing, 2001.

Misulia, Charles. *Columbus, Georgia, 1865: The Last True Battle of the Civil War*. Tuscaloosa: University of Alabama Press, 2010.

Nelvin, David, and the editors of Time-Life Books. *The Civil War: Sherman's March, Atlanta to the Sea*. Alexandria, VA: Time-Life Books, 1985.

Official Records of the War of the Rebellion. Vol. 38, ser. 1, pts. 1–4. Washington, DC: Government Printing Office, 1898.

O'Neill, Charles. *Wild Train: The Story of the Andrews Raiders*. New York: Random House, 1956.

Ransom, John. *John Ransom's Andersonville Diary*. New York: Paul S. Eriksson, 1986.

Scaife, William R. *The Campaign for Atlanta*. Saline, MI: McNaughton & Gunn, 1993.

———. *The March to the Sea*. Atlanta: William R. Scaife, 1993.

Secrist, Philip L. *The Battle of Resaca*. Macon, GA: Mercer University Press, 1998.

———. *Sherman's 1864 Trail of Battle to Atlanta*. Macon, GA: Mercer University Press, 2006.

Segars, J.H., ed. *Life in Dixie during the War*, by Mary A.H. Gay. 1892. Macon, GA: Mercer University Press, 2001.

Sherman, William T. *Memoirs of General William T. Sherman*. New York: Charles L. Webster & Co., 1891.

Smedlund, William S. *Campfires of Georgia's Troops, 1861–1865*. Kennesaw, GA: Kennesaw Mountain Press, 1994.

Strayer, Larry M., and Richard A. Baumgartner, eds. *Echoes of Battle: The Atlanta Campaign*. Huntington, WV: Blue Acorn Press, 1991.

Tucker, Glenn. *Chickamauga: Bloody Battle in the West*. Indianapolis: Bobbs-Merrill, 1961.

Warner, Ezra J. *Generals in Blue: Lives of the Union Commanders*. Baton Rouge: LSU Press, 1964.

———. *Generals in Gray: Lives of the Confederate Commanders*. Baton Rouge: LSU Press, 1959.

Watkins, Sam R. *"Co. Aytch" Maury Grays—First Tennessee, or a Side Show of the Big Show*. Wilmington, NC: Broadfoot Publishing, 1994.

OTHER RESOURCES

Andersonville Prison (http://www.georgiaencyclopedia.org/nge/Article.jsp?id =h-789&hl=y)

Andrews Raid (http://www.georgiaencyclopedia.org/nge/Article.jsp?id =h-711&sug=y)

Atlanta Campaign (http://www.georgiaencyclopedia.org/nge/Article.jsp?id=h-2713)

Battle of Chickamauga (http://www.georgiaencyclopedia.org/nge/Article.jsp?id =h-642)

Battle of Kennesaw Mountain (http://www.georgiaencyclopedia.org/nge/Article .jsp?id=h-3115&sug=y)

Black Troops in Civil War Georgia (http://www.georgiaencyclopedia.org/nge/Article .jsp?id=h-783&hl=y)

Capture of Jefferson Davis (http://www.georgiaencyclopedia.org/nge/Article.jsp?id =h-640&sug=y)

Civil War: Atlanta Home Front (http://www.georgiaencyclopedia.org/nge/Article.jsp?id=h-824&hl=y)

Civil War Heritage Trails (http://www.georgiaencyclopedia.org/nge/Article.jsp?id=h-829&hl=y)

Civil War Prisons (http://www.georgiaencyclopedia.org/nge/Article.jsp?id=h-3182&hl=y)

Cyclorama (http://www.georgiaencyclopedia.org/nge/Article.jsp?id=h-825&sug=y)

Fort Pulaski (http://www.georgiaencyclopedia.org/nge/Article.jsp?id=h-610)

Georgia Civil War Commission (http://www.georgiaencyclopedia.org/nge/Article.jsp?id=h-1150&hl=y)

National Civil War Naval Museum at Port Columbus (http://www.georgiaencyclopedia.org/nge/Article.jsp?id=h-2712&hl=y)

Secession (http://www.georgiaencyclopedia.org/nge/Article.jsp?id=h-1085&sug=y)

Sherman's Field Order No. 15 (http://www.georgiaencyclopedia.org/nge/Article.jsp?id=h-3353&sug=y)

Sherman's March to the Sea (http://www.georgiaencyclopedia.org/nge/Article.jsp?id=h-641)

Ten Major Civil War Sites in Georgia (http://www.georgiaencyclopedia.org/nge/Destination.jsp?id=p-59&hl=y)

Wilson's Raid (http://www.georgiaencyclopedia.org/nge/Article.jsp?id=h-3356&sug=y)

Women during the Civil War (http://www.georgiaencyclopedia.org/nge/Article.jsp?id=h-2719&hl=y)

For more information about the Civil War in Georgia, search the New Georgia Encyclopedia website at www.newgeorgiaencyclopedia.org.

Index

Swanton, Benjamin, 97
Swanton House (Decatur), 47, 97
Sweeney, Honora, 141
Sweeny, Thomas W., 97
Sweetwater Creek State Conservation Area (Douglas County), 47, 108–9
Sydney Lanier Cottage (Macon), 130, 146

Tanyard Creek Park (Atlanta), 46, 76
Taylor, Robert, 135
Taylor-Grady House (Athens), 130, 135
Tennessee Campaign (1864), 26–27, 109
Terry's Mill Pond (Atlanta), 79, 88
Texas (railroad engine), xix, 10, 87
Thomas, George H., 4–6, 14, 16–17, 52, 64, 75–76, 217
Thomas County Historical Museum (Thomasville), 173, 177
Thomas R.R. Cobb House (Athens), 130, 135
Thomaston (Upson County), 120–21
Thomaston-Upson Archives, 113, 121
Thomasville (Thomas County), 175–76
Thomasville Prisoner of War Camp, 173, 177, 205
Thompkins, Haviland, 108
Thornburg, C.E., 159
Thunderbolts (Athens), 137
Ticknor, Francis O., 123
Tidwell, M.M., 109
Tisdell, Robert, 194
Toombs, Robert A., xix, 84, 136, 156–58
Toombs Oak Marker (UGA, Athens), 136
Tracy, Edward Dorr, 145
Treaty of Indian Springs (1821), 56
Troiani, Don, 80; *Allatoona Pass*, 34
Troup Hurt House (Atlanta), 80, 85, 87
Tullie Smith Plantation House (Atlanta History Center), 73
Tunnel Hill (Whitfield County), 3, 10–11
Tunnel Hill, Battle of (1864), 3, 10–11
Tybee Island (Chatham County), 198–99
Tybee Island Museum and Light Station, 187, 199
Tyler, Robert C., xiii, 118–19, 221

UGA Hargrett Rare Book and Manuscript Library (Athens), 136
Ulysses Davis Folk Art Collection (Beach Institute, Savannah), 194
Uncle Tom's Cabin (Stowe), 203
Underground Railroad, 198. *See also* slavery
University of Georgia (UGA; Athens), 130, 134, 136
U.S. Army Corps of Engineers (Cartersville), 3, 32, 35
U.S. Army Signal Corps Museum (Fort Gordon), 154, 165
U.S. Arsenal (Augusta), 154, 162
USCT (United States Colored Troops). *See* blacks
Utoy Creek, Battle of (1864), xx, 46, 91–94, 219
Utoy Primitive Baptist Church (Atlanta), 46, 93

Valdosta (Lowndes County), 178
Vallandigham, Clement, 78
Van Den Corput, Maxillian, 19
Varnell (Whitfield County), 3, 9–10
Vaughan, Alfred, 66
V.B. Hargis House (Kingston), 27
Venable, Samuel Hoyt, 101
Village Inn Bed & Breakfast (Stone Mountain), 100
Vinings (Cobb County), 65–66
Vining's Station, 47, 66
Vinson, Carl, 150
Virginia (*Merrimac*; CSS), 123
Vulcan Battery (Bird Island), 198

Walker, James, 5
Walker, W.H.T., 46, 79, 88, 163, 219
Walker, William S., 86
Wallis, Josiah, 56
Wallis House (Kennesaw), 47, 56
Walnut Creek, Battle of (1864), 142–43
Walthall, Edward C., 90
Ward, William T., 19
Ware, Edward, 137

About the Authors

An Atlanta native, Barry L. Brown received a masters of heritage preservation from Georgia State University in 2005. He works for the Georgia Department of Economic Development in Heritage Tourism. Brown lives in Stone Mountain Village with his son Brendan and his cat.

Gordon Richey Elwell has had a lifelong interest in the Civil War that began with a visit to the Atlanta Cyclorama at the age of ten. He has since retired from the Centers for Disease Control and now teaches research methods for Central Michigan University's off-campus masters program in Atlanta. His PhD in business administration is from Georgia State University.

Elwell has also retired from the Georgia Army National Guard, where he served as command historian. He currently is historian for the all-volunteer Georgia State Defense Force. He has published more than twenty journal articles on management and military history. *Crossroads of Conflict* is his first book-length publication. "Sherman's Atlanta Campaign and March to the Sea is a fascinating study of management, as well as stirring history," says Elwell. He lives in Canton with his wife Brenda.

www.chickamaugacampaign.org